W9-BGW-490

Reviews of the Italian edition of
Economists and the Environment

'A very well constructed book. Its brisk rhythm makes it readable. Its theoretical contribution is relevant. And the overall result is widely accessible. In short, a book not to be missed.' *Management*

'This book makes clear the blinkers social science today tends to wear when it faces – or, more frequently, avoids – the most alarming problems connected with the (modern economy's) production and consumption processes.' *Ecologia*

'A vehement protest against the present methods of economics and the attention they pay to the numbers rather than to the ecological crisis in which we are involved.' *Ricerca e innovazione*

'Economics can no longer be kept apart from ecology. The fact that it is, is the subject of this book by Carla Ravaioli in which the reader will find 28 outstanding experts in economics – some of the most famous in the world – being interviewed and challenged by her.' *Corriere della sera*

'This book focuses our attention on the disconcerting ignorance of environmental problems that most economists display ... Subjected to Carla Ravaioli's arguments, a number of Nobel laureates in economics cannot hide their embarrassment when confronted with problems they have never faced before.' *L'Unita*

'Is the basic problem of humankind – the deterioration of the biosphere – overlooked by current economic research? The statements of some of the leading economists collected in this excellent book of interviews by Carla Ravaioli offers an answer to the question. Economists have shut themselves away in a vicious circle dominated by the production and consumption process.' *La Republica*

About the authors

Carla Ravaioli is a well-known Italian author, feminist and former member of the Italian Senate. *Bête noire* of the macho tendency in Italian society, her most influential books (in Italian) include: *Women against Themselves* (Laterza, 1969); *In Obliging the Male* (Bompiani, 1973); *How Much and for Whom? The Culture of Change* (Laterza, 1982); *A Time to Sell and a Time to Utilize* (Angeli, 1986). Several of her books have also been published in other languages, including Greek and German.

Paul Ekins came to economics from an extensive involvement in green politics, initially as General Secretary of the UK Green Party. He is Director of The Other Economic Summit (TOES) and active in the New Economics Foundation – both of which organizations are seeking to bring economics into line with late 20th century realities. A Research Fellow at Birkbeck College, University of London, he is author of a number of important books, including *The Living Economy: A New Economics in the Making*.

Publisher's note

This book's illuminating portrait of the wide range of views towards the environment currently held by many of the world's leading economists makes fascinating, and often deeply disturbing, reading. One of Carla Ravaioli's skills has been to render accessible to non-economists the complex nexus of issues where economics and the environment inevitably intersect and which economists have – or, as shown by her cogent and close questioning in these interviews, often have not – reflected upon adequately.

For those readers who would like to proceed to a more exhaustive, synoptic overview of the state of mainstream economics as a discipline, we have included a second part by Paul Ekins, the noted environmentalist and economist. Inevitably more technical in its language and analysis, this important contribution makes clear the central failings of the currently dominant attempts on the part of economics to grapple effectively with the challenges to its modes of reasoning thrown up by environmental problems. Paul Ekins also demonstrates the absolutely central importance of our acceptance – whether we be ordinary citizens, professional economists, or the politicians and public servants who formulate policy – of the notion of environmental sustainability, embedded in a much more profound understanding of the relationships between the environment and the economy. He concludes with a powerful indication of the implications thereof for a fundamental refashioning of much of economic thinking as it now exists.

ECONOMISTS AND THE ENVIRONMENT

Carla Ravaioli

translated by
Richard Bates

with a contribution by

Paul Ekins

Zed Books
LONDON AND NEW JERSEY

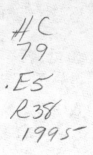
Economists and the Environment was first
published in Italian under the title *Il pianeta degli
economisti ovvero l'economia contro il pianeta* by
ISEDI, Turin, in 1992. This English edition was
first published by Zed Books Ltd, 7 Cynthia
Street, London N1 9JF, UK, and 165 First
Avenue, Atlantic Highlands, New Jersey 07716,
USA, in 1995.

Cover designed by Andrew Corbett.
Set in Monotype Bembo by Ewan Smith,
London E8.
Printed and bound in the United Kingdom by
Biddles Ltd, Guildford and King's Lynn.

A catalogue record for this book is available from
the British Library.

US CIP data is available from the Library of
Congress.

ISBN 1 85649 277 X cased
ISBN 1 85649 278 8 limp

To Claudio Napoleoni

CONTENTS

FIGURES

x

ABOUT THE PARTICIPANTS

Abel Gezevic Agambegian Russia. Born in Tbilisi (Georgia) in 1932 and a member of the USSR's Academy of Sciences since the age of 32. From 1955 to 1961 he worked in the State Committee for Labour problems. From 1966 to 1985 he was the director of the Institute of the Economy and Organization of Industrial Production of Novosibirsk. In 1985 he became economic adviser to President Gorbachev; he is considered to have been one of the architects of perestroika. He is at present Rector of the Academy of Economics of Russia. His main interests currently are labour relations, incomes and standards of living, and economic planning.

His main works are: *Zarabotnaia plata v SSSR*, Moscow, 1959; (with V.F. Mayer) *Primenenie matematiki i elektronnoi teknniki v planirovanii*, Moscow, 1961; (with Granberg) *Analiz mezhotraslevykh sviazei v SSSR*, Moscow, 1968; *Perestroika economiki v SSSR*, Moscow, 1988.

Interviewed 8 June 1991

Elmar Altvater Germany. Born in Monaco in 1938, he is currently Professor of Economics, Political Sciences and Sociology in the political science faculty of the Freie Universitat of Berlin. Actively engaged in the defence of human rights, he is concerned with the analysis of social and political systems. Since the 1980s he has been studying the international financial system.

His main works are: *Gesellschaftliche Produktion und ökonomische Rationalität*, Frankfurt, 1969; *Die Weltwährungskrise*, Frankfurt, 1969; *Inflation, Akkumulation, Krise*, Frankfurt, 1976; *Vom Wirtschaftswunder zur Wirtschaftskrise*, Berlin, 1979; *Alternative Wirtschaftswunder zur Wirtschaftskrise*, Berlin, 1979; *Alternative Wirtschaftpolitik ienseits des Kapitalismus*, Wiesbaden 1983; *Sachzwang Weltmarkt*, Hamburg, 1987; *Die Zukunft des Marktes*, Hamburg, 1990.

Interviewed in Berlin, 7 Ocotober 1991.

Gary B. Becker USA. Born in Pottsville, Pennsylvania, in 1930. Since 1970 he has been Professor of Economics and Sociology at the University of Chicago. He is considered the first person to have produced a neoclassical analysis of discrimination in labour markets, and had devoted himself to the theory of human capital and of time allocation by economic agents, laying the basis for a neoclassical interpretation of extra-economic phenomena.

His main works include: *Human Capital*, New York, 1964; *Economic Theory*, New York, 1971; *The Economic Approach to Human Behavior*, Chicago, 1976, *A Treatise on the Family*, Cambridge, Mass., 1981.

Interviewed in Stanford, 7 February 1991.

Mercedes Bresso Italy. Born in San Remo in 1944. She has taught in the Faculty of Political Sciences of Turin University. She is currently Professor of Economics at Turin Polytechnic. She is a member of the Piedmont regional council and ISPE consultant. A specialist in environmental economics and in natural resources who is close to the theories of bioeconomics of Georgescu-Roegen, she argues the necessity for a stronger connection between economics and life sciences.

Her main books are: *Pensiero economico e ambiente*, Loescher, Turin, 1982; (with others) *Il turismo come risora e come mercato*, Angeli, Milan, 1984; *Analisi dei progetti e valutazione di impatto ambientale*, Angeli, Milan, 1985; *Ambiente e attività produttive*, Angeli, Milan, 1991.

Interviewed in Turin, 6 June 1991.

Herman E. Daly USA. Born in Houston in 1938. He has run courses at the University of Ceará in Brazil and at Yale University, USA, and is currently Professor of Economics at Louisiana University and Senior Economist in the Environment Department of the World Bank. His special interests are the problems of economic growth and population increase, and the relationship between the economy and the environment. He is widely known as the theorist of the necessity of a steady-state economy.

His main works are: *Steady State Economics: the Economics of Biophysical Equilibrium and Moral Growth*, San Francisco, 1977; *Economics, Ecology, Ethnics: Essays Toward a Steady State Economy*, New York, 1980; (with J. Cobb) *For the Common Good: Redirecting the Economy Toward Community, the Environment and a Sustainable Future*, Boston, 1991.

Interviewed in Washington, DC, 16 February 1991.

Milton Friedman USA. Born in New York in 1912. Awarded a Nobel Prize in 1976, he is the most important representative of the famous Chicago school. He was Professor of Economics at Chicago from 1946 to 1976, and he was an adviser to former US President Ronald Reagan. Nowadays he is President of the Hoover Institution at Stanford University. He has worked in a variety of government and research institutions. His celebrity is mostly a consequence of his monetarist theories, which inspired the economic policies of many Western countries from the late 1970s on. His studies on the function of consumption, on unemployment and on stabilization policies are also very important.

His principal works are: *Essay on Positive Economics*, Chicago, 1953; *A Theory of the Consumption Function*, Princeton, 1957; *Capitalism and Freedom*, Chicago, 1962; (with A.J. Schwartz) *A Monetary History of the United States 1867–1960*, Princeton, 1963; *The Optimum Quality of Money and Other Essays*, Chicago, 1969; *Price Theory*, Chicago, 1976; (with R. Friedman) *Free to Choose*, New York, 1980.

Interviewed in San Francisco, 6 February 1991.

John K. Galbraith USA. Born in Iona Station (Canada) in 1908. Professor at Harvard University from 1934 to 1939 and president of the American Economic Association from 1948 to 1975, he performed important tasks in the US administration during the Kennedy presidency, and was ambassador to India from 1961 to 1963. He is one of the most internationally celebrated personalities in the field of economics. The analysis of modern industrial societies, which according to his theories do not conform to Keynes's competitive model, the predominant role of the large enterprise, and the critique of a production system largely based on needs induced by the interests of big business, are among the most important of the many themes he has developed.

His main works are: *American Capitalism: the Concept of Countervailing Power*, Boston, 1952; *The Affluent Society*, Boston, 1958; *The New Industrial State*, Boston, 1967; *The Age of Uncertainty*, Boston 1977; (with Stanislav Mensicov) *Capitalism, Communism and Coexistence*, Boston, 1988.

Interviewed in Boston, 31 January 1991.

Nicholas Georgescu-Roegen USA. Born in Constanza (Romania) in 1906, he graduated in mathematics at Bucharest and in statistics at Paris. He devoted himself to economics only after he met Schumpeter at Harvard in 1934. He was a teacher at Bucharest University and held important offices in the Romanian administration until 1946, when he moved to the USA. He subsequently taught at a number of US and European universities. From 1960 to 1972 he occupied the chair of economic theory at Vanderbilt University, where he is now Emeritus Professor. Endowed with enormous knowledge in the fields of science and philosophy as well as of economics, he established the basic principles of bioeconomics.

His most important works are: *Analytical Economics: Issues and Problems*, Cambridge, Mass., 1966; *Entropy and the Economic Process*, Cambridge, Mass., 1971; *Energy and Economic Myths: Institutional and Analytical Essays*, New York, 1976; *Economics of Natural Resources: Myths and Facts*, Tokyo, 1981.

Interviewed in Nashville, 13 February 1991.

Emilio Gerelli Italy. Born in Milan in 1929, he is Professor of the Science of Finance and Financial Law, and director of the Institute of Finance of the University of Pavia. He is interested above all in problems of public finance, particularly in the Italian experience, and in problems of environmental economics. He is director of the *Revista di diritto finanziario e scienza delle finanze*. He is adviser to the Italian environment ministry.

His main works are: *Economia e tutela dell'ambiente*, Il Mulino, Bologna, 1974; (with J.P. Barde) *Économie et politique de l'environment*, Paris, 1977; *Per una politica della spesa pubblica in Italia*, Angeli, Milan, 1978; *Per la riforma della finanza locale*, Il Mulino, Bologne, 1981; (with others) *Ascesa e declino del business ambientale, Dal isinquinamento alle tecnologie pulite*, Il Murino, Bologna, 1990.

Interviewed in Rome, 18 October 1991.

Frank H. Hahn UK. Born in Berlin in 1925, he moved to England in the 1930s. He has taught in Birmingham and London, and since 1972 he has been Professor of Economics at Cambridge University. Strongly critical of monetarism and neoclassical macroeconomics, he is considered one of the greatest economists working today. His main preoccupations are the theory of general economic equilibrium, money in the modern market economy, and the question of involuntary unemployment.

His main works are: (with K. Harrow) *General Competitive Analysis*, San Francisco, 1971; *Money and Inflation*, Oxford, 1982; *Equilibrium and Macroeconomics*, Oxford, 1984; *Money, Growth and Stability*, Oxford, 1985.

Interviewed in Cambridge, 9 May 1991.

Volkmar Hartje Germany. Born in Cologne in 1947, Professor of Development of Territory at the Technische Universität of Berlin, he is in charge of the consultations for a number of German government departments concerning ecological policies and economic assistance to the Third World. The integration of environmental concerns into concrete political projects in favour of developing countries, structural changes in industry and the economy of territory are integral to his line of research.

His main books are: *Beihilfe sum Überleben, Umwelt und Ressour-*

censchutz in der bilateralen Entwicklungshilfe der BR Deutschland,
Frankfurt, 1982; *Theorie und Politik der Meeresnutzung*, Frankfurt,
1983; (with K.W. Zimmerman and A. Ryll) *Ökologische Modern-
isierung der Produktion: Strukturen und Trends*, Berlin, 1990.

Interviewed in Berlin, 7 October 1991.

Albert O. Hirschman USA. Born in Berlin in 1915, he moved
in the 1930s first to Italy and then to the USA to escape the
persecution of the Jews. He has taught at the universities of Yale,
Columbia and Harvard. Since 1974 he has been Professor of
Social Sciences at the Institute for Advanced Studies at Princeton
University. He is concerned with the structure of international
trade, the problems of socioeconomic development, and the
relationships among economics, politics and ideology. His work
is distinguished by its interdisciplinary approach.

His most important books are: *The Strategy of Economic Develop-
ment*, New Haven, 1959; *The Passions and the Interests: Political
Arguments for Capitalism before its Triumph*, Princeton, 1977; *Shifting
Involvements: Private Interest and Public Action*, Princeton, 1982.

Interviewed in Rome, 26 April 1991.

Christian Leipert Germany. Born in Neustadt in 1944, he works
at the International Institute for Society and the Environment in
Berlin. His main interests are the relationship between the
economy and the environment, and the analysis of a possible
ecological conversion of the existing productive system. He has
studied the evaluation of ecological damage, the defensive costs
of Germany, and above all, the incorrect use of GNP as a
macroeconomic indicator of a country's well-being. On this basis
he has theorized the necessity for a different form of national
accounting.

His principal works are: *Unzulänglichkeiten des Sozialprodukts in
seiner Eigenschaft als Wohlstandsmass*, Tübingen, 1975; *Alternative
Ökonomie und ökonomische Theorie*, Frankfurt, 1980; *Die Aufnahme
der Umweltproblematik in der ökonomische Theorie*, Frankfurt, 1989;
*Die heimlichen Kosten des fortschritts. Wie Umweltzerstürüng das Wirts-
chaftswachstum fördert*, Frankfurt, 1989.

Interviewed in Sienna, 12 April 1991.

Wassily Leontief USA. Born in St Petersburg in 1906. He was
awarded a Nobel Prize in 1973. Resident in the USA since 1931,
he has held various administrative positions; since 1980 he has
been a consultant to the UN on development programmes. He
has taught at Harvard and in 1975 became Professor of Economics
at New York University. His name is connected with the
elaboration of the theory of input-output analysis and with the

application of the methods of econometrics to economic analysis.

His most important works are: *The Structure of the American Economy 1919–1929*, Oxford, 1941; *Essay in Economics*, Oxford 1966; *Input–Output Economics*, Oxford, 1966; *The Future of the World Economy*, Oxford, 1977; *Military Spending: Facts and Figures, Worldwide Implications and Future Outlook*, New York, 1983.

Interviewed in New York, 26 February 1991

Edmond Malinvaud France. Born in Limoges in 1923, he has been director of the Ecole Nationale de la Statistique et de l'Administration Economique, president of the International Economic Association, and director of the Institut National de la Statistique et des Etudes Economique. Since 1987 he has been a member of the College de France. In his work he has considered all the most important problems of modern economics at the levels of both theoretical analysis and econometric methodology.

His main works are: *Méthodes statistiques de l'économetrie*, Paris, 1964; *Leçons de théorie macroéconomique*, Paris, 1969; *Théorie macroéconomique*, Paris, 1981; *Mass Unemployment*, Oxford, 1984.

Interviewed in Paris, 15 May 1991.

Juan Martinez-Alier Spain. Born in Barcelona in 1939, he has been a research fellow at St Antony's College, Oxford, and visiting professor at the University of Sao Paulo in Brazil and at the Freie Universität in Berlin. He is currently Professor of Agricultural Economics at the Università Autonoma in Barcelona. He has studied agricultural economics but is mainly known for his work on the relations between the economy and the environment.

His most important books are: *La estabilidad del latifundismo*, Paris, 1968; *Labourers and Landowners in Southern Spain*, London, 1971; (in collaboration with V. Stolcke) *Cuba, economia y sociedad*, Paris, 1972; *Haciendas, Plantations and Collective Farms*, London, 1977; *L'ecologisme i l'economia Historia d'unes relacions amagades*, Barcelona, 1984; *Ecological Economics: Energy, Environment and Society*, Oxford, 1987.

Interviewed in Barcelona, 18 September 1991.

James E. Meade UK. Born in Swanage in 1907, he was awarded the Nobel Prize in 1977. After working in the British administration during the Second World War, he taught international economics at the London School of Economics from 1947 to 1957, and then at Cambridge University until his retirement in 1974. His studies in the theory and politics of international trade are of great importance, as is his work on the application of economic theory to the formulation of economic policies. Despite his neoclassical background, he argues for the necessity of public intervention in the economy for the benefit of the weakest classes.

His most important books are: *Theory of International Economic Policy*, Oxford, 1951–55; *Principles of Political Economy*, London, 1965–1976; *The Intelligent Radical's Guide to Economic Policy*, London, 1975; *Stagflation*, London 1982–83; *Agathotopia: the Economics of Partnership*, London 1989.

Letter of 27 May 1991.

James O'Connor USA. Born in Newton, Massachusetts, in 1930, he is Professor of Sociology and Economics at the University of California in Santa Cruz. An outstanding representative of neo-Marxism, he has made a considerable contribution to the reformulation of Western Marxist thought. The dynamics of social and production relations, the relationship between public expenditure and private profit, and more recently the problem of the environment are the concerns to which he has particularly devoted himself. He is editor-in-chief of the review *Capitalism, Nature, Socialism*, which has given birth to a network of European sister reviews.

His main works are: *The Fiscal Crisis of the State*, New York, 1973; *The Corporations and the State: Essays in the Theory of Capitalism and Imperialism*, New York, 1974; *Accumulation Crisis*, Oxford, 1984; *The Meaning of Crisis: a Theoretical Introduction*, Oxford, 1987; *Capitalism, Nature, Socialism*, Santa Cruz, 1988.

Letter of 6 August 1991.

René Passet France. Born in Begles in 1926, he is Professor at the Université de Paris 1, where he directs the Centre Economie Espace Environment. His main concerns are economic analysis and, during the last twenty years, economics and the environment; notably, he confronts ecological subjects from the point of view of energy and the relationship between the natural sciences and economics.

His principal works are: *Introduction aux mathématiques de l'analyse économique*, Paris (1. *Une approche nouvelle*, 1970; 11. *L'analyse des relations entre phénomènes économiques liés*, 1970; 111. *La mésure des variations corrélatives*, 1971; *Analyse économique structurale et problèmes de décisions*, 1977; *L'économiques et le vivant*, Paris, 1983; 'Prevision à long terme et mutation des systèmes économiques', *Revue d'économie politique*, n. 5, 1987, pp. 532–55.

Interviewed in Paris, 17 May 1991.

David W. Pearce UK. Born in Harrow in 1941, he has been director of the Centre for Economic Research into the Public Sector at the University of Leicester, and Professor of Political Economy at the University of Aberdeen. Since 1983 he has been

Professor of Economics at University College, London. His work is concerned with the relationship between the economy and ecology, and he is particularly interested in the use of cost–benefit analysis to determine the value of environmental resources, and the economics of natural resources and energy sources.

His main writings are: *Cost Benefit Analysis*, London, 1971; *Natural Resources Depletion*, London 1975; *Environmental Economics*, London, 1976; (with A. Markandya and E. Barbier) *Blueprint for a Green Economy*, London, 1989.

Interviewed in London, 8 May 1991.

Paul A. Samuelson USA. Born in Gary, Indiana, in 1915, he was awarded the Nobel Prize in 1970. Professor of Economics at the Massachusetts Institute of Technology since 1947, he was an economic adviser to presidents Kennedy and Johnson. His work covers almost every field of economic dynamics, the analysis of the conditions for stability, the theory of consumption, welfare economics and international economics. Many aspects of his impressive work have become obligatory reference points for economists worldwide.

His most important works are: *Foundations of Economic Analysis*, Cambridge, Mass., 1974; *Economics*, New York, 1948; *Collected Scientific Papers of P.A. Samuelson*, Cambridge, Mass., 1966, 1972, 1977.

Letter of 7 February 1991.

Stanislav Sergeevic Shatalin Russia. Born in Moscow in 1934, he is a member of the Academy of Sciences of the USSR. He played leading roles in the public administration of the USSR, and has been Professor of Mathematical Methods of Economic Analysis in the Faculty of Economics at Moscow University. He became well known as a consultant to Mikhail Gorbachev and Boris Yeltsin and as the author of the famous '500-day plan' for the transition from a planned economy to a market economy. His main interests are economic–mathematic models, and the methodology of economic planning.

His main writings are: *Voprosy economiko-matematicheskogo modelirovaniia*, Moscow, 1973; (with Cao Pinna) *Consumption Patterns in Eastern and Western Europe*, Oxford, 1979; (with E.T. Gaidar) *Ekonomicheskaia reforma: pricini, napravlienia, problemi*, Moscow, 1989.

Letter of 11 November 1991.

Herbert A. Simon USA. Born in Milwaukee, Wisconsin, in 1926, he was awarded a Nobel Prize in 1978. He is Professor of Government and director of the Department of Industrial Direction at Pittsburgh University. His most important contributions have been in the field of decision-making processes within economic organizations (particularly companies).

His main works include: *Administrative Behavior*, New York, 1947; *Models of Man*, New York, 1957; (with J.G. March) *Organizations*, New York, 1958; *New Science of Management Decision*, Englewood Cliffs, 1960; *The Sciences of the Artificial*, Cambridge, Mass., 1968; *Models of Bounded Rationality*, Cambridge, Mass., 1982.

Interviewed in Pittsburgh, 21 February 1991.

Robert M. Solow USA. Born in New York in 1924. Awarded a Nobel Prize in 1987. Since 1973 he has been Professor of Economic Theory at the Massachusetts Institute of Technology. From 1960 to 1963 he was adviser to President Kennedy. Neoclassical in orientation, he has mainly been concerned with the problems of macroeconomics, the theory of long-term growth, the nature of unemployment, the use of the Earth and the role of non-renewable resources.

His main works are: (with R. Dorfman and P. Samuelson) *Linear Programming and Economic Analysis*, New York, 1958; *Capital Theory and the Rate of Return*, Amsterdam, 1965; *Growth Theory: an Exposition*, Oxford, 1969; *The Labor Market as a Social Institution*, Cambridge, Mass., 1990.

Interviewed in Boston, 31 January 1991.

Luigi Spaventa Italy. Born in Rome in 1934, he has taught at the universities of Palermo and Perugia. He is Professor of Political Economy in the Faculty of Statistical, Demographic and Actuarial Sciences of the University of Rome. He has been an independent left member of the Italian parliament in two legislatures, and is president of the Commissione scientifica per il debito pubblico. He has worked on various themes of theoretical and applied economics, particularly on Italian economic development and the long-term effects of public debt.

His works include: *Appunti di economia politica*, Rome, 1976; *Nuovi problemi di sviluppo economico*, Turin, 1962; (with F. Giavazzi) *High Public Debt: the Italian Experience*, Cambridge, 1988; *La teoria dei giochi e la politica economica*, Bologna, 1989.

Interviewed in Rome, 18 June 1991.

Paolo Sylos Labini Italy. Born in Rome in 1920, he has taught at the universities of Catania and Bologna; from 1961 to 1990 he was professor of the Institution of Political Economy in the Faculty of Statistial, Demographic and Actuarial Sciences of Rome University. He is a member of the Accademia dei Lincei. His contributions to the study of oligopoly and his analyses of the relations between wages and prices in various forms of market are both important.

His main works are: *Oligopolio e progresso tecnico*, Einaudi, Turin, 1961; *Sindacati, inflazione e produttività*, Laterza, Bari, 1972; *Saggio sulle classi sociali*, Laterza, Bari, 1974; *La forze dello sviluppo e del declino*, Laterza, Bari, 1984; *Le classi: sociali negli anni '80*, Laterza, Bari, 1986; *Nuove tecnologie e disoccupazione*, Laterza, Bari, 1989.

Interviewed in Rome, 14 June 1991.

Immanuel Wallerstein USA. Born in New York in 1930, he has taught at Columbia University and at McGill University and is now a professor in the Department of Sociology at the State University of New York, where he directs the Fernand Braudel Center for the Study of Economics, Historical System and Civilization. A renowned expert on global capitalism, he is distinguished for his interdisciplinary approach and the global perspective through which he confronts the problems of economic evolution in the modern era.

His most important works are: *Africa: the Politics of Independence*, New York, 1961; *The Modern World System*, New York, 1975–1980; *The Capitalist World-Economy*, London, 1979; *Historical Capitalism*, New York, 1983.

Interviewed in Paris, 16 May 1991.

Milos Zeman Czechoslovakia. Born in Kolin in 1944. He is a member of his country's parliament and president of its financial committee. A futurological economist interested in the sociological, psychological and environmental aspects of economics, he has published around 120 studies of the methodology of futurological research, particularly in the field of simulation. Unpopular with the former Czechoslovakian regime, he was repeatedly expelled from institutes where he was working and obliged to work at a diverse range of jobs in order to make a living.

His most important work is: *Nafe Pofttotalitni Krize a Jeji Mozna Vychodifka*, Prague, 1991.

Interviewed in Prague, 10 October 1991.

PART ONE

CHAPTER I

QUESTIONS WITHOUT AN ANSWER

For some time now we have been familiar with the idea that the crisis of the environment is basically an economic problem.

Confirmation of this comes regularly every year from the report of the Worldwatch Institute. In its information about our planet's precarious state of health, the main cause of this ill-health, along with the constant increase in world population, is given as the production levels and methods of our economic system. This assessment is more or less openly confirmed by all the most authoritative analyses on the subject, drawn up with growing frequency by the United Nations, the World Bank, the Organization for Economic Cooperation and Development (OECD), the World Wildlife Fund and international scientific conferences.

Governments, too, in their policies implicitly demonstrate that they regard the environmental question as essentially connected with economics, whether by taxing the industrial processes that cause most pollution, by seeking to contain energy consumption, or by taking concerted action at international level to reduce the use of chlorofluorocarbons.

The political parties now talk publicly of the environment as an economic problem, and it is standard practice for them to include proposals for the 'ecological reconversion of the economy' in their manifestos. Industry, too, seems to be in agreement, with more and more companies either committed to lowering the toxic levels of their production processes to avoid fiscal sanctions (while eagerly publicizing the wholesomeness of their products), or discovering with enthusiasm the new business of the recovery, recycling, transport and treatment of waste, and so on.

So, the ecological crisis is an economic problem. But if it is, if this is the only way to make sense of the increasing imbalance of the world's ecosystems, and if this is the right approach for trying to control and contain it, a series of questions automatically follows, which so far have received no reply.

Why is it that economics textbooks, whether for technical institutes or at university level, generally consider the question of the environment, when they do consider it (a very recent trend), in a brief additional chapter as a marginal subject, totally unrelated to the general treatment of the principles and methods of the subject? Why is it so rare to come across an article on ecology in economics magazines and journals, whilst in most articles dealing with questions directly connected with the various forms of pollution there is not even the slightest hint of the danger to the environment? Why is the environment mentioned so rarely in those forecasts for the short-term trends in the economy that the press usually issue each New Year? Why is it that one can read on the same day, and perhaps even in the pages of the same newspaper, not only cries of alarm about the unsustainable levels of air pollution of our cities (mainly caused, as is well known, by car exhaust emissions), but also equally alarmed cries that the automobile market has been in the doldrums for a few months?

Why is it that the constant appeals for an increase in gross national product (GNP), higher productivity, greater competitivity, new markets to explore, old markets to exploit more effectively and so on (an everlasting refrain in the speeches of politicians the world over) are never considered alongside that variable that is so decisive for our survival – the capacity of the natural environment to tolerate all this? Why is it that the opening of a market economy in China and Eastern Europe, and the many aid programmes for the Third World, are greeted in the business world as opportunities for lucrative transactions, whilst no one seems to bother about the consequences for the environment? Why is it that for all the insistence on limits and the need to adapt our behaviour and thinking to the finite nature of our planet, not just by environmentalists, but also by a now widespread ecology-conscious public, we seem to impose no limits on our economic activity, or seem even to be unaware of the need for limits?

I had been wondering about these questions for some time before I began work on this book. But the most intriguing question concerned the silence of the economists. I am not an economist. I am not even a professional environmentalist, nor can I boast any full-time involvement with the subject, even if I have taken a direct interest in the subject on various occasions. I am simply someone who has been observing over recent decades the gradual deterioration of the world, and has noted that this process has been accompanied by the growth and triumph of consumerism and productionism. This society has become more and more overloaded with enormous quantities of things for sale, which sometimes seem to have no very obvious use, existing merely as things to be sold, having no identity beyond their status as goods. Nothing seems able to resist the predominance of the market as a perfect and irreplaceable social synthesis, the only rational possibility, to which all our decisions must be adjusted. Meanwhile the responses offered in the name of the environment have seemed feeble, partial, fragmented, incoherent and completely inadequate.

Many serious thinkers have expressed reasoned criticisms along these lines: Dahrendorf, Illich, Severino, Touraine, Offe, Giddens, Lasch, Louhman, Morin, Guattari, Rubbia, Popper, Gorz ... one could go on.

So what about the economists? Do they really have nothing to say?

I was aware that there exist quite a few environmental economists, who are convinced that economics and the environment are extremely closely related and belong to a single system, and that neither the problems of the environment can be dealt with, nor other troubles avoided, unless we intervene in the organization of the economy. These economists have been for some time directly involved in the attempt to devise production methods and processes that could satisfy all the various requirements of an advanced modern society without endangering the essential continuity of the human race. I knew that among them were a growing number of researchers from many countries who have formed a group known as ecological economics, and who are formulating radical questions about their subject, considering it in relation to other disciplines, and questioning its centrality within our socio-political system. But I also knew that most of them were relatively unknown as economists, almost all of them were young, and they were often on the fringes of the academic world.

It was not them I was curious about, but the most famous economists, the Nobel prizewinners, the government advisers, the star names at all the most prestigious international meetings, those who are invariably consulted and interviewed whenever there is an upturn in the economy or a crisis. It is they who, in developing economic thought at the highest theoretical level, are consequently responsible for the whole conceptual system that governs the day-to-day management of the economy, dictating policy decisions at every level of the business world, conditioning the behaviour of everyone in industry, commerce, finance, and the trade unions, and directing political decisions at national and international level.

Today we are facing something that has no historical precedents, that is visible to everyone, the evidence of which is a degradation that knows no geographical boundaries, a complex and terrifying danger either potential or already upon us. The growing pollution of air and water, increasing deforestation and desertification, the reduction of the ozone layer and global warming are already more than just potential threats.

On the other hand, environmentalists today are becoming more and more experienced and aware, and can count among their numbers university teachers from many different faculties, staff of the United Nations (UN), and the World Bank, and government ministers and parliamentarians the world over, people who cannot possibly be accused of the extremism, radicalism and lack of precision that have tainted some sectors of the green galaxy. They are all agreed that the greatest threat to the equilibrium of the environment comes from the way the economy is organized, and almost all of them blame in particular the quantity of goods produced, and in doing so call into question one of the mainstays of our economic activity: ever-increasing growth and accumulation. If the diagnosis is accurate, it amounts in effect to an epoch-making epistemological break with the past, which throws doubt on old certainties that have been fundamental throughout the history of *homo faber*. This diagnosis also induces doubts about the value of time-honoured rules such as the 'laws' of the market and of profit; it clears away the abstractions of economic theory, bringing them up against the unavoidable physicality of the real world; it also imposes a complete new interpretation of such left-wing slogans as 'progress', 'development' and 'needs'.

Is it possible to be a world-famous economist and take no interest in all this? Can one be a distinguished representative of a branch of knowledge that more and more is becoming a reference point for society, and make no contribution to a subject of such fundamental importance, if only to issue a denial and demonstrate that the diagnosis is unfounded? How can one fail to realize that the world needs economists who are ready to tackle all the most urgent problems, and that the environment is one of these?

Spurred on by these questions, I at last decided to go and take a look at the situation for myself. I decided to talk to the most famous economists in the world, and pose my questions to them. Who better placed to provide answers?

'The environment? But Professor Friedman is an economist!' The secretary could hardly believe her ears and seemed almost indignant when I telephoned her to ask for a meeting on this subject. Were such responses evidence of a resolute resistance on the part of the most celebrated names in economics to any contact with ecology?

'No,' Franco Modigliani assured me as he courteously refused an interview. 'There are many problems I have never given any attention to. The environment is just one of them.' Might this be a confirmation of my worst suspicions about the top economists' total ignorance and lack of interest in the subject?

'But I'm not a specialist in environmental problems,' many of them objected, trying to head me off in the direction of 'a colleague who is interested in energy' or 'a brilliant pupil who is publishing his thesis on externalities'. What was I to make of all this? That these economic luminaries, or many of them, considered the environment to be an insignificant sector of their subject, of interest only to a few specialists?

Nevertheless they agreed – nearly all of them – to meet me, and of those who did, all readily consented to a discussion, which frequently turned the interview into something closer to a debate, if not an argument. A positive symptom, perhaps: was it a first hint of interest in questions that otherwise most of them continue to regard as having nothing to do with them?

What follows will make clear the positions of the people I spoke to. These positions range from frank indifference to the ecological danger, to a fairly realistic and adequate assessment of it; in some of the contributions there were even at times traces of a passionate involvement in the issue. But, with few exceptions, none of these, the most celebrated names in economics had any detailed knowledge of the problem as it is now understood in the most highly qualified environmental circles, and, in particular, of the interdisciplinary approach that even the general public has now become aware of in analyses of the question.

A significant number of these economists admitted that they had never read a single book on the subject of the environment (with the exception, generally, of a few texts dealing with the strictly 'economic' aspects of the question, such as taxation, energy, prices, market reactions), and that they owed what knowledge they have to the newspapers. Given that most of the press present a sensational and alarmist treatment of the subject, focusing on the most eccentric and highly coloured aspects of the ecology movement, rather than giving full and accurate reports, it is not surprising that the economists' opinions on the environment question often seem conditioned more by the positions of fundamentalist green extremists than by more serious research. This in turn explains and offers a sort of alibi for their distance and scepticism, and is another reason for their lack of interest.

In the same way, almost all of the celebrated economists I spoke to admitted complete ignorance about the theories and lines of action suggested by the most famous environmentalists in the world. In some cases I had to fill in the gap by offering a sort of crash-course in ecology in the course of the interview. Clearly, too, hardly any of them knew anything at all, beyond the vaguest hearsay, about the existence of that 'counter-economics' or 'economic counter-culture' whose founding fathers are Georgescu-Roegen, Boulding and Kneese, and which has a significant number of followers among the younger generation of economists. This is the 'ecological economics' I mentioned earlier, which has been questioning the whole approach to economic theory. As a result it hardly seemed worth asking certain questions that this new economic logic suggested, as it seemed so unlikely that they would meet with any fruitful response.

While planning this book, I had decided to interview the main representatives of ecological economics as well as the most distinguished mainstream economists. This decision was dictated partly by the need to offer as complete a picture as possible. But it was also made because it seemed proper to allow the reader to make a comparison between two different methods of considering economic problems, that are in some ways so distant one from another, but yet – as more than one of the new-style economists hoped – that can to some extent be integrated with each other, and that in the future ecological evolution of the world are destined to confront or even clash with each other.

From my very first meetings with the 'greats' of official economics, this task seemed to me more necessary than ever. I began to realize that if the 'new' economists are aiming for an interdisciplinary approach that would restore *homo oeconomicus* to a richer and more complex reality as a living being – subject to the laws of biology as well as those of the market, the focus of the most diverse relationships of which the monetary dimension is only a part – traditional economists too, in completely different ways and for completely different reasons, seem to be moving in a similar direction.

When faced with problems relating to the environment, the traditionalists tended to move the argument towards non-economic areas: the population explosion, the safeguarding of individual freedom and democracy, the need to educate people in different forms of behaviour, and the rediscovery of ethical values. In one way or another they implicitly admitted that the traditional parameters of economics are not adequate to answer environmental questions; thus, paradoxically, they too ended up reaching out towards human and social horizons much vaster than those usually found in university departments of economics. Despite this, however, they continued to avoid the knottiest environmental problems and are still extremely far away from the interpretations of ecologists. So much so that at times one seems to glimpse between the lines two completely different visions of the world: in the first, economics is the universal science to which all other disciplines are subordinate; in the second, economics is only one form of knowledge among many, and the interrelation between the various subjects is the essential epistemological key.

I mentioned above my desire to give as full an account as possible. To this end the selection of interviewees was governed by the aim of presenting as representative a panorama as possible of the different positions and fields of interest, from which one could expect to derive different ways of dealing with the environmental question. I tried also to bear in mind the sometimes significant differences of approach among those economists specifically involved in the subject of the environment. For all that, I am fully aware that this work is far from being exhaustive. That would have required far more space and labour, and would perhaps have been beyond the scope of a single author.

I am equally aware that these pages cannot lay claim to any academic value. This is a work of journalism, which makes no claims to provide answers, but seeks only to make some contribution to our knowledge of the environmental problem.

I wish to express my keenest gratitude first of all to the twenty-eight economists who kindly agreed to grant me some of their time to answer my questions; then to my friends Giovanna and Bruce Ames, Roberto Cullino, Edwin Morley-Fletcher, Giovanna Ricoveri, Gianni Riotta, Amalie Rothschild and Osvaldo Sanguigni, who have in various ways contributed to the difficult task of organizing this work. I feel a particular debt of gratitude to the warmth and encouragement of Lucio Gambi, who read the manuscript with intelligence and patience and offered much valuable advice, and to Mercedes Bresso, who, in addition to giving me an extremely interesting interview, was of great help in the choice of people to listen to, and in the general presentation of the book.

The interviews took place between the end of January and early November 1991. Some of them, for different reasons, could not be held face to face, but were conducted in writing. In these, inevitably, there is a lack of the conversational immediacy that characterizes the others.

CHAPTER 2

LET'S NOT EXAGGERATE

While sorting out and arranging the texts of the interviews that make up this book, my eye fell on a news item: 'State of emergency in Mexico: do not leave your homes'.[1] The level of air pollution in the city, according to the newspaper, was 340 points, 240 more than the established tolerance limit; the government seemed to have no defensive system other than asking the 20 million inhabitants of Mexico City to stay indoors.

The news story was not particularly surprising. It was already common knowledge in 1987 that deaths due to respiratory diseases caused by air pollution in the urban areas of Mexico were calculated as over 100,000 a year. It is the dramatic record for a phenomenon present to a greater or lesser extent in all the world's great metropolises, and which casts a threatening shadow over the future. At the end of the World Conference on Climate Change, held in Geneva in November 1990, the seven hundred international scientists present were in complete agreement that if there is no significant decrease in emissions of carbon dioxide, in a few decades' time the increase in the earth's temperature will cause damage to all forms of life.

Air pollution is just one of the innumerable aspects of the current ongoing environmental degradation. One might imagine that it would be difficult not to have a reasonably clear sense of the risk: one needs only to look around or give the most casual attention to the daily news – one needs only to be alive. And yet this is not always so. The proof lies in quite a few of the answers I received from the world's most famous economists to a fairly general question concerning their overall estimate of the ecological crisis.

What follows below is a generous selection of those answers, freely juxtaposed in a sort of imaginary round table. It is a useful way of anticipating their various positions.

---

1. *Il Manifesto*, 30 October 1991.

Becker There are two aspects to the problem. One concerns the way in which society affects the environment, and that is the function of many variables, including the degree of industrialization of society. The other concerns how society reacts to environmental changes. Usually, richer countries are less tolerant of defects in the environment than are poorer countries. The richer countries are willing to spend money collectively to correct some aspects of it.

So you think the green movement is in part responding to a genuine problem and in part overreacting. But is it a real danger or not?

Yes, it's a significant problem: some effects of industrialization, such as the by-products of chemical activity, or the refrigeration techniques that make use of chlorofluorocarbons, or the emissions of carbon dioxide that produce the greenhouse effect, though that's much more controversial. Yes, all this is a real problem. But it has certainly been exaggerated.

Hirschman I have no specific knowledge of the environmental problem. Obviously, I'm aware of its existence, and I find it very alarming. It's a problem that concerns not only the industrialized world, but the developing countries as well. In certain cities of Latin America such as Santiago, São Paolo and Mexico City there's a serious risk to people's health. But, strangely enough, the problem concerns the countries of Eastern Europe even more. There's a tendency to blame capitalism for environmental damage, but now we find that in the socialist bloc the situation is much worse. That's because in capitalist countries there is such a thing as public opinion, which can make itself heard and influence governments, and force governments to do something. In Eastern Europe this was not allowed for by scientific socialism; it did not exist. The problem of the environment is serious, without any doubt. But how to deal with it is another question. There are many interests involved, some of them powerful, and there are many different needs ... Some measures are absolutely out of the question, such as eliminating traffic ...

Gerelli I am with the optimists. While it is true that the situation is often very serious at both the local and the global levels, there is growing political interest in the environment, both nationally and internationally. There have been interesting practical decisions concerning the use of economic instruments, such as the decision of the EEC to tax energy and gases responsible for the greenhouse effect. And whilst I'm no worshipper of technology, we cannot underrate the importance of one or two immensely significant innovations that would have considerable beneficent effects if they were used on the environment.

But are the new technologies normally used for ecological ends, or to improve productivity, increase production, promote competition, and so on?

Well, yes, certain forms of technology can also have negative effects for the environment. But we have to remember that the most advanced technology is making less and less use of materials. Optical fibres are used instead of copper, the notorious plastic cans are getting thinner and thinner, radios have transistors instead of valves, and so on. All this means fewer resources per product unit and is extremely positive.

Simon Yes, it's a serious problem, made up of many problems. Basically it's a matter of how we can plan our society so as not to damage or exhaust the resources that we and other living creatures need. How dangerous it is depends on what timespan you take. Nothing disastrous is going to happen in the next few decades. We can put off the risk if we learn what we need to learn to find solutions to the problems.

Spaventa In economic terms it is an old problem of externalities, social costs which are different from private costs. This is a problem which little by little has become quantitatively much more important. Anyone who has not made a specific study of the question can only steer a middle course between the exaggerations and underestimations.

Does steering a middle course mean regarding the problem as serious?

I think so, yes. But that is a newspaper reader's opinion. I have read absolutely nothing specific on the subject. I know no more about this than the man in the street.

Shouldn't you be interested, as an economist, in knowing more about it?

I'm already extremely taken up with a series of other subjects, and given that other economists are working specifically on this subject − and working well, I think − then I'm prepared to trust any suggestions they come up with. In any case, there is a growing interest among economists in environmental problems, but I don't think it will be easy to find convincing solutions.

It seems as if you are delegating the question to colleagues. Does that mean that for you the environment is a specific field of study which doesn't concern the economy and economics as a whole?

You must remember that economists are becoming more and more specialized. And in any case I don't trust these grand, world-embracing visions. I don't think it is any use at all to make general pronouncements when I don't have any specific knowledge of the problem.

Meade The question is: what will happen to human society over the next century? That will depend on a very complicated network of feedback relationships between demographic developments, industrial and economic developments, technological developments, biological and ecological developments, and psychological, political and sociological developments. In each of the many subdivisions of each of these separate fields, experts are confronted with difficult specific problems which they have yet to solve. But in addition to these specialized problems there remains the basic problem of how the developments in these various fields react upon each other. We need to see the system as a whole if we want to confront the question of our survival. Unfortunately, our present intellectual atmosphere of expert specialization means that it is precisely in this kind of general vision and in interrelations of this kind that we are weakest.

Friedman The environment movement consists of two very different parts. One is the traditional conservation groups, who want to save resources etcetera. The other is a group of people who fundamentally aren't interested in conservation at all, and who aren't primarily interested in pollution. They're just long-term anti-capitalists who will take every opportunity to trash the capitalist system and the market economy. They used to be communists or socialists, but history has been unkind to them, and now all they can do is complain about pollution. But without modern technology, pollution would be far worse. The pollution from horses was much worse than what you get from automobiles. If you read descriptions of the streets of New York in the nineteenth century ...

So you're not convinced that production causes pollution?

No, of course not. Private industry tends to reduce pollution, not increase it, because it's in the manufacturer's interest to use fewer resources to produce more. It's the consumer that causes pollution. Industrialists are just intermediaries. They meet the demand of consumers.

So business has no interest in producing and selling?

I'm not saying that. I'm saying that it's the consumer who causes pollution, asking for goods and services that create problems for the environment. If he doesn't like this he only has to change his behaviour and redirect production. He's free to do it.

But is the environmental problem a very grave one or not?

No, it's not very grave. There are very different priorities in our country.

And in the world?

I don't think you can give a global answer. It depends. In Mexico City it is a very grave problem.

So it is a problem?

In some places.

Samuelson The problem of the preservation of the environment remains a serious one, and we can't rely on the mechanisms of the market to solve it.

Wallerstein It's a very serious problem. We're reaching the point where we are exhausting certain resources or they are becoming extremely expensive. But this using up of resources is only half the problem. The other half is the problem of pollution. In the process of using everything we create dirt or poison or waste, all of which are increasing. These are wounds inflicted on nature, dangers to the health not only of human beings but of all living species. Something has to be done about the problem, but that is a very expensive proposition. Furthermore, it's clear that with an expanding world population and an expanding world level of production, the problem has to get worse and worse, and geometrically worse and worse. It's been a problem for thousands of years, but it's only become a serious problem very recently, which is why people have begun to get concerned about it.

Agambegian I think it is a key problem for our future. Some months ago we tested public opinion throughout Russia, asking people to indicate what they regarded as the most important problems: food, health, crime, the environment etcetera, and the environment was regarded as the most important of all. This was so throughout my country, not just in those areas most seriously affected by pollution. People realize the environment influences their health and that of their children. This is very clear to them now.

Sylos Labini It's a very serious problem, with two distinct aspects. One is the exhaustion of resources, and that's the less worrying. If we run out of a certain mineral we can always replace it with another. The other is the progressive deterioration of the environment, and this is an extremely serious problem, for which there are no ready-made solutions.

Leontief It's a very big problem. How dangerous? It's difficult to say. Even in the United States, which is a rather conservative country and very influenced by business, they have realized this ... Because something is done about the environment when important people are affected by it. At first, rich people can move out of the cities and they're not affected, but finally global warming will reach them too. When pollution reaches a certain level it makes no distinctions between rich and poor ...

Malinvaud The problem of the environment is linked to the vast increase that has taken place in human activity on the planet, whose combined causes are the increase in population and the increase in per capita production. A transformation of this kind, with the consumption of resources and the resulting harmful by-products, is absolutely unprecedented in human history. But we need to distinguish between ecological problems at a local level and at the global level. We have known how to deal with local problems for some time now. Mining engineers in Europe began dealing with air and water pollution in the last century, and even today these unpleasant factors are being handled satisfactorily by economists. Global ecological problems are a more recent phenomenon, even if they are substantially connected to long-standing worries economists have had about resources. First of all the question was, will the Earth be able to sustain humanity? Later, will coal, petrol and energy be sufficient to sustain production? Today the question is, isn't human productivity in excess of what the planet can tolerate?

What do you think?

I have no clear ideas, only very serious doubts. We have no certainties, only a strong probability that halfway through the next century the problems will have exceeded any threshold of tolerance.

Well, we can be certain about some things. There are already extreme situations.

No, if we study the facts scientifically, we have no certainty at all as to what the consequences will be, though it's true the probabilities point in a certain direction. We must start thinking about solutions immediately.

Martinez-Alier Overall, the situation is deteriorating. There have been improvements in some local situations, such as air pollution in some American or north European cities, but elsewhere things are getting worse all the time, as on the Mediterranean coast, or in the forests of Africa ... Global problems, such as global warming, are getting worse and worse, and nothing so far has been done about them.

O'Connor   Global ecology is getting worse. More cities are deteriorating than not. Rural conditions have never been as bad as they are today. Unemployment is greater and work conditions are worse. There is more poverty, disease, starvation and misery than ever before in human history. Inequality of wealth and income between and within nations is greater. In some respects environmental conditions are better in the North. In the South, with a few exceptions, the picture is very grim. To the degree that things are better, we have social movements to thank, not the state primarily, and certainly not capitalism. But the labour, environmental, feminist and urban movements have had to struggle in an economic climate of unrelieved cost cutting. Capitalism's obsession with reducing costs of production, speeding up the turnover of capital, and expanding credit spending to keep consumerism alive have hurt the environment, urban conditions and individual well-being for well over a decade. This hyper-capitalist conjuncture has reduced the effectiveness of the environmental and other social movements, which have also shot themselves in the foot by remaining single-issue or relatively narrow movements. I mean that all those who are fighting capitalism and the state on a thousand local fronts have not yet joined together to develop an overall strategy. They are not yet political movements capable of challenging the centre–right and right-wing governments that rule most of the countries in the world, not to mention the International Monetary Fund. This also limits the type and degree of their criticism of the existing state of affairs, as well as their proposed remedies. Until they get together politically, the best we can hope for is tenuous piecemeal reform.

Hartje   There is a whole series of 'nonconventional' pollutants which we are just beginning to identify, and which the process of development is worsening. Climate change is a typical example. Then there are a number of pollutants whose effects we still don't understand, and the continual increase in the consumption of resources. How long will the environment go on being able to provide an ecological basis for human life? Or, in other words, how much time do we have to deal with the problem? If you think of environmental policy as a process that starts with the definition of the problem and ends with doing something about it, we are still in the first phase. The major question is whether the evolution of environmental policy will be fast enough to catch up with the problems and deal with them.

   And what is your answer?

   Oh, I've no idea at all. If you think of the prognosis for climate modification, which will become catastrophic in fifty or eighty years time ... And don't forget that the industrialized countries can move quite fast, but the developing countries need time before people start taking on board the environmental question. Mainly because they are poor and have other priorities, but also because most of them do not have democratic institutions, or are very young democracies, still fragile and not very efficient.

Shatalin The problems of the environment are the gravest that mankind has had to face in recent decades, and their significance will grow with each passing year. Ecosystems formed over thousands and millions of years are now undergoing enormous transformations and becoming unstable because of increasing anthropogenic influence, not only at local level, but to a greater extent on a global scale. In fact, the gravest environmental problems – nuclear weapons and nuclear energy, depletion of the ozone layer, global climatic change, ocean pollution, disposal of waste, etcetera – are no longer the problems of individual states but concern us all. Ecological well-being cannot be achieved on a country-by-country basis: one has only to think of the examples of the Chernobyl catastrophe and the oilfield fires in the Gulf War. Awareness and responsibility by all states are required for the destiny of every living creature on our planet.

Galbraith With the exception of the risk of nuclear war, the question of the environment is the most serious problem in the world.

CHAPTER 3

ECONOMICO MA NON TROPPO

Consumption, resources, production per capita, the market, taxation, industrialized countries and developing countries: the concepts that have emerged in this first approach to the question of the environment, the very terminology used by my interviewees, are typical of the way economists talk. There was no shortage either of explicit appeals to some of the branches of economic theory that had obvious relevance to aspects of the environment. All this would seem to indicate unequivocally that even economists who have never taken any professional interest in the environment, or who at any rate have never taken up any public position on the subject, consider the question as essentially economic.

Nevertheless, the opinions that emerged when I posed the question directly were by no means in agreement. 'It's a political question', '... a population question', '... a philosophical question', '... a problem for technicians'. Some of the arguments offered, all of them containing a grain of truth (it is no accident that complexity and an interdisciplinary approach are among the leading characteristics of environmentalists' thinking), gave an irresistible sense of evasiveness, as if the speaker were trying to wriggle out of shouldering his responsibilities with an affirmative answer. There was even an attempt to justify a lack of interest by defining the subject as insufficiently sophisticated, lacking intellectual elegance. A significant number of my interviewees, however, including many who have never dealt personally with these subjects, recognized uncompromisingly the substantially economic nature of the environmental question, and its undeniable relation with economics. Some even hinted at a timid *mea culpa*.

Hahn I think it's a political rather an economic problem. The economic aspects of the question are rather trivial, and come down to Pigou's theories of externalities and so on. The only interesting problems are in the international political sphere. That is where the major questions of the environment can be faced and studied. The rest is a matter of technical problems: energy, deforestation and so on, where detailed knowledge is required.

Do you mind if I ask what you know about the environmental question? Have you read any of the many books on the subject?

I have read some books on nonrenewable forms of energy, and I was at the Helsinki Conference. Nothing else. I know no more about the environment than the average educated person. I do know that Professor Solow's son, who is a geophysicist, does not believe in the ozone layer hole. But I can't claim any technical knowledge at all.

The ozone layer, nonrenewable forms of energy ... these are serious problems, but there are many others. The environmental problem is made up of very many problems.

My own view is that the greatest environmental problem, from which most of the others come, is population. If I were interested in the environment, my first task would be to take drastic authoritarian measures to stop the population explosion. I don't think any of the other things will work until the population is halted.

Yes, this is certainly one of the major causes of the Earth's ecological crisis. But to come back to what you said just now about the question being more political than economic, it's true that certain decisions, particularly at international level, are inevitably political, but decisions about what if not economic matters? What we know, and what environmentalists underline, is that the greatest environmental degradation has been contemporaneous with the explosion in productivity.

If you want to do something serious about the environment it's costly. Who's to bear the costs? Reducing pollution by x per cent costs something. You can use taxes, licences, standards, and all that, but you need the will to introduce these measures and to decide who is to bear them. That is essentially a political will, which involves an internal redistribution, whereby some people will be better off and some people worse off, and an international redistribution between the undeveloped and the developed countries – because Third World countries want to industrialize, they want to grow their crops so they get rid of forests. For them not to do it you'd have to give them hefty subsidies of one kind or another. And these are political decisions that have to be taken.

But political decisions about economic questions ...

Well, politics and economics are interrelated very closely, but it's politics that decides things in the end. I'll give you an example. About fifteen years ago in England we had a very high-powered economic commission to decide the site of the third London airport, where it would cause least pollution by noise and so on. A very good cost–benefit analysis was done, and a particular spot was found to be about five times as suitable as any of the others. The government did not accept it and chose another, because the spot chosen was full of middle-class supporters of the government. There are endless examples of this kind. Economic problems? Yes, of course. Economically we could deal with the question, but that doesn't mean anything will be done. And I believe that nothing will be done until there's a very serious crisis.

So we have to wait for the catastrophe?

Catastrophe is a word one should use with a certain amount of discrimination. It's used too much. In relation to the environment too. A catastrophe would be the death of a hundred million people ...

So you don't regard the environmental problem as very serious at the moment?

I'm not in a position to judge. As I've said, I don't have enough technical knowledge of the subject. For example, I'm a member of the American National Academy of Sciences, and they have committees on this, which do not produce unanimous reports. They differ a good deal. We don't have scientific certainty on the subject.

Don't you think that the lack of scientific certainty on some aspects of the question is often a good alibi for doing nothing?

Well, it may be. But it's also a serious matter. How can we do anything without firm bases?

Simon   I don't think it's correct to describe it as an economic problem. Global warming, for example, is essentially a technical problem.

But the pollution that causes global warming is a result of production. And now the most reliable analyses from the environmental commissions of the UN, the World Bank and the OECD state that if production continues at the present rate, the risk to the environment will reach unsustainable levels. Should economists be concerned about this or not?

I think we are more concerned about it than you think. And there are many economists now who specialize in the subject of the environment. But how much we produce and in what way doesn't concern economists. It's a moral problem, not an economic one. Economists are not preachers; economics is the scientific study of how a certain part of society works, but they are not responsible for it. They can say what happens if we produce less, but they can't decide it.

Shatalin   The problem of the environment is to a great extent an economic problem, although one should not disregard the moral aspect. An unpolluted environment is a global human asset, and every human being should be ensured the right to enjoy it. Every human being should feel responsible for its preservation.

Leontief For me it is basically a technical problem.

Not an economic one?

I do not distinguish between *technical* and *economic*. One of the troubles with modern academic economics is that we work in isolation. Human economy and technical matters, though they have their own characteristics, are part of a single system, that of human society. The economic system is essentially a social system, whose basis is the production and consumption of various goods, material and immaterial. Since this involves use of natural resources on a very large scale – and particularly since the Second World War the size of this apparatus has increased immensely – it is bound to affect the environment, not only in exhaustion of resources, but also in pollution and climatic change. My feeling is that economists are wrong in their analysis of the modern economic system, with their emphasis on the problems of enterprises and the price system. But many of the relations between economic activities and the environment were not even noticed until recently. Even sixty years ago we did not know that the steel industry produced polluted water. Only now have we begun to discover these things and be concerned about them.

Wallerstein I'm unhappy with the distinction between *political*, *economic* and *social* as categories. But if you mean, 'Are the problems of the exhaustion of resources and pollution the result of a certain way of handling the economy' then, of course, that is the crux of the problem. Every problem of pollution, or almost, could have been handled by spending a certain sum of money at a certain moment in time. But people didn't want to spend that money. So it's a question of 'Whose economy?' The person who controls a production process doesn't want to spend *his* money on solving the pollution problem, though he would have no objection to other people spending their money on it. In short it's a problem for the owner of the production process and a problem of time: people don't want to spend now even if that means they have to spend twice as much in fifty years time. Postponing the expense means that it increases, but in a strictly economic sense, if you postpone the expense, you save your own money.

Putting it bluntly, everyone thinks of his own interest ...

But that's the name of the game. The aim of our economic

system is to accumulate capital. To accumulate capital you have to produce something at a cost inferior to the future sale price. Every manufacturer tries to reduce his costs in every possible way, and one of these is to 'externalize' them: i.e. make someone else pay them. The problem of the environment is the result of the fact that someone makes someone else pay his production costs by leaving out the clean-up cost and the non-pollution cost. If I have a factory, and during the work process something falls on the floor I hire someone to come and clear it up, and I include this cost in my balance. I don't imagine that someone else ought to pay me for keeping my factory clean. But if I throw my waste in the river, I externalize the cost. At this point the state can arrive and say, 'Hey, what the hell are you doing? You can't use a public river as a drain.' But if the state doesn't say it, and neither does anyone else, I have no reason to worry about how I get rid of my waste, which is very expensive. In short, no one has an economic incentive to solve the problems of the environment. It's done only if there are precise laws and social pressure.

That's what's happened recently.

Yes, indeed. Environmental groups have come along and said, 'Enormous costs have been externalized for hundreds of years and no one has ever said anything. We have now realized this and we want to internalize them.' And the manufacturers start yelling, 'This messes up my balance sheets. If you put all these pollution costs on my shoulders I'll go bust.' And it's true. In economic terms it's true.

O'Connor The environmental problem is cultural, social, ideological and political, but it is fundamentally an economic problem. The material production, distribution, exchange and consumption of human beings are the physical activities that transform nature. This is basic materialism. Any other line is idealism. Of course, changes in cultural values, for example, can lead people to develop a different relationship with the environment, for example ride their bikes to work. But these cultural changes are explicable mainly in terms of material changes, for example, patterns of industrial location that shorten the distance between home and work, making it possible to commute by bike. One of the greatest obstacles to a socialist, or red, green movement, in my view, is the idealism of so many strains of environmentalism.

Bresso Undoubtedly the root of the environmental problem is economic. The real crisis of the environment was caused by the Industrial Revolution. Of course, even before then there may have been imbalances, such as the large-scale deforestation in the Mediterranean area, caused by excessive sheep farming and the spread of arable land, but these were crises of a very specific kind and could be resolved. The whole of the pre-industrial economy was based on the use of renewable resources, and so it was an organic part of the productive cycles of the living world, where the producers are the vegetable life and the consumers are all the animal species. In other words, in the most natural way imaginable, agricultural societies, exploiting and respecting this system, were based on a cyclic economy.

The cycle was broken with the advent of the industrial economy, which began to make use of nonrenewable resources, such as metalliferous and nonmetalliferous minerals, fossils which could not be reproduced in human time, and little by little synthetic substances too, which were also derived from nonrenewable resources. Agriculture too, an activity necessarily linked to the natural cycles, began using more and more nonrenewable inputs. So the whole economy of industrialized societies is an open cycle: resources are no longer withdrawn from a renewable flow, but from a fixed stock, the exact quantity of which we do not know, but which definitely is limited; and these resources are restored at a higher level of entropy, in a form unfit for human use. In short, the causes of the ecological imbalance of the planet are directly connected to two principal characteristics of the industrialized economy: it is an open economy, in which resources cannot be restored to the previous state; and it is an economy based on continual growth, on accumulation that is aimed at growth, and increase in production means an increase in entropy and degeneration.

None of my other interviewees had any serious reservations on this basic point – that the ecological crisis is fundamentally an economic question.

At this point, we come back to the question that was the starting point for this investigation, and that has already popped up here and there: why do almost all of these economic luminaries ignore the environmental problem in their work? Why does economics in general, at both the theoretical and the practical level, pay so little attention to a subject that is to all intents and purposes a part of it?

Many of the replies I received tended either to justify or deny this.

Gerelli There is very little justification for the accusation that economists have disregarded the subject of the environment. One of my pupils has recently documented very fully how in Italy many researchers at the turn of the century, from Pantaleoni to Cossa and Einaudi, studied questions of the environment, such as the protection of forests and property rights for mineral resources. These studies were very perceptive, if unsystematic. The same is true of the classical economists, from the chapter on the stationary state by Mill to Malthus and some parts of Smith. Marshall actually suggested a tax for the protection of the purity of the air. It's true that in the past there was none of the systematic and organic treatment you can find today, but you must bear in mind the physical and social conditions of the period.

Actually, when I asked the question, I was thinking of the important names of today, now that the environmental crisis is being seen more and more as having fundamentally economic causes.

But, like it or not, research today means specialization. Take me: there are some extremely important monetary questions, but I have to confess that I haven't studied them in any depth. The same is true for most academics ...

Shatalin Soviet economic science pays considerable attention to environmental problems. The category of optimal or objectively preconditioned assessments, introduced into economics by the Nobel prizewinner L.V. Kantorovic, made researchers reconsider the problem of monetary assessments of natural resources and components of the environment. For the last three decades these scholars have elaborated the methodology of economic (monetary) assessment of natural resources, of damage from pollution, of the efficiency of environmental protection measures, of waste technologies, etcetera. A number of these theoretical ideas were tested at the stage of feasibility studies; others were tested as pilot projects in various regions of the country. For the last few years the efforts of economists studying environmental problems have focused on elaborating economic mechanisms to control the threat to the environment that could be tied to the monetary structure of the economy and adapted to the transition to a market economy. The first practical realization of these efforts is the enactment of mandatory payments for environmental pollution (air, water, waste, stockpiling, etcetera). I would add that no other country in the world has such a comprehensive monetary penalty system.

Hartje The environment established itself as a problem in the seventies. Economists who had been active for twenty or thirty years went on dealing with the problems they had dealt with up till then. And then, there are many important problems in economics that have nothing to do with ecology.

But can the problems be completely separated? Ecologists say they can't ...

I think that if you really want to get to the bottom of a subject, understand it fully and professionally, then you must concentrate on that. Take inflation: understanding the mechanisms connected with production and international markets, being absolutely familiar with how the banking system works, discovering how you can control the drives towards inflation – all this doesn't leave much time for other interests. Sure, I wouldn't want to justify an economist who completely ignored the relation between economics and the environment. But I wouldn't be very surprised. Some are completely ignorant about political repression in the Third World ... But not just economists – scientists and literary men too.

Hahn The truth is that the most prominent economists have different agendas. There are very many really difficult economic problems that we still need to tackle to understand how society works. And we all recognize that from the economic point of view the environment is not a difficult intellectual problem. Yes, there are interesting aspects of the subject on a factual level, but otherwise they are elementary matters. In general it is an undergraduate exercise.

A subject that concerns the survival of the planet ...

I think you're exaggerating. The planet will survive, I'm sure of that.

Agambegian In our research institutes there are departments whose function is the study of the environment. Not only that but we are involved at an international level too. Each year we organize a conference on the economic problems of the environment; in 1990 it was held in Washington, with a large number of participants from all over the world, and in October 1991 it will be held in Moscow. Close collaboration between the economists of different countries on these subjects is very important, because, yes, I agree with you: the problem of the environment is mainly an economic problem. While it's true that we should bear in mind that physics, biology and health care are also involved, the socioeconomic aspects of the problem are certainly the most important.

If that is the case, all economic decisions should take account of possible effects on the environment ...

Yes, and that happens ...

Does it really happen in the Soviet Union? Always?

No, not always, but sometimes. You're right, economists tend to play down the importance of the environmental problem. But it's a new problem; twenty years ago nobody knew anything about it at all. And in our country there was also the problem of censorship. Writing about the effects of pollution or discussing the ecological imbalances that could be seen in this or that state of the Soviet Union was forbidden. These questions have come to light only since the switch towards democracy and perestroika. The slowness of our economists to deal with the question is also due to this.

Solow   A few economists – not many, it's true – are working on this subject. It is gradually becoming a specialization.

From the outside it doesn't seem like it. Apart from a few environmental economists, all the others, particularly the most famous, really don't seem very interested in the environment.

Yes, I think you're right. But perhaps we shouldn't blame economists when people in power all over the world are more worried about the European monetary system or competing with the Japanese than the environment. If our political leaders gave a high priority to environmental issues, then there would immediately be courses on environmental policies being taught in the universities. Not only is the environment not a political priority, but in the US (and I imagine in Europe too) you hear people saying that we can't compete with the Japanese because we have more stringent environmental regulations, and so they can produce more cheaply than we can. And as a result we build factories in Mexico or Brazil because they don't have environmental regulations.

But are economists trying to put the environment on the political agenda?

All economists who deal with this subject will tend to have the same prescription, the same answer. And the prescription is a very unpopular one, which people and politicians do not like to hear. What is the message? We produce things for useful purposes, food, automobiles and so on, and in the process something happens that is very bad for the environment. Can we eliminate this effect? Forbid certain products, ban the use of pesticides, for example? We wouldn't have enough wheat. The same would happen in other sectors. No, economists prefer to use fiscal measures. If pesticides cost more, farmers will use them less. If gasoline costs more, people will use the automobile less. So if an activity has an environmental cost, the polluter should pay, and that revenue should go towards the environment. But how does a politician or an ordinary person react to this? 'What you are proposing is immoral; if someone does something wrong you cannot allow them to buy the right to go on doing it.' But can you react to an economic problem with a moral argument?

Isn't this a convenient alibi for politicians?

Sure.

Sylos Labini In point of fact economists were the first to face the question, even if in a fragmentary and discontinuous way. The first was Pigou, in a book published in 1909 called *Economics of Welfare*, which had a great influence on me when I was young. He was the first to bring out the process of external diseconomies, the damage that one factory can cause to other factories or to the environment in general. But at the beginning of the century the problem was a very limited one, and Pigou's argument was of theoretical interest. Then things started to change. If there is a systematic increase in industrial production, as has happened in the course of this century, then the crisis becomes explosive. Five per cent, 4 per cent, 3 per cent ... it seems nothing. But even an increase in production of 3 per cent, progressively accumulating, can have unimaginable consequences. The fact that production has increased twenty or twenty-five-fold in the course of the twentieth century means that there has been a proportionate increase in all the fumes, waste and poisonous substances produced. In situations like this, there are what I call 'critical thresholds'. First critical threshold: awareness of the problem. Second critical threshold: starting to take adequate measures. We have passed the first threshold now. How much time passes between the first and second threshold depends on many factors, above all, society's maturity. Economists are often dragged along in society's wake; they arrive later.

But most economists, even the most famous, seem to display very little interest in the problem. They don't even seem to have reached the first threshold.

Yes, I know ...

For example, in the big international meetings, in the world conferences on economic problems, is there ever any mention of the risk to the environment?

Very rarely. But usually they are meetings devoted to very specific subjects. For example, if the subject is monetary problems, obviously no one brings up the environment. Conferences on development would be the most suitable forum, given that it is the by-products of development that are damaging the environment. But such congresses are very rare. What you say is true, though: economists aren't sufficiently interested in this subject. Which is perfectly understandable. One can't become an environmentalist at the drop of a hat. I regard the question as a very serious one, but I would never dream of setting myself up as an expert.

What about internal and international economic decisions, including the most important ones? Are they ever considered alongside the environmental condition of the countries concerned?

Rarely, very rarely.

Pearce The attitude of economists towards the environment is changing. In the last twenty years there have been a number of first-rate studies of it.

I have already interviewed many of the most famous economists in the world. With a few exceptions, they know practically nothing about the environment. And they are quite frank about it.

No, they don't know much about it, you're quite right. But there's a reason for that. They suffer from a form of conditioning: economists do not like any subject that does not appear to be very rigorous, where the statistics are often difficult to get and very vague and often not easy to manage. And the profession doesn't like interdisciplinary work. Anyone who works in an interdisciplinary way is considered a bad economist. The other problem is that our profession is not interested in communication: it makes no effort to translate what it has to say into a language that people can understand, it tends to lock itself up in an ivory tower. The success of *Blueprint*[1] is due to the fact that we tried to explain economic concepts to the general public. But the profession regarded it as unacceptable as a piece of academic output; it was regarded as a sort of popular novel. Only now are some of them starting to have second thoughts.

In the public sector how are things going now regarding concrete economic decisions?

In the public sector the environmental problem is becoming more and more a factor in economic decisions.

Does 'more' here mean often, sometimes or rarely?

No, not very often. But things are changing here very fast. In the UK we are asking every government ministry to adopt methodologies for integrating the environment into their decision making, whether they are making decisions about roads, health, education, energy, defence, it doesn't matter. They have to tell us how they are going to make those changes. Gradually we are getting these ideas pushed through into practical decision making. Of course, a lot of things will not happen, but in the political world you go three steps forward and one back, or even two back.

You are talking about public decision making. But don't you think the same factors should condition private economic decisions too?

Absolutely.

That doesn't happen, though.

Not enough, no. But again, it's changing. Take certain detergent

---

1. David Pearce, Anil Markandya and Edward Barbier, *Blueprint for a Green Economy*, Earthscan, London, 1989.

companies. I know one where they have made a revolution in the way they are treating the environment. They have a completely new environment division in their company, they are looking at all the processes they use, all the environmental impacts, and they are changing some of the processes and products. And so are many other companies, especially in the chemicals sector. Companies will go green if they see a good reason to go green.

And if they have to choose between profit and the environment?

They will choose profit. But let's not forget, sometimes the two things coincide. There is now strong pressure from consumers and more and more from governments too. And the pressure can come from unexpected sources. Sometimes the source of the pressure is the employees, who say they don't want to work for a company that isn't green.

Bresso The truth is that up until now economists have taken very little interest in the environment. It has been considered a specialist subject, like many others, with the result that it has been left to a few specialists. So much so that it has become a sort of ghetto, a 'Red Cross economics', with a few members of the profession repairing the damage done by others. Without exception, the big names, the Nobel prizewinners, have never taken any direct interest in the subject. And when they have compiled their textbooks, their analysis has been limited to the obvious consideration that there are externalities, that is, negative effects external to the production process, and has taken for granted that internalizing the effects could solve the problem – taking action afterwards with norms, bans, and taxes. But none of the most famous economists have faced the question at a theoretical level, trying to pinpoint the root of the problem or understand when the human economic system became detached from that of the cycles of nature.

Of course, economists were under no obligation to suggest practical solutions, but they should have pointed out the problem, and underlined the urgency and gravity of the situation. The gravity of the question is undeniable, quite apart from the present state of affairs, because it is a fundamental one. That is, it's not just one person's mistake or the fault of those naughty manufacturers. It is the result of a choice made by the whole of humanity, which in the long term could not fail to come into conflict with the stability of the ecosystems.

Daly I've been asking myself for a long time why the major economists have taken so little interest in problems of the environment. I don't have a good answer. But they have gotten into this disciplinary organization of knowledge in which economics abstracted from the physical world and focused on exchange, exchange value and monetary transactions. All you've got is this little model of transactions which you treat as if it were the whole world, forgetting on the one hand the physical dimension of goods and services and on the other the moral dimension, subordinating all ideals of justice to profit. So economic thinking is based on a double abstraction. All these people who have made their great reputations by manipulating this abstract model of exchange value – probably very honest people and working in good faith – are not dealing with the real world any more.

Is this a particularly noticeable tendency of recent decades?

Absolutely. This has been above all Reagan's policy. But now the scale of human economics has reached a point where we can no longer abstract ourselves from the biophysical world. For the moment no one seems to have noticed, but it will have to happen soon.

What about the young who are studying economics now, are they aware of the need for change?

I would like to be able to say yes, but the discipline has been controlled so tightly that the present generation of economists are cloning themselves with the young. I'm not at all encouraged by what I see of the young economists. There are some students who attach great importance to certain values and take up a critical position, but they soon find there is no place for them. There is a selection process of a very negative kind. I think environmentalists should organize demonstrations in front of the Massachusetts Institute of Technology (MIT) Department of Economics and say, 'Do you realize the world needs your help while you carry on playing your mathematical games? Why don't you look around you and do something that is useful to society?'

O'Connor Economists typically are mouthpieces of capitalism, and since the capitalists are not yet seriously interested in reforming their economic system and way of life in rational, ecological directions – which would also bring about social and economic justice – the economists are not interested in reforming their theory. Most economists respect private property and banks as sacred institutions, and don't discuss at all what are the basic causes of the environmental crisis, that is to say the production process and the self-expanding nature of capitalism.

Economists theorize markets, and there are no markets for hazardous waste products, clean air, genetic diversity, wetlands, healthy ocean habitats and so on, including a planet fit to live on. All the economists can come up with are obscene plans to auction off pollution licences, licences to kill. Resource economists do not have the theoretical apparatus to deal with the fact that future generations have no say about the exploitation now of nonrenewable resources, and that present generations can find no forum in which to express themselves on the subject. How can I know whether or not my purchase of a pound of beef will result in more methane production in California or more destruction of ecologically fragile land in Guatemala or neither? Does my purchase of a car lead to more ecologically destructive strip mining, urban congestion, and toxic leakage in undermaintained petrochemical plants? I guess so, but I have no way of knowing without doing first-hand research. If I buy tuna fish produced by a company that advertizes itself as 'saving the dolphins', am I ruining the fishing ecology for small Mexican boats that cannot afford to abandon gill nets, and am I thus contributing to the centralization of capital in the fishing industry? And so on. Economists don't ask these questions. On the other hand, an economic theory always arrives a generation or more late to deal with the real economic problems.

Martinez-Alier Explaining the allocation of resources through market transactions is the basic idea of economics, an idea that is no use at all when we have to decide on long-term allocation, because that means measuring the future, which is the main interest of ecologists. We can't have transactions with people who haven't been born yet. In the same way mathematical models on the exhaustion of resources are no use, as are discussions on whether Pareto's optimum has been reached. So economists avoid the subject, as if it didn't concern them, as if it were a sort of sociology of the future, or a branch of the history of science, or a form of ethics. And so they get rid of the question.

Hirschman Environmentalism deals with things that are difficult to link with traditional economic categories. And economists have a powerful resistance to dealing with subjects that don't fall within their categories. That's why they have created the concept of external diseconomies, to bring these subjects back into the theory of the market.

Galbraith A friend of mine once said that economists are 'determined little thinkers'. Many of them much prefer to avoid problems like this, and prefer to do small mathematical equations on the nature of price making under conditions of imperfect competition. But you shouldn't worry too much about that. If they talked all the time about the environment they wouldn't add much to the discussion. No, I take that back, they should talk much more about it, but some of them wouldn't add much.

Wallerstein Economists don't want to discuss the environment and they can't. Resolving the problem of externalizing costs, internalizing costs, is something that undermines their whole ideology.

Georgescu-Roegen If they were to take a serious interest in it they would have to say the opposite of what they have said up until now.

CHAPTER 4

OUR GOD, THE MARKET

An administrator in Los Angeles recently suggested setting up, along the main arteries of the city, public booths containing an apparatus that would supply pure air containing the correct proportion of oxygen. The outlay of 25 cents would guarantee a few minutes' relief from the bad effects of smog.

I don't know if the proposal was ever put into effect, but it is in any case indicative of a fairly widespread tendency in the United States: you have to pay for anything that is ecologically guaranteed in the same way as you pay for any activity that is ecologically harmful, pay for the environment as well as for the pollution of it, put a price on and sell resources that had always been regarded as free until then. The next step is to trust to the mechanisms of the market, which will immediately put in train a reduction in the consumption of products that cause pollution, and so lower the threshold of environmental risk.

Following this logic, and taking it to its extreme, there have been devised what are known as 'pollution coupons'. These are in effect transferable pollution permits, and their use has been warmly recommended in some quarters. Armed with these, the polluter purchases the right to go on polluting, but he can sell his permit to another polluter when technical improvements allow him to eliminate or reduce significantly the damage he causes to the environment. The incentive to do this, according to the supporters of this method, is the chance of recouping the cost of the permit. The same applies to the second purchaser, and so on, from one polluter to another (until pollution the world over has been eliminated?).

There is a vast literature in support of this thesis. The market and how to use it for ecological ends is in any case understandably one of the subjects on which the debate is fiercest, not only between traditional economists and environmentalists, but also between the various orientations of environmental economists.

It is not only a matter of a demand for control of the market, something regarded as necessary by the great majority of my interviewees. The doubt that emerges is whether it is permissible to put a price on risk to the environment rather than taking steps to reduce it; whether the internalization of environmental costs should not be social rather than monetary; whether the use of typical market parameters, instead of safeguarding the natural environment, is not little more than the purchase of an artificial succedaneum (like the Los Angeles pure-air machine). Does it make sense to think in terms of a minimal response or adjustment of our behaviour, to seek a bolt hole within the present economic mechanisms, when we are in the presence of a problem that, if faced seriously, requires a semantic leap, a new way of looking at things?

The natural and most convinced paladin of the market as an instrument of salvation, even for the environment, is the famous founder of the Chicago School.

Friedman   The free market and political freedom are inextricably linked in Western democracies, and they are based on respect for the right to private ownership. Ecological values can find their natural space in the market, like any other consumer demand. The problems of the environment, like any other problem, can be resolved through price mechanisms, through transactions between producer and consumer, each with his own interests.

You are the famous theorist of deregulation. In the 1980s your theories were very influential and applied almost everywhere, but the environmental situation has got strikingly worse.

Not at all, it's not true that that my ideas were applied everywhere. Perhaps by the airline companies, that was the only case in the United States. And it's not true that the environmental situation is getting worse. The air today is cleaner in most of the United States.

Maybe. But there's not only the air of America to clean up ... It's true that some local situations have been resolved, but new problems are arising everywhere, and there has been no solution for the most serious problems which concern the whole of the planet ...

You can't eliminate pollution completely. You have to choose the lesser evil and leave it to the market, which will open the way for that. For example, we could eliminate smog by closing the factories and leaving the automobiles to rust in the garage. But we can be pretty sure that the consumer wouldn't be happy about that. In the same way the inhabitants of a highly polluted city would prefer to breathe clean air, but obviously the advantages of living in a city outweigh that preference. And perhaps it wouldn't even be a good thing to solve completely the problems of smog, because that would attract more people to cities that are already overcrowded, like Los

Angeles. In short, by natural means and perhaps quite unconsciously a choice of priorities is created which the mechanisms of the market express.

But there are many other environmental problems ...

Of course. Take oil, for example. Everyone says it's a limited resource: physically it may be, but economically we don't know. Economically there is more oil today than there was a hundred years ago. When it was still under the ground and no one knew it was there, it wasn't economically available. When resources are really limited prices go up, but the price of oil has gone down and down. Suppose oil became scarce: the price would go up, and people would start using other energy sources. In a proper price system the market can take care of the problem.

But we know that it takes millions of years to create an oil well, and we can't reproduce it. Relying on oil means living on our capital and not on the interest, which would be the sensible course. Don't you agree?

If we were living on the capital, the market price would go up. The price of truly limited resources will rise over time. The price of oil has not been rising, so we're not living on the capital. When that is no longer true, the price system will give a signal and the price of oil will go up. As always happens with a truly limited resource.

Of course the discovery of new oil wells has given the illusion of unlimited oil ...

Why an illusion?

Because we know it's a limited resource.

Excuse me, it's not limited from an economic point of view. You have to separate the economic from the physical point of view. Many of the mistakes people make come from this. Like the stupid projections of the Club of Rome: they used a purely physical approach, without taking prices into account. There are many different sources of energy, some of which are too expensive to be exploited now. But if oil becomes scarce they will be exploited. But the market, which is fortunately capable of registering and using widely scattered knowledge and information from people all over the world, will take account of those changes.

Take the pollution of the sea. The Mediterranean, for example: I suppose you know the terrible condition it is in now, full of phosphates, oils and plastic. What can the market do?

All you have to do is put prices up. If, for example, all the Mediterranean countries want to stop the sea being polluted with phosphates, all they have to do is tax phosphates. This would bring in money and reduce the phosphates.

So you think that some government action is necessary and some taxes should be imposed?

Listen, I'm not an anarchist. I believe that government has a role. First of all it has to guarantee the rights of ownership, and impose taxes when a situation cannot be resolved through private transactions. The problem is that government tends to intervene beyond the desirable limits, and very often in the wrong way, imposing the wrong kind of taxes and regulations. There is only one real remedy: set the right prices.

Equally convinced of the utility of the market as the principal instrument for the reclamation of the environment was Becker, even if he recognized that its pure application would meet with difficulties.

Becker   In theory it's possible, but sometimes the problem is the value to put on the negative effects of certain activities.

But do you think it is possible to internalize all the real costs without deregulating the market? For instance, a big truck. If you calculate air pollution, acoustic pollution, consumption of limited resources, paving over of land to build freeways and so on, does it make sense in the end to use it?

You'd have to ask people what value they put on the bad effects you've listed, and calculate the internalization on that basis. We could also cut down trucking activity, but that would increase the cost of goods, and people would wonder if it was worth reducing the noise and all the rest of it but pay more for the goods. It means choosing between people's various interests.

The great majority of the other positions were relatively in favour of the market, oriented towards the combining of market forces with government measures and intervention. But within this general tendency there was a great variety of opinion.

Gerelli   The market is a very efficient mechanism, but on its own it would be harmful to the environment. For it to be of use for ecological purposes it needs modifying, making use of what is called 'market simulation'. That means introducing factors that tend to make products and processes that cause pollution cost more, and those that are compatible with the environment cost less. This can be done in various ways. The purest instrument, if I can put it like that, is the use of transferable rights of pollution, which are already in use on a limited scale in the United States, but which have not yet been introduced in Europe. The other instrument is taxation, widely applied already in such countries as Sweden, Denmark, Holland and Germany, particularly where energy is concerned, but with the tendency to expand into other sectors too. But we still have a very long way to go; let's say that 98 per cent of the journey is still ahead of us. But we've taken a few steps, above all because action should be taken when there is some understanding of the subject; and here I see one or two important signals, such as the recommendation of the OECD for the use of these economic instruments, and the partial change of philosophy in the EEC Commission, due in part to the Italian presidency.

So, with certain modifications, the market can be very useful. But is it enough?

No, it isn't. I've underlined the importance of this type of intervention because up to now it has been ignored, and we have relied almost exclusively on direct regulation. This has sometimes been successful, but not always. But there's no doubt at all: the best way to halt and also forestall environmental degradation is a judicious mixture of market simulation and government control that introduces standard limits of acceptable pollution but threatens legal action if these are not respected.

But don't you think that in many cases it is the market pure and simple that prevails, unconditioned in any way, with private interests unrestrained by any limits? Take the case of Italy. A drop or so of rain above the seasonal average in autumn, and the result is devastation, landslides, and natural catastrophes, caused, as everyone knows and as the Minister for the Environment has publicly stated, by a crazy policy for land and transport, which favours the roads at the expense of the railways, and involves road building out of all proportion to the limited area of our country.

In this case, too, a mixed strategy is necessary, in the sense that we need to make public transport efficient, and able to compete in the market. So long as the trains fail to run on time and lose the goods they carry and so on, the railways are not an acceptable alternative.

But isn't this inefficiency due to the state of neglect of the Italian railway system, which is the result of definite political decisions?

Yes, there has been a political choice in favour of the motorways, which is also visible in motorway tolls, road taxes and so on, which are absolutely insignificant for lorries. Of course, it's easy to say we should adopt a policy that would lead to a switch to public transport, but this would also have social effects. Apart from anything else, the road transport lobby seems to be very strong and for the moment public intervention cannot do anything about it. Here too a complex strategy is necessary in which economic instruments should have their importance. Not just the private, but also the social cost should be paid by those who use certain resources such as the roads.

Hartje   I'd like to know how many economists would be in favour of abolishing all safety regulations and trusting completely to the market. Take a highly carcinogenic substance such as plutonium: I don't think even Friedman would want to propose tradable permits for plutonium. If we go beyond ideological positions, which are often a strong presence in the debate on the environment, and we look for a pragmatic solution to the various problems, then we cannot give up government regulation. It's only if market mechanisms are disciplined in this way that they can be effective. But I think this is the position of the majority of economists, in Germany at least: that we need to opt for a mix of the market and publicly fixed controls.

Pearce   Completely free markets are the enemy of the environment. However, in some cases that indispensable rule of the market that is competition can be a positive factor, because keeping production costs down means a minimum use of raw materials and energy. And that is totally lacking in planned economies, which have in any case failed completely towards the environment for a thousand other reasons. So the philosophy is that neither free markets nor centrally planned economies work. Use the best of the two.

Sylos Labini   If we put all our trust in the market, everything will go to pot. It's true, we shouldn't make the market into a bogey, but it's just as wrong to think of it as an automatic panacea. The market is useful in many cases, and even the transferable pollution coupons, which many people regard as scandalous, are acceptable. But where genuinely poisonous products are concerned, such as certain pesticides, prohibition is the only course.

Spaventa   It's not really a matter of trusting in the market. One introduces mechanisms that are market simulators, through taxation or incentives or pollution rights. One creates artificially a nonexistent part of the market.

Samuelson   Market mechanisms alone cannot be counted on to solve the environmental problem which economists classify under the heading of 'externalities'. Governmental regulations and policies are mandatory.

Leontief   Relying on the market alone is nonsense. The invisible hand of the market cannot protect the natural environment from the destructive effects of economic growth. I visualize society as a sailing-boat: private enterprises are the sails that move the boat and are essential. But you also need the government with its hand on the rudder. Reagan raised the sails, caught the wind and went down to the cabin to drink cocktails. The boat will go on the rocks in this way. In Russia it was the opposite: the sails were down, and the rudder doesn't work if you're not moving. Private enterprise will thrive for a long time, following the selfish interests that move humanity, but there are also social interests, such as the environment. And for this you need government, humanity's greatest invention.

But some positions were even more clear-cut.

Hahn   There is nothing in economic theory to suggest that the market could solve problems such as the environment. The market can improve the situation, through policies such as taxation, licences and so on. But it is government that is making such policy decisions, not the market.

Malinvaud   These are questions that the market is absolutely incapable of dealing with. For example, I can't see how the mechanisms of the market can induce refrigerator manufacturers not to use chlorofluorocarbons, which are apparently so bad for the ozone layer. It would mean giving up a technology that allows them to produce at a relatively low cost and to sell well.

Hirschman   Government intervention is necessary. The only people who think differently are the market-freaks, most of them neoclassical economists. They are so fond of certain market patterns where everything functions wonderfully, is perfectly balanced, like Pareto's optimum, that when they are faced with something in the real world that doesn't work like that, they feel miserable. And then they insist that the difference isn't really very serious, that the market always finds the right balance.

Wallerstein   The market does not touch environmental factors and has no interest in them. It doesn't deal with any such problem and never has. In matters of environment the market would move in the opposite direction. If I have three producers of chemicals, and one of them, without any legal obligation, decides that he will pay for the elimination of toxic waste from his factory, and the other two say they won't, obviously the one who does will go bankrupt fairly soon. So the market will push in the directly opposite direction from handling any ecological problem whatsoever.

The most radical objections naturally came from the world of ecological economics, beginning with its leader.

Georgescu-Roegen   Mainstream economists have formed a sort of circle to protect the dogma that the market knows what it's doing and prices will take care of every problem. This is just an economic fantasy, and the state of the environment is proof of this. Whales are in danger of extinction precisely because the price of their meat, their oil and their skin is that of the market. The Brazilian forests are being despoiled precisely because of the 'fair price' of their wood. Don't get me wrong, I don't want to see the market disappear. There are many areas where it has a role to play, but I want to eliminate it from the environment. Restrictions are necessary for the environment, but legal restrictions: saying, 'You must not dump your waste in that river because you are polluting it, and if you do you'll go to prison.' A fine is not enough, because you can always pay a hundred dollars and go on polluting. But if it means imprisonment, you'll stop.

Leipert   Let's say right away that environmental goods are a typical example of public goods, which cannot be divided in parts and sold on the market. For example, a tree or a species is part of a local ecosystem, which is part of a regional ecosystem, and this in turn is part of a network of ecosystems in the whole country, the continent, the world. And all these ecosystems interact with each other in such a complex way that they constitute together a single, indivisible, collective, public good, which belongs to the human race. It's self-evident that the fate of a public good, its conservation, maintenance and use cannot be left to the decisions of the market. Another very important point for us environmentalists is the inter-generational question. Since the generations to come cannot in-fluence the decisions made today, although these will have serious consequences for the options open to the people of the future, then it's up to us, to the present generation, to take responsibility for these decisions. And this is another problem that the abstract amorality of market mechanisms is quite incapable of handling.

This doesn't mean that the market has no function in solving the environmental question. When the state fixes pollution levels or imposes taxes, it is relying on the effects that market mechanisms will have. An adequate approach to ecological problems requires a close relationship between market mechanisms, government de-cisions, and decisions of another kind – social decisions. This is one of our number one priorities: creating not just new and cleaner technology, but new social technology, a social base that knows how to use the market correctly. The market as it functions today is terribly anti-economic and destructive to nature. Think of our transport system, for example, where the private car is central. The motorist pays only a tiny part of the social and ecological cost that private transport involves. Things would be very different if products that harmed the environment in any form were taxed at a proper rate, and so had a higher market price. This is the sort of action we should organize, coordinating public administration bodies and private individuals.

Bresso There is no doubt at all: the market as such, as a self-regulating mechanism, cannot concern itself with free goods, which are of common ownership, part of the inalienable heritage of humanity as a whole. Certain recent tendencies of putting on the market rivers, seas, and so on, through an attributed ownership, are just absurd. It's no accident that these things belong to the state, and have been declared as such for reasons that everyone has agreed in considering fundamental and true. But there's another reason why the market cannot resolve environmental problems, and it's a fundamental reason. The basis on which the market functions is that of added value. Anyone who produces something, adds value to it, utility to the raw materials he transforms, and when he puts the product on the market he asks a price higher than the value that was invested at the beginning. The consumer will then either buy it or not, depending on the quality of the product, so there is a retro-action from the consumer to the manufacturer. Conversely, use removes value, the goods are transformed into waste, which has no market value and is destined to go back to the environment. But the environment cannot refuse to 'buy'. The environment is, however, the heritage of a community of living human beings, who have the duty to protect it in order to protect themselves.

Recently, though, we have seen the creation of a market for waste material.

That's true, but even in this case, so far as the protection of the environment is concerned, the mechanism of the market does not function beyond a certain limit. For example, if a manufacturer produces poisonous waste and hands it over for a certain sum to a waste disposal company which then simply throws it all in the nearest dump, or in public water, this is economically very efficient. It obtains a maximum profit with a minimum of labour. No consumer wants to know how you got rid of that waste; no buyer refuses the offer. So public controls are necessary. Taxes, standards, emission rights – everything that the market can do has to be part of a comprehensive public policy.

Passet   There is a tendency to think that the market can resolve everything. As if what was in question was the malfunctioning of the market and not its very functioning as the cause of the degradation of the environment. The belief is that if the market functions well then the environment will automatically function well too. As if a good norm for environmental reproduction could come into being spontaneously, through the logic of the market and its variables. This is just absurd. Take any renewable resource, a forest for example. The reproduction norm for a forest is not economic but physical: it is the rate of growth and renewal of the forest. For the forest not to be used up what is taken away must not exceed that rate. In other words, the limit is not economic but biological and natural. The great mistake of neoclassical economics, which is the dominant form of economics today, is believing that the market can spontaneously regulate, in monetary terms, the management of natural resources and at the same time guarantee their reproduction. The argument just doesn't hold water. The course to follow is the very opposite: the economy should make use of the norms of reproduction of the natural environment and its logic. And once a rule has been established in this way, then everyone should be forced to respect it, and respect it in the way most consistent with economic efficiency. Because, as resources are scarce, the problem of rational economic behaviour is still the same: we must not waste resources, but manage them rationally.

In this context the debate on the instruments to use to internalize costs – taxes, subsidies, pollution rights and so on – is very interesting. My view is: if you think you can regulate the reproduction of the biosphere using these means, you're wrong. But if you think that when we have ensured the reproduction of the biosphere through certain norms this debate can be of use in defining the best means to respect the norms and modify our economic behaviour, then yes, I agree. It doesn't mean trashing our whole economic policy, but modifying it. It means realizing that economic instruments on their own cannot regulate anything; we have to modify them to modify our behaviour, so that it respects the needs of the environment.

Daly   There's a lot that the market can do. It can allocate a given amount of resources among alternative uses within the economic system. What it seems to me it cannot do is determine the total volume of resources we bring into the economic system from nature and eventually expel back into nature as waste. So the market is a very useful but limited instrument: good for handling optimal allocation of resources, but not for their optimal scale, for determining how big the total economy should be relative to the ecosystem of which it is a part.

To decide these things we need all sorts of information about such factors as population size, resource use per person, times of resource availability and so on, factors that have so far been continually increasing at a rhythm that nature cannot tolerate. And so limits have to be fixed – and the market is absolutely unable to do this. Those limits have to be collectively set and imposed, through social decisions that cannot be just the sum total of individual decisions. Once the limits have been set, the market can reflect them in prices, so that we can have individual decisions and a different allocation of resources.

The other problem the market has difficulty with is distribution. A fair distribution of resources between peoples is an ethical question, which the market cannot deal with. So we have to set ethical limits for the distribution of goods, and scale limits to respect environmental capacity. It's unfortunate that many partisans of the market don't seem to realize that, and treat us as opponents of the market, which is just not true. Really the market has many good points: it's decentralized decision making, it's the opposite of bureaucracy and centralized control. But in order to have all these advantages you can't treat the market as a god, able to do everything.

Martinez-Alier The idea that the market can solve everything is the conviction not only of traditional economists but also of orthodox environmental economists such as those you find in magazines like *Environmental Economics and Management* and *Environmental and Resource Economics*. Their line consists in separating the question of resources from the question of externalities, and in trying to bring externalities into the market, either by creating a market for externalities or by imposing taxes. But it's absurd: externalities are by definition effects that cannot be measured by the market. And they make no attempt either to discuss future externalities – obviously, because it can't be done. Of course, some problems can be dealt with through tax/price mechanisms, but many others can't. Take the production of carbon dioxide, which is closely related to economic growth, to the continual increase in the quantity of oil burned: what can the market do about that? Don't forget that there are two main tendencies in our economy: increased efficiency and increased production. Efficiency has increased greatly and will continue to do so, and the thrust of the market is very effective in this area. But growth means oil burning, which means more pollution and further exhaustion of resources. And even if there were no increase in consumption in absolute terms because of a significant improvement in efficiency (in Japan, for example, energy consumption has gone down slightly in spite of economic growth), even in this case the level of production is so high that the world just cannot tolerate it.

Altvater   The rationale of the market defines as value only those things that can have a price, that can be sold to produce profit, that are goods. And this excludes all sorts of things. For example, a tree has value because it can be sold, and so it is separated conceptually from the forest whose value consists in being an agglomeration of saleable trees without any value for the market in itself. Consequently it can be left to rot, as happens in many tropical countries. Given this, how can we consider the market able to resolve the problems of the natural environment?

CHAPTER 5

A VISIBLE HAND, PLEASE

As we have seen, government intervention is regarded by everyone, with greater or lesser emphasis, as an indispensable instrument for managing the environmental crisis. For several decades now, governments have been trying to deal with this problem, and provisions and measures of various kinds and of varying degrees of seriousness have been passed practically everywhere. The result has often been a sort of hyperlegislation, with national and local regulations, international conventions and agreements, EC norms and directives piling up. Not only are these not always compatible with each other, but they are often not rigorously applied.

What do we have to show for all this? Can we hope that these actions are getting to the root of the deterioration of our ecosystems? Or are they merely patching-up operations, dealing with the symptoms while leaving the disease itself untouched? Here too the judgements of the economists I met reveal a range of different opinions. There is, however, one element that all their answers had in common: dissatisfaction.

Friedman   I've already said, government action is sometimes necessary. But the problem is that most governments today have gone way beyond the limits that are desirable. Not because government is bad, but because it often doesn't know how to use its power, and it certainly doesn't use it in the most efficient way. I think governments create more pollution, not less. Take the policies that try to control the growing of food, limiting fertilizers and pesticides. The people who have promoted the campaign against this type of industrial intervention in agriculture are the usual groups who are always ready to seize any opportunity to denigrate the capitalist market system. They have shown a total lack of respect for the facts: Bruce Ames has done a remarkable job demonstrating that there are more dangerous poisons and carcinogens in nature than in these synthetic products. The same is true of air pollution. Of course we have problems here, I don't deny it, but again many of them arise

43

from government intervention. The so-called Clean Air Act is a monstrosity.[1] It's not going to make the air any cleaner, it's simply going to impose heavy costs on industry to conform to arbitrary standards. It's absurd to have the same standard in New York and Los Angeles and North Dakota. There are one or two good elements in that law which permit people to trade with one another the emissions they can make, but it enormously increases government regulations with very little effect on the cleanliness of the air.

When you were an adviser to Reagan you were against fixing strict standards ...

No, I'm not against imposing strict standards of pollution; I'm against imposing techniques for avoiding pollution, like requiring people to fit scrubbers and so on. A scrubber might be expensive and inefficient. In this way you force people to spend a lot of money badly. On the other hand if you say 'You have to pay a tax,' the company has an incentive to reduce emissions in the most efficient way, and it will do it in the most economic way. It's not a question of imposing standards, but how you impose them.

Becker On the environment, governments do some good things and some bad things. And when they do bad things, they worsen the problem rather than improve it. The truth is that governmental behaviour is the reflection not just of the seriousness of a problem but also of the power of various pressure groups. This happens wherever there are organized interest groups. That's true with the environment issue too, which is becoming an arena that is used to strengthen the competitive position of certain groups. We can see this in some of the US policies on the type of coal to be burned, which effectively favour companies of the north-east at the expense of those of the south-west, which have been punished as a result. Measures of this kind go under the name of environmental policies, but they are really something else. And there are many cases of this kind.

There are good policies too, like the Clean Air Act, which tend to operate on two fronts, cleaning up pollution and avoiding it. We need to both block and, if possible, reduce existing pollution on the one hand, and prevent further pollution on the other. We need to reduce the output of pollutants such as chemical waste and garbage, and toxic gases, but we need also to reduce inflow, to take action so as not to worsen the situation, before it gets really dangerous. Is

---

1. The Clean Air Act is a US federal law for the control of atmospheric pollution.

there a greenhouse effect? Who knows? Scientists are very uncertain about this, but if there is, the real worry is not the current situation but what could happen if pollution goes on increasing.

We need to take this very seriously, without attacking industry the way some green fanatics do; we need to worry about the environment without forgetting all the benefits we derive from products that cause pollution. Perhaps we need to accept the fact that production involves a certain amount of pollution, and what we should try for is to pollute in the most efficient way, so to speak: that is, so that a certain level of pollution allows the maximum production. It's not a moral argument, it's an economic argument. There's also the problem that environmental policies conflict with the contradictory desires of people, who want clean air, good health and so on, but also more goods.

Solow Government policy for the environment has been going very slowly, but some progress has been made. In the United States and some European countries we no longer allow cars to emit anything they want into the environment. It's not enough, but it's better than nothing. And getting an adequate environmental policy is very difficult, because there is a lot of resistance among politicians. If they went to their electors and said, 'From now on you can only drive 5,000 miles a year,' there'd be a revolution. But there would not be a revolution if you told people there would be a fee for disposing of your car. I think they'd understand, because it is a necessary measure, and the sooner the better. But politicians tend not to be very courageous.

Spaventa Some foreign countries have taken certain steps. Much more than we have. The air in New York is much more fit to breathe than the air in Rome, and so is the air in most European cities. They have catalytic converters, lead-free petrol, and so on, things we still haven't got round to. Our choices, unfortunately, are conditioned by heavy production taxes. All the mistakes made in this field, diesel buses, road rather than rail transport, and delay in the application of catalytic converters have been the result of conditioning factors that have nothing to do with the choices themselves – if our governments are ever capable of making these choices. Everything is made worse in Italy by the myopia of our governments, which is also due to institutional problems.

On the other hand our governments could only deal with the Italian situation, not the more worrying problems that concern the whole planet.

Well, let's solve our own problems first. Let's not fall into the temptation of thinking only in terms of the largest issues, or we'll never get anything done.

In the meantime the damage to the environment is growing terribly fast. Exponentially, I should imagine.

Leontief We must be realistic about this. Very strong measures might have a bad effect on the economy. I think we are fortunate that there are people passionately concerned about the environment. But very often they are not realistic enough. Before you take measures you must understand what is happening. It requires very detailed research, and study of the effects on the environment of present and future economic activities. Five years from now, technology will be different, and choices between alternative technologies must take the environment into account. And this is something only governments can do.

Samuelson Public intervention in the field of the environment has been inadequate so far. Depolluting is not enough: we must restrain pollution. Raising the cost of polluting production processes by means of taxation is one of the most useful policies. But since environmental problems do not respect the boundaries of nation-states, in principle an optimal solution would presuppose the existence of a world government – which of course does not exist and is not just around the corner. Even those nation-states that have an effective concern for the environment are up against the 'free rider problem'. Those who fail to share the common costs are not penalized, and the costly improvements contrived by the few affluent regions that are environmentally motivated can be easily wiped out by the self-interested actions of the rest.

Galbraith When an environmental problem happens in the United States one of two things happens. If it doesn't seem particularly urgent, we have a Presidential speech about it, or a speech by some other public official. If the problem seems quite urgent, then it's proposed to do some research on it, which is a long-term response. We have an elementary policy, and some results have come of this. In the Environmental Protection Agency in Washington there are quite sincere and responsible people.[2] In the short run I want to see all countries, and in particular the advanced industrial countries, make an exact analysis of their environmental situation, and then

---

2. The Environmental Protection Agency is the central agency of the US government for environmental protection.

take a range of measures, because the problem is complex and multi-faceted: sometimes by prohibiting a product, sometimes taxing its consumption, sometimes, as in the case of chemical waste, reclaiming past environmental damage, sometimes controlling waste disposal, particularly nuclear waste. There is also a form of pollution that doesn't affect health but offends one's sense of the beauty of the countryside. I mean the uncontrolled use of land, which has greatly damaged our landscape and countryside.

In Italy we are all too familiar with this kind of damage to the environment.

I have never been to Italy without thinking about this. When I was first there fifty years ago, many parts of Italy were much more beautiful than they are now. To say nothing of the ancient monuments that are at risk. But we have not yet had the kind of global policy that the situation calls for. On something like acid rain, the greenhouse effect, the gap in the ozone layer, we have so far done very little. The tendency of the government was to say 'We take it very seriously, we'll make some more studies of it.' But the fact is we can only have a global policy for the environment if we have a global authority.

All over the world, you mean?

That's not necessary, because polluting is done mainly by the advanced industrial countries and much less by poor countries. I want to see the industrialized countries develop an overall environmental policy. The UN in particular could take a lead. Its doing that has been handicapped in part by the weakness of the UN, but also because the strongest countries in the UN are the greatest polluters.

Pearce Governments have been very very slow, because they are very cautious. And for a very simple reason: they understand something that the public often does not understand, which is that you do not get environmental improvement for nothing. You have to pay for it, and governments are reluctant to introduce policies for fear that when they present the bill, then people will not pay, and they will not be re-elected. And this is more or less true: no party can win an election by promising higher taxes, even for the environment. But I think that governments must make people realize that the environment has, and must have, a price. This is the most important policy to follow.

Meade Nowadays there is a greater general appreciation of the need to do something to confront the environmental crisis than there was twenty or even ten years ago. But much too little has in fact been done and very great changes in environmental policies are needed.

Among the different measures so far proposed, which ones do you favour?

I strongly advocate (and have always advocated) the use of taxes and the price mechanism in all those cases in which it is administratively possible to proceed in that way: pollution of the atmosphere through the burning of fossil fuel; the congestion of road space through its free use for traffic and for parking of vehicles; the disposal of waste in rivers; the use of fertilizers that indirectly affect water supplies, and so on. They are all problems that can be tackled by charging the polluter. It's that type of provision that I support rather than subsidies to nonpolluters. To tax the private car, for instance, rather than subsidize the public bus, is more useful as a means of both reducing road congestion, and also raising a substantial revenue. But in some cases it may be essential to control the actual quantity rather than the price of a pollutant, that is, to fall back on direct controls, restrictions and regulations. This does not necessarily mean the abandonment of the price mechanism.

Wallerstein Governments are worrying mainly about clean-up, internalizing some external costs, but this covers perhaps 10 per cent of the present pollution problem. It's something, but I guess it involves a very modest percentage of national budgets. Something is being done too to prevent pollution, like the laws requiring cars to have devices to reduce smoke pollution ...

But meanwhile the number of cars is increasing all the time, and so the problem remains more or less the same ...

Yes, that's it exactly.

Daly It seems to me that certain countries of northern Europe such as Denmark, Sweden and the Netherlands have done a better job ... In the United States all sorts of important things haven't even been considered so far. The most urgent is to tax energy and gasoline to bring our energy prices up to European levels. If gasoline cost more, there would be a big saving in energy and it would encourage research into more efficient technology, which would consume less with the same performance. As well as that, the revenue could be used to reduce our deficit and introduce a system of greater social equity, and correct the terrible inequality of income distribution that we have seen in the Reagan administration. Unfortunately many people support present policy and it won't be easy to change it.

Leipert   Governments have taken some measures, but very few and often wrongly. They have created ministries for the environment, but the environment is never a priority. They have passed laws to fix standards, but standards everywhere are too low, and this allows the production and accumulation of more damage. Most of all, it is the approach to the problem as a whole that is misguided: it is a curative approach, which tries to repair the damage that has been done, while we need a preventive approach that avoids creating damage, and makes it difficult to create damage. But that requires developing a different economic system, a social and ecological market system. Nature must no longer be free for anyone; each individual must understand that the quality of the environment will correspond to what he or she has paid. For example, if we impose a new tax ten times higher than the present one for the breaking down of certain kinds of waste, there will be an interest in inventing new methods and new technology to avoid waste accumulation.

Bresso   The overall judgement has to be negative. There is a sort of race, which cannot be won, between the demand for environmental quality and the destruction of the environment. Faced with the progressive worsening of the environmental situation, societies, particularly those with a notable level of prosperity, express growing demands for a better quality of life, and governments respond by trying to patch over the most serious damage. This works to a certain extent, but they can never keep up with the pace of the degradation, which goes on increasing, in spite of the objective increase of government investment in the field of the environment, and all the norms and regulations and laws. There is a growing willingness to pay for a clean environment (paying, perhaps, also in terms of giving up things and reducing consumption, etcetera) but it is still lagging behind the burdens the environment has to bear, which are linked with growth in production.

Passet   But do you really think there is an environmental policy anywhere? There are provisions, lots of them, which are accumulating. And they are by no means negative measures: they deal with this or that problem, improve situations here and there. But this isn't a policy: it is just patching up. The question is much more serious. It means effectively rethinking our whole economic system. And there are signs that this truth is starting to be recognized, even by those who govern us. The Montreal agreement, the decision not to exploit the Antarctic ... I wouldn't talk about victories, but they are certainly positive symptoms. And there are signs of change among manufacturers too. It's true, they are the polluters, and they often pour scorn on those who are concerned about the environment. But there are also some, quite a lot in fact, who have accepted the idea of spending something on the environment. Obviously they will then try to make a profit out of ecological expenses, publicizing their products as clean and so on. But I see nothing wrong in this: if it's possible to make money out of products that are less polluting, why not? What I can't accept on the other hand is the flourishing of what are known as 'eco-industries', something I find completely nonsensical. As if half of industry is involved in polluting the planet and the other half in purifying it, and what the world needs is both of them making a profit. This is a perfect example of the gap between monetarism and the real world. From a monetary point of view an economic system working like this would give incredible results.

In your view, do the decision makers on environmental matters — politicians, ministers, local administrators, big managers — have some sort of awareness of the problem?

Let's say that they have a vague general idea about it. This is already a step forward. A few years ago they knew absolutely nothing. Even today they know next to nothing, but they do know that the problem exists, that it's topical and in the public eye, that it's becoming a big political subject. And even the politicians take some sort of interest in it, especially when elections are in the offing. They have to, because public awareness of this subject is growing rapidly. Twenty years ago, when I started holding courses on environmental economy, the students looked at me as if I was some sort of a freak. They had never seen an economist talking about biology before, and they'd never heard anything about the subjects I dealt with. In those days I thought making people aware of the problem would be a much slower process than it has been, even if it's still much slower than it should be.

So it all hangs on which is going to advance more quickly, the degradation of the environment or people's understanding of the problem?

Exactly.

O'Connor   A well-known businessman recently announced: 'We're now seeing throughout much of Europe that green is becoming less extremist. Thatcher has taken a great interest in it and so has Bush. Green has become very mainstream.' The first and most basic fact in many discussions of government intervention is that the problems of our time are global. Conditions in the North are better in some respects than they were ten years ago, worse in others. But I believe that a state-by-state, region-by-region 'before and after ecological restoration' comparison would yield a very mixed picture. In the South conditions are almost all worse. Governments in the North, with a broad array of environmental and social regulations, have pushed capital to the South, where the conditions of the environment and of work are terrible and regulations are weak. To some degree, therefore, governments in the North have simply displaced environmental and social problems to the South.

Moreover, many good environmental regulations are not enforced and/or are unenforceable. As a rule, governments in the North are reluctant to impose extra costs on the industries which are at the forefront of productivity and production of surplus value. Nevertheless, there is a growing market for pollution control equipment; Europe spends about $50 billion each year on environmental protection. Germany and Japan have better environmental regulation than in the past, but of course they can afford it because of their strong export positions.

Some political scientists argue that liberal democratic states can go so far and no further in regulating capital and environmental planning. While liberal democracy provides a milieu in which social movements can identify problems, disseminate information, agitate for reform, etcetera, elected legislatures do not seem to be able to agree on anything, and wait for important initiatives to come from the executive, which has to pay attention first and foremost to the needs of capital. And the executive (administration) is very good at hiding information, lying, blocking solutions, etcetera, which is why, in my opinion, we need much more democracy within the state or administration.

Martinez-Alier The error of governments is that of thinking that economic instruments such as taxes and incentives are sufficient for a policy for the environment. They have their uses, but these are very limited. It is impossible to handle problems like that of growth in this way. The United Nations Conference on Environment and Development, scheduled for June 1992, was supposed to be a great opportunity for facing these serious international problems. Well, it seems that it will produce a treaty on biodiversity and another on the rainforests, along the lines of the Montreal treaty on the ozone layer. But it doesn't look as if there will be a treaty on the greenhouse effect, a problem that brings out the gulf between rich and poor in a way that cannot be denied, the relation between income and the production of toxic gases being so clear. It's something everyone can see and understand: we cannot continue to pump gas into the atmosphere without causing harm, whether in terms of climatic change or something else. But there'll be no mention of this at Rio. None of the big ecotechnocrats from Washington will say anything – in deference to the rich countries.

CHAPTER 6

PRODUCING GROWTH

Can a species continue growing in number and at the same time increasing its per capita consumption at the rate that the human race is at present without placing its own and many other creatures' survival at risk? This is one of the crucial questions posed by environmentalists, and it has already been raised incidentally here and there in the contributions above.

A few figures will illustrate the reasons for the question. In the last hundred years the production of goods has increased fiftyfold. Since the end of the Second World War the human race has consumed more goods than in the whole of human history up till then. Let us take the object that more than any other is the symbol of consumerism, the car: the number of cars parked or moving along the world's roads has tripled in the last ten years to reach the present figure of 400,000,000. And then there is oil, the basis and motor of the whole production process: 20,000 oil tankers, with a capacity ranging from 100,000 to 700,000 tons of oil, are sailing the world's seas at any given moment.

Growth is in any case a natural part of the very accumulation mechanisms of our economic system, and is taken for granted by everyone at every level of that system. The consensus is that growth, if its level is to be satisfactory, must be of the order of 3 to 4 per cent a year. If the gross national product (GNP) increases by a mere 1 to 2 per cent, let alone decreases, then a chorus of alarmed voices is immediately heard, talking of recession, unemployment, and crisis. No one seems to take into consideration the fact that a growth in GNP of 4 per cent a year is the equivalent of a doubling of production (of goods, consumption, waste and pollution) in eighteen years, and that even a modest 1 per cent growth leads to the same result in seventy years.

If these figures are read in the light of population forecasts, which speak of a world population of 8 billion in the year 2025 and more than 11 billion in 2050, then it is not excessively pessimistic to ask if the human race can reasonably continue on a path of exponential growth in production. On the other hand, impartial sources, however cautiously, are casting doubt on growth as an unqualified good. One of these, the OECD, has declared that 'increases in personal income as a result of economic prosperity are no longer synonymous with an improvement in individual quality of life'.[1]

But some assessments of the situation are much more radical. Dennis L. Meadows, one of the authors of the much-criticized yet in many respects prophetic MIT report to the Club of Rome in 1972, announcing a new study by the same group which will appear on the twentieth anniversary of the first, said, 'In 1991 our researches have demonstrated that the global system is above any sustainable level.'[2]

Most of the criticisms of consumerism by environmentalists begin from this premiss. The first economist systematically to question the myth of unlimited growth was Nicholas Georgescu-Roegen, the father of bioeconomics, a theory which, using interdisciplinary methods, analyses economic processes as concrete and living processes, and, as such, subject to physical and biological laws, which impose limits that cannot be surmounted.

Georgescu-Roegen The irreversible diminution of natural resources is not only a constant factor in the increase of prices; it is something far more than a mere economic problem, one that touches the sphere of bioeconomics. The only reasonable bioeconomic programme is to choose conservation as a system: on the one hand taking action to reduce the rate of world population growth, and on the other accepting quantitive restrictions; instead of maximizing our rate of production we should minimize our future problems.

In what way are our future problems connected to the rate of production?

According to the law of entropy, what is hot is cooling down continually and irreversibly, and what is cold is tending to heat up, and the result is the progressive degradation of matter within a closed system like ours. The root cause of scarcity, and hence of economic value, lies in the degradation of energy and raw materials through entropy: the use of highly concentrated mineral resources with low entropy transforms them into high-entropy matter, which

1. 'OECD List of Social Indicators', cited in *AAVV, La società ecologica*, Franco Angeli, Milano, 1990, p. 87.

2. Dennis L. Meadows, 'Developing Visions of a Sustainable World', speech given at Rome on 22 Ocotber 1991 at a meeting arranged by the Aurelio Peccei Foundation.

is disordered and so no longer reclaimable. Like any other vital process, the economic process is irreversible. This imposes very clear limits on all living creatures, including *homo sapiens*. These limits are not only on the resources we can use today: they concern our very chances of survival. Ours is a very distinctive species which has equipped itself with exosomatic organs, more and more refined tools and instruments, from the first stone hammer to the spaceship, but which, in spite of everything, remains subject to the laws of biology. Prometheus's gift of fire was not an unmixed blessing. We are dominated today by this growthmania: we produce an enormous amount of extremely short-lived objects, we go on inventing new machines and appliances, gadgets of every kind, and spreading larger and larger cars all over the planet, and the throwaway mentality we reveal in our use of paper, glass, metals and plastic is responsible for a monstrous waste of low-entropy materials and a continuous and growing contribution to pollution and environmental imbalance.

Many people count on new technology to improve the environmental situation ...

It's time we gave up this delusion. Those who believe in the miracles of technology don't seem to understand that there is no new recipe for providing extra energy and materials beyond those available in our solar system. After Prometheus I who gave us fire and Prometheus II who gave us the steam engine, we need a Prometheus III. A safe nuclear energy perhaps? Or a solar energy which doesn't consume more than it produces? For the moment we have neither one nor the other. We can't rule out the possibility that something of the kind will be invented in the near future, but neither can we rule out the possibility that we'll have to wait centuries for it.

And in the meanwhile?

In the meanwhile 'conservation' is the only logical response. Conservation means reducing consumption to the point where we use the minimum vital resources compatible with a reasonable possibility of survival for the human race. It means adopting an austerity programme, but not going back to nature or to a pre-industrial society, a proposal that some people have wrongly attributed to me. We should first of all give up all kinds of instruments for killing ourselves, which means stopping the production of armaments; then we should get out of the throwaway mentality, and start producing goods that are as long-lasting as possible; we should stop eating more than we need, spending more than we need, lighting, heating, cooling more than we need; we should cure ourselves of the morbid passion for extravagant and useless objects and stop following fashion, which Galiani in 1750 defined as a disease of the human mind. But, and this is important, it is the rich countries who should take the lead in putting this programme in action, not the poorer ones. All the same, the poorer countries, which are overpopulated and have the highest rates of population growth, should make the greatest effort to halt that growth.

Do you see any concrete possibility of a programme of this kind being put into effect?

Unfortunately my programme runs up against two big difficulties. First, no human being is willing to give up his luxuries voluntarily. Second, it is not a programme for a single city or nation, but something that requires the participation of everybody in a world organization that administers the use of resources. And so far, in spite of all the international meetings, I haven't seen any sign of this happening. Perhaps the human race will continue running towards its own extinction, with its economic system separate from, if not opposed to, its own interests.

Does this mean that environmentalists can do nothing?

On the contrary. We must try to convince people, carry out what I call 'oecologia militans'. We must have the courage to say what people don't want to hear. We are living dangerously, and we must say this clearly. And to those who say we do not have definite information on the effects of pollution, global warming, climatic change, etcetera we must reply, 'We know enough to be certain that it is essential to change our way of life.' But who can go round saying these things? Politicians? The government? No, it's up to us ecologists. 'Oecologia militans' is the recipe.

The theories of Georgescu-Roegen, to which other famous 'grand old men' of environmental economics, such as Kenneth E. Boulding and Allan V. Keene, have adhered, are generally followed by the ecological economists, the most innovative group among those who have studied these problems.

Bresso   Growth in production is the crux of the problem, because there is no such thing as activity that has zero impact on the environment. One can try to use clean technology, improve efficiency and so on; but the more raw materials we withdraw from the earth, the more we have to put back into the earth; and however well they are treated, that means entropy and degradation. Take the example of a fairly simple and closed ecosystem such as a valley in the Alps. If I install two or three ski systems, respecting ecological regulations as much as possible, then I can hope to preserve some sort of quality in the environment. But if I build ten, and set up factories at the bottom of the valley, and rows of cheap houses, with a corresponding increase in population, traffic, water consumption, etcetera, then I have placed an unsustainable burden on the environment.

But that's exactly what is happening all the time the world over ...

Exactly. This is the great difficulty economics is faced with today, one to which we have found no solution. As they are organized now, economic systems regress as soon as they halt. It's not just a question of physical but mental ecology. Growth has become a kind of drug, which has corrupted our minds.

Martinez-Alier To go on thinking and planning in terms of unlimited growth is absurd. And the economists are mainly responsible for this: they have no other suggestions to make, and they impose it in politics, where they have absolute intellectual hegemony. Faced with the damage to the environment, they place their hopes in technological progress to solve everything, which can sometimes be genuine, but is more often unreal or completely unfounded, as in the grotesque episode of cold fusion. But the social-democratic parties bear a great deal of the responsibility too; ever since 1945 they have adopted Keynesian theories as a panacea. Everyone will better his position with growth: this is the only thing they believe in. And they have to believe in it, as they don't want to hear any talk of distribution as an instrument for dealing with the inequalities of the world, the only instrument that would be ecologically acceptable.

But can you see any possible solution?

Well, I think that present consumption patterns must change. Take the car: it cannot become a universal good. Today there are 400 million cars in the world. If, as is forecast, world population reaches 10 billion, the same level of private cars everywhere that we have in the rich countries would mean 4 billion cars, ten times the number of today. That would mean ten times the consumption of petrol, carbon dioxide, waste, highways and asphalt, and so on. If the rural populations in countries such as India, Brazil and China were to decrease by 5 per cent, with the consequent movement to the towns, then Shanghai would have 150 million inhabitants. You only have to look at Mexico City today to see that this is not going to work, and that Western patterns of consumption would be impossible. It's not just a matter of resources, but of functionality. I think people will understand this, just as they have understood that smoking is harmful. University students today don't smoke.

But the poor smoke more and more, and there are a lot of them in the world. Aren't you afraid the same thing might happen with the car? People in Eastern Europe and the Third World want a car and everything else that is part of a Western lifestyle ...

That's true. But there are also traditions that pull in the opposite direction. In India, for example, there is a Gandhian tradition which isn't oriented towards consumerism and owning cars. In Europe, too, anarchists have often been vegetarian ... Perhaps traditional cultures of this kind can be recovered. And I think that large-scale environmental movements will be formed, not so much in the rich countries as in the Second and Third Worlds.

Daly   The equilibrium of our planet's ecosystem is threatened by unlimited growth, which means it is threatened by our very economic system. When I was talking about what the market can do, I mentioned its inability to fix an 'optimal dimension' of resources, which can only be the result of collective or government decisions.

You are in fact very well known, both among environmentalists and elsewhere, as the author of a theory that introduces this very concept of 'optimal dimension', something nonexistent in traditional economic theory.

Yes. My socioeconomic theory is based on the steady-state principle.

Can you describe it briefly?

By 'steady-state' I mean an unaltered reserve of natural wealth and a constant population. Obviously these two quantities, capital and population, do not remain constant by nature: people die, wealth is spent or consumed and depreciated ... But they can be kept constant if the rate of influx (births, production) and outflow (deaths, consumption) are balanced. My theory of a steady-state society means that the optimal dimension would intervene to safeguard the environment so that, once the level of production judged to be optimal had been reached, the influx would be adjusted to the outflow, and growth would be arrested, because beyond that limit it would become anti-economic.

That limit that is continually being ignored now ...

That's right. Our economic system pursues unlimited growth with unlimited optimism as a response to our unlimited needs, and presupposes the existence of a world equally unlimited, which, as we all know, it isn't. We are in effect destroying the planet, and we sell this destruction as progress, or, at best, the inevitable price of progress.

So we have to set limits to growth. But by what criteria should they be fixed?

I would make a distinction between growth and development. Growth is a quantitative increase in material and energy flows, and is part of the physical dimensions of the economy. Development is qualitative change, the expansion or realization of potential, an increase in prosperity achieved through better understanding of means and ends. A growth economy gets bigger, a developing economy gets better. An economy can develop without growing, or grow without developing. A sustained steady-state economy does not grow but is free to develop. It is not in any way static, as you might think, but forces us to think of the effects of changes of scale and think in terms of a scale that is ecologically sustainable.

In concrete terms how can an economy of this kind be organized?

As I said, it's a matter of collective decisions about the overall scale of input of resources in the economic process. It means limiting the input of resources, energy in particular, through taxes and so on. Once we have fixed these limits the market can deal with the micro questions of allocation: how many cars to manufacture, how many bicycles, how many air conditioners. That is the beauty of the market: decisions don't have to be taken.

What instruments do you have in mind to actualize this project? National or international bodies?

So far my colleagues and I have only thought in terms of national decisions, because there are policy-making institutions at national level. At international level we have very weak institutions. Now that leads to a problem, because if a country seeks to follow a path of sustainable development, it will have to internalize all the external costs, so its prices will be higher, and it will lose out in free-trade competition with other countries. So there is a conflict between sustainable development and free trade. We must learn to move at international level too. I think it would be useful for individual countries to adopt a certain amount of protection so as to pursue a sustainable economy at national level. Of course, this will be seen as an attack on the sacred cow of free trade, in which economists have a sort of religious faith. I think the time is ripe for a re-examination of the question of free trade and the extent of economic integration.

Coming back to your proposal for a steady-state society, I suppose you know that Georgescu-Roegen, the father of ecological economics, is very critical of your theory. According to him, even at current production levels with no further growth, the destruction of the planet is inevitable.

I know. And fundamentally he is right. There really is no such thing as a steady-state society in the long run. But that's a very long run indeed, and before that all sorts of other things can happen. My proposal isn't offering a model for society that has to last forever. There's a huge difference between thinking in terms of fifty years and in terms of five hundred years.

I wonder how realistic it is to think that a steady-state society can be achieved. Economic growth continues to be the main, undisputed objective and natural goal for all politicians, business people and economists ...

That's right. I have no reply. What's going to happen? The damage to the environment is real. We are already suffering the consequences of the greenhouse effect. The dangers posed by the hole in the ozone layer are getting more and more serious, like the population problem and the food problem. The world is full of people who are dying of hunger. We may end up paying a terrible price. We can only hope that people change and wake up to reality. Some people are waking up and starting to realize what is happening ... centres for ecological economics are springing up. We must continue the battle without expecting miracles.

A fair number of the most distinguished mainstream economists, faced with the exponential growth in production and the spread of consumerism in the past, particularly in the years of the boom, expressed publicly their doubts, aware of the risks and of the ecological and social imbalances that could follow. What is their view now?

Paul Samuelson, in the editions of his celebrated treatise on economic theory that appeared in the seventies, devoted a few highly significant pages to environmental problems.[3] In these he placed the accent firmly on quantity of production as the decisive factor in ecological equilibrium. He criticized the 'cult of growth pure and simple', the 'craziness of excessively rich life-styles', and insisted on the need to opt for 'less quantity and more quality', wondering if Americans would ever be prepared to accept a cut of two thirds in their standard of living for the sake of a constant world income. Twenty years later, twenty years characterized by continuous and insistent growth in production and an explosion of ostentatious consumerism, his position seems moderate.

Samuelson It is a mistake to identify the problem of pollution, solely or exclusively or even mainly, with the industrialized nations and their high GNPs per capita. Poor populations with high birth rates feel they must perforce burn dung and strip native forests, so Utopian improvements by the affluent could easily be submerged by the future trends among the impoverished regions.

I am an environmentalist, but I am fearful of 'sentimental environmentalists'. GNP in North America, Europe and the Pacific Basin cannot realistically be expected to be frozen; nor is there realism in proposals that the global GNP be held constant while nations of less

3. Paul A. Samuelson, *Economics*, New York, 1948.

than average affluence are accorded the surpluses formerly enjoyed by the nations above the average.

Mere increase in production is not the essential enemy of the environment. Technical methods differ in what molecules they unleash and withdraw from the fossil fuels our ancestors inherited. Whereas fission as an energy source might improve the stratosphere, atmosphere and water resources in comparison with the combined use of fuels such as wood, coal and oil, the use of fission might accentuate the danger of nuclear war. The trade-offs are grave, and agreements among citizens in our democracies are hard to come by.

Galbraith, in his work The Affluent Society,[4] *was one of the precursors of the critique of consumerism, of the production of goods which, as he lucidly observed, was becoming an end in itself rather than serving human happiness, and of societies that were more and more identifying success with the production of goods and income. His opinion has not changed, yet he offered his recipe with great prudence.*

Galbraith Clearly the continuous increase in production is damaging to the environment. But I want to be practical, and saying we should stop economic expansion just isn't. Therefore I concentrate my attention on how we minimize the adverse effect of increasing production on the environment, and not on the fact of increasing production as such. Moreover, there's a practical political question here. People who are concerned with the environment are generally from the more fortunate communities, and I'm not at all persuaded that those who have a high standard of living should lecture the poor on reducing their consumption of goods.

'Isn't the quantity of production in excess of what the planet can bear?' As we have seen, Malinvaud formulated this question as part of his general evaluation of the problem of the environment. But faced explicitly with the question of growth in production, which environmentalists indicate as one of the cruxes of the planet's ecological crisis, and faced with the hypothesis of a reduction in consumption, with the change in living patterns that would entail, his response was extremely evasive.

Malinvaud It's a problem that goes beyond the economy. It's more of a social problem, which concerns the way we live now ...

Yes, but growth in production is one of the rules of the present economic system, and the great majority of economists regard it as indispensable.

---

4. John K. Galbraith, *The Affluent Society*, Boston, 1958.

Not the economists, the politicians ...

OK, the politicians, but the economists too ...

As I've already said, there is a great deal of uncertainty. If we bear in mind the great fears of the past, Malthus, the oil crisis, we may take a calmer view. However, there is a serious probability that what has so far been a false alarm could become reality. And if that is true, then the whole of society has got to start dealing with it, and immediately. I'm a moderate, I have a simple life, I have never believed that happiness is linked to economic growth. Obviously, if I look at the young, I can't deny that there is a lot of waste. But this isn't a problem for economists.

But isn't waste written into the form of our present economic system? Isn't it connected to and a function of the exponential growth in production?

No, no, no. The economic system could easily adapt itself to a different way of life.

But accumulation, which is a basic category of the present economic system, requires an increase in production, and so of consumption, whether useful or not, doesn't it?

It requires an increase in productivity. And that is not necessarily the same as an increase in production. It could mean working less.

Would you like to see a general reduction in working hours?

What I would like to see is people realizing that our grandchildren might have much less than we have today, and that we have to take decisions about this. If this isn't done, well, in that case I'm a doom merchant. But it's a matter of changing not the economic system, but the whole conception of life and the functioning of society ...

Which the economic system is one of the bases of.

Yes, well, no one's saying that the economic system functions perfectly.

So you're saying that we need to take radical measures, but so far we have taken only marginal measures?

I didn't say we had to take radical measures ...

You may not have used that word, but when you say you're a doom merchant if we don't make adequate provisions ...

I was talking of probabilities. Obviously, in my view we have to bear these in mind. But they are decisions in relation to which I have no more competence than any other member of the planet. It all depends on people: will they get used to the idea of giving up something they consider good?

So on the whole we need to reduce consumerism and the growth rate?

I don't know, we must wait and see. The population explosion is another explosive factor, and has just as serious effects on the environment as the growth in production ...

Among the leading economists we can, at least, find one man whose opinion has not substantially changed over the years: since 1972, to be precise.[5]

Meade Given the structural pattern of the economy, pollution and the exhaustion of natural resources depend and will depend in the future on the absolute level of total economic activity. This means that it is necessary to restrain both the rate of growth of population and, at least in the developed countries, the rate of growth of consumption per head. This points to the need for a fundamental change of emphasis in economic policies in the rich countries. In general, attention needs to be paid to a more equal distribution of what is produced rather than to a boosting of the growth of production.

Not everyone, however, was as worried by the idea of a continual exponential growth in the production of goods as by the arguments of the environmentalists who talk of the need to reduce consumerism, the production of superfluous goods, the waste of energy and raw materials.

Friedman Who is to decide what is superfluous? Proposals of this kind mean that the citizen should not be free to make choices about his ordinary everyday behaviour, that others should decide for him what and how much to consume.

Environmentalists are aware that it is a very difficult problem ...

It's not difficult, it's immoral. It's contrary to the values of freedom we believe in, according to which I decide for myself, and I'm responsible for the effects of my choices on other people, and I pay for what I get from others. Your question means wanting to substitute individual responsibility with bureaucratic responsibility.

Believe me, all environmentalists consider this problem, but they consider another problem too, which concerns the well-being of citizens as much as their freedom to consume: is the Earth a limited entity or not?

Of course.

So can a limited entity support unlimited growth in production without catastrophic consequences for everyone?

I don't know how much the Earth can support, and you don't know either. Nobody a hundred years ago would have thought it could support what is being produced now. There is an appropriate regulatory institution, the market, in which prices are adjusted to real costs: it's an automatic process which will place limits on itself,

---

5. James E. Meade, *The Theory of Economic Externalities*, Institut Universitaire d'Hautes Etudes Internationales, Geneva, 1973.

with full responsibility lying with population, and without anyone imposing limits from outside.

But environmental degradation is increasing terribly, and the market doesn't seem to be doing anything about it. On the contrary, the so-called 'laws of the market' foresee a continual expansion of production of all types of goods, and so of pollution. Cars, for example. Automobile manufacturers look to the East and the Third World as enormous new markets to be exploited. Do you think it's possible to give a car to every inhabitant of the Third World? What will the consequences be?

I don't know, I don't know. I'm sorry, but you're talking about countries that have been managed so badly they can't even afford the car. But if they are better governed and they open up to the market, why not?

Take an overpopulated country like China, for example. A car for every Chinese?

If the Chinese want the automobile, and I hope they do, they will create the conditions to have it. Apart from anything else, China has resources that are enormously greater than those of Western countries, but industrial efficiency in China is a fraction of ours. If they really develop and reach the necessary income level, and start to buy automobiles, the price of automobiles will come down.

And the pollution, the traffic, the waste? I'm thinking of the situation as it is in Mexico City or Palermo ... Enlarging the automobile market to the whole world would mean aggravating a situation that is already very serious. I use the car as an example, but I could mention any other product.

Why don't you think of well-run cities such as San Francisco, the cities of New Mexico or Wisconsin or Arizona? ... That's the American way of life. Do you think it's a bad way to live?

I believe, and so do the environmentalists, that there are limits, beyond which it becomes bad.

But it's not up to you to decide. It's up to individuals on the basis of market mechanisms. This talk about waste and superfluous goods means basically that some people are worse than others and they don't deserve to have what others already have. And I find this immoral.

So you think we can go on producing more and more ad infinitum?

I don't know, I don't know. The question has no meaning. If we look at the past we see that every prediction about limits turned out to be wrong. All I know is that we have an institution that can stop us going too far: if we go too far the market will stop us through the price mechanism.

So you're not at all worried about the environment?

Not at all. We have many problems in our society. The environment isn't the most serious one.

While not denying that growth has bad side-effects, Becker too was inclined to believe that the instruments available would be able to deal with them.

Becker Apart from the mechanisms of the market, which, along with taxes, can do a lot, new technology, such as the electric car, which we are working on now, can do an immense amount. Besides, I believe we can induce people to change their behaviour through democratic means: in some ways this is already happening. So let's not get alarmist about this, and let's take with a pinch of salt the prophets of doom, who will certainly be disproved by the facts.

But are you saying that production doesn't cause pollution?

Of course it does, to a certain extent it causes pollution ...

And so the exponential growth in production is bound to cause a similar growth in environmental degradation ...

I don't think it's correct to say that a growth in production determines a proportional growth in pollution. We can bring in all sorts of innovations that greatly reduce pollution, materials used up till now can be substituted, machinery can be invented that uses less energy ... In some cases garbage is a problem, and we need to intervene heavily with taxes, but on the whole we shouldn't even call it waste any longer: collecting empty bottles, reusing and re-cycling are a new source of wealth today. Of course, we need to develop policies that encourage all this. But reducing pollution is possible.

Perhaps it is possible to contain each individual act of aggression on the environment, but the worrying feature is their increasing number. Can the planet resist a series of attacks that may be less serious, but which are growing in number? For example, if you burn your finger, you hurt yourself but you get better; if you burn your whole body, you die. This is what the Earth is risking. Because it is surely undeniable that the situation is worsening rapidly. I remember, the first time I saw tar on a beach, twenty or twenty-five years ago, I had no idea what it was. Now all the beaches of the Mediterranean are covered with tar.

Yes, I understand ...

And that's not all. Often even the clean-up appliances pollute: the filters, scrubbers, and chemical substances for dispersing oil slicks, and so on. We have a twofold production of goods that pollute and goods that remove the pollution – which in turn cause further pollution themselves during production, or clean up in one way and pollute in another.

Yes, there's no question, some of them do that. Pollution has increased a lot. Perhaps we need to make distinctions: the oceans, for example, aren't owned by anyone and the externalities have increased, while in other parts of the world the water has gotten better. But yes, I think that's true, there *has* been an increase in pollution. Its consequences in terms of health so far have been limited: on the whole the world's population is getting healthier, not less healthy. We have to make a policy. The question is what should be the criteria. We must do things in a balanced way without panicking, because, yes, pollution has got worse, but the world isn't going to hell, it hasn't gone to hell. But we have to make a policy. Some people say, 'Well, we're rich, let's stop the poor countries that want to become rich from improving their position.' But then pollution would affect other countries ... it's an international problem. We now have international agencies trying to reach international agreements. Perhaps the best way is to balance the benefits and the costs. I don't think it does any good to dramatize or exaggerate the problem as many environmentalists do, who have been unwilling to face any proposal different from their own.

Don't you think that, given that, economists should take more interest in the environment?

Yes, but they're starting to. I'm president of an international association and in the near future we're having a congress devoted entirely to the environment. But you're right, yes, we should do more.

The environmentalists' condemnation of consumerism and waste, and their consequent demand for changes in lifestyles, which Friedman dismissed with such contempt and horror, left others uncertain too – even some of those who were seriously concerned about the condition of the environment and who were active proponents of corrective measures.

Spaventa   A new lifestyle? No, I really don't think it's possible.

I know it's difficult, I know no one is in a position to decide who needs what, and what our real needs are, and so on. But all the same, the greatest damage to the environment has coincided with the greatest explosion in productivity and consumption.

I don't know.

But is there a problem or not?

It's a problem with no solution, except using authoritarian methods which I can't accept.

Perhaps something could be thought out at international level? Some people – James Meade, for example – suggest that we should reduce consumption in the West and increase it in the Third World ...

Oh, come off it. How? From a macroeconomic point of view it's obvious: the Third World needs aid, let's give them capital and consume less here, and concentrate our exports on those countries. Then they'll start the same kind of production and consumption habits as we have. We can hardly deny them a refrigerator, can we?

Yes, but wait a moment. It's one thing giving everyone a refrigerator, it's quite another making a refrigerator that only lasts a few years, and that can't be repaired because the spare parts aren't produced, and which, according to the television, has to be new or it's no good. Result – you have to buy another.

I realize the problem exists. It's undeniable that there is a significant element of waste. But this is a moral judgement, and these sermons against consumerism just don't convince me. How we are to solve the question economically I don't know, and neither do the environmental economists.

But does it make sense to think that we can go on producing at this rate, polluting here, purifying there, while inevitably the ecological condition of the planet goes on getting worse?

You and I are on two completely different wavelengths. You're saying, 'Oh God, what a mess!' I'm saying, 'Let's take things one at a time. First of all let's do something about the pollution in Rome.' What is beyond a doubt is that governments should do more than they do. Apart from anything else, disarmament now should free resources which could be devoted to the environment. Using the peace dividend in this way would be a great opportunity, if governments were sensitive to the problem.

Hahn I am rather hostile myself to this consumerism argument. A great deal of what is called consumerism is a humane improvement in people's lot.

That's true. But not all of it …

No, but a great deal. I don't believe in the idea of a new model. There have been many attempts to change human nature. The most recent was Mao's, and it wasn't very successful. All we can do is try to improve society a little, but not change it. This is true for the environment too. And if, as people say, there is a catastrophe, something will be done.

Wouldn't it be better to prevent the catastrophe?

Yes, if we knew how to …

If we don't think about the problem we'll never know how to.

No, no, no. Let me quote Russell. He said that the secret of decent academic work is to ask the right questions. The right question is one for which you can conceive of an answer.

I'm absolutely convinced that we need to ask the right questions about the environment, but I know that very few people are trying to do so. And on the whole the economists aren't among them.

Look, we can do quite a lot with local problems, but it's the global problem that we can't handle. It's a question of poor countries, a very bad distribution of wealth in the world, and we know the causes of all this, but there's no way we can do anything about it. It's like a sort of natural phenomenon. I think Malthus was right: what happens when you get this enormous growth in population? Disaster. What can you do? It's nothing to do with a lack of knowledge. Not always, anyway. Often it's sheer lack of will to do what we all know is necessary. For example, we should make massive transfers of capital towards the underdeveloped countries, but we're just not willing to do it.

Apart from anything else, aid of this kind to the Third World would mean a serious worsening of the situation of the environment.

Of course it would. And what are you going to do about it? This isn't economics …

One suggestion is that we should try not to reproduce in the vast area of the Third World the economic model of Western countries, which can be seen now as extremely dangerous for the planet and for the human race itself.

So what kind of model would you like to see then? Look, I know India. They need hospitals, houses, quite ordinary things before they begin to think of lipstick and motorcars … And that is a huge piece of growth. But every time you build a hospital or a motorcycle or anything, you pollute. Industrialization is inevitable and pollution will increase. This is not an intellectual question at all, it's not a question of not knowing what to do, it's a question of there being over one thousand million Chinese who want to live freer lives, work less hard, go to the cinema, have cars and explore their own country, and then go to Italy and see Venice. These are natural desires …

And absolutely legitimate. But if these desires are satisfied to the extent they have been in the West, then this will be the end of the world …

I think you're too pessimistic. It's a race between knowledge and development. For example, if we can succeed with nuclear fusion the whole problem changes completely.

But it's not just a matter of energy. Think of what one car per person would mean: 5 billion cars … is there the physical space for them?

The market can do something about that. Obviously if there were billions and billions of cars, the price of petrol would hit the roof, and this would automatically lower the demand for cars. But we should think of other possible forms of technological development, small electric cars, for example, which would carry just one person ... I think we have too little imagination. There are scientific possibilities we cannot even conceive of today. And then, I just don't believe in catastrophe. Of course, the environment is a serious problem, but I don't believe there's going to be a catastrophe. Apart from anything else, there are also other possible catastrophes of a geological kind, a new ice age, changes in the level of the sea, flooding ...

Which could be caused by global warming ...

It could be. But it could also happen on its own, because the inclination of the earth in its orbit round the sun changes. All sorts of things can happen ... My guess is we'll survive.

Sylos Labini   I've said it many times before and I'll say it again: systematic industrial development, which has had a fiftyfold overall increase in total volume in the last hundred years, can have terrible effects on the industrialized countries themselves. It's obvious the developing countries should follow a different way from the one we have pursued in the West.

You've written that 'we need to set in motion a gradual but radical transformation of the apparatus of production and the organization of our cities; otherwise the catastrophe can be put off but not avoided'.[6] You have spoken of 'forms of consumption that are not only useless but harmful', and have explicitly stressed quantity of production as the prime cause of the huge proportions the environmental problem has assumed.[7] I imagine you agree with the environmentalists who talk about the need to reduce consumerism, waste, superfluous production ...

First of all, let's rule out decrees of any kind. The problem of the environment needs to be faced and resolved, but not with authoritarian methods. Authoritarianism should always be rejected, even in alarming situations, because we risk leaping out of the frying pan into the fire. But let's face it, the greens with their sermons aren't much use either. You can't be preached into saving. There are other ways, and taxation is certainly one of the most efficient. I've been saying for ages that we should raise the price of petrol, tax it heavily. Let's not forget that the greatest technical advances in energy saving were made after the oil crisis. Not that this means blocking development. That shouldn't be our aim – it can't be an aim for our

---

6. Paulo Sylos Labini, *Nuove tecnologie e disoccupazione*, Laterza, Bari, 1989, p. 207.

7. Ibid.

civilization. Development needs partly to be slowed down – and that doesn't worry me at all – and partly modified. It means finding the optimum between these two actions, maintaining a balance. But I repeat: no decrees or models imposed from above.

Simon Growth is certainly a problem, not only for us but for the whole world. I've spent a lot of time in China, and I don't think you'd be very warmly received if you told them they had to stay at their present standard of living because their factories make too much smoke. The problem is not preventing human beings from being too productive, but how they can be productive in a way that is harmonious with the environment. It's a big problem and we haven't found a solution yet. It's the problem of pollution, new energy sources and dealing with waste. It's the problem of the five billion people in the world today becoming 10 billion. Increasing production depends on the fact that we want comfortable lives and we don't know how to decide how many people there should be in the world.

You are an economist who is also interested in the psychology of consumer behaviour. Don't you think it should be possible to reduce consumption by influencing the behaviour patterns and the psychology of people?

Changing people's basic attitudes is very difficult. There have been two major experiments in our lifetime intended to make new people, in Russia and in China, and no one thinks they changed people very much. The question is how we can produce without destroying the environment. Some significant changes are already taking place: people are starting to want more services rather than more material goods. So the problem can partly take care of itself. The best way to convince people to consume less is to put a price on goods that measures not only the cost of production but also the effect on the environment.

Taxation, then?

Yes, but also pollution standards, making energy more efficient, and inducing people to buy the best kind, regulating industry's consumption of electricity, and setting up a commission to look into this. There are a lot of things we can do, but I don't believe there is one single solution to problems of this kind.

You have made a study of limited rationality.[8] Does a society that wastes so much seem rational to you? Take the overheating of buildings in winter and the excessive air conditioning in summer. They have gone so far now that instead of eliminating discomfort, which would be the natural thing to

---

8. Herbert A. Simon, *Casualità, razionalità, organizzazione*, Il Mulino, Bologna, 1985.

*do, they make us suffer the cold in summer and the heat in winter – all
this when energy is one of our major problems.*

Personally, I'm sympathetic to what you're saying. But you're
telling me about the things people do that you don't like. But
people who keep their houses at a temperature of 72 degrees like
them that way ...

*But they have to open the windows all the time, and in summer they
have to put a pullover on if they don't want to catch a cold ...*

Sometimes, yes, that's true. There's a lot of human irrationality.
Do you have a good prescription for getting rid of it?

*What about fixing by law maximum limits to heating and air con-
ditioning? But to stay with this subject, although it is just one of many ...*

Laws like this have been attacked in some European countries.
Individuals are different: some like it hot, old people need to be
warmer ...

But if we can fix standards for pollution, why not for central heating?

That was done during the oil crisis. I think only a limited number
of problems can be solved in this way. I'm not considered an
orthodox economist but I do think taxation can achieve many
environmental goals without setting limits by law. If we impose
what I call 'full-cost pricing', which includes the cost of the environmental damage of what is consumed, in many cases people will
consume less.

Solow   I agree that our society is too consumption-oriented. Take
the car as an example. Using the car to go a few metres is profoundly
wrong. And I'd still say that if cars didn't cause pollution, if they
were made of paper and vanished into thin air when they were used
up and replaced. It's a bad habit that I'd like to see changed. I use
the car very little myself: I go from my home to the campus on
foot, using public transport. But this is a cultural problem; it's got
nothing to do with the environment, which is an economic problem.

And at an economic level what do you suggest to combat consumerism?

I don't think there's just one way of dealing with environmental
problems. But raising costs is a big help in many cases. For example,
one of the most serious problems in the United States is how to
deal with waste: how to get rid of old automobiles, for example.
We have 100 million automobiles driving round in the United States
and every year a few million of them die. So there's thousands of
tons of metal to be disposed of in some way. The economist's way
of dealing with it is this: we estimate what it costs society to dispose
of an automobile. Suppose it's $500. Whenever you buy a car, you
pay an extra $500 in tax. When you dispose of it, if you can show

you recycled 50 per cent of it the government gives you $250 back plus interest, if you manage to recycle all of it you get the whole $500 back. But if you leave it on the streets or take it to the garbage dump, then you have paid the entire social cost. There is another advantage to a policy of this kind: automobile manufacturers have a strong interest in producing cars that can easily be recycled.

And this would reduce production too ...

In part. But mainly of things that are a burden to the environment in favour of things that are not. In short, I want to organize the economy in such a way that things that do not damage the environment cost less, and increase environment-friendly production. Books, for example. It's true, there's a problem with the paper. But we can design a tax that will get paper recycled. And perhaps people would start reading books instead of driving back and forth in their cars.

But this means changing people's mentality and habits completely ...

Anything we do to improve the environment requires a change of mentality. I don't think it will take that much time to get across to people who have lived in a market economy, a capitalist society, that you must pay for what you consume, including your consumption of the environment. But I don't think the environmentalists have better answers than we do. People who are used to living in advanced countries don't want to consume less, they don't want a simpler life. No one wants to go back to the candle, but they do want to have less pollution. This is a contradiction we cannot ignore. So it's perhaps a matter of substituting rather than reducing, changing the composition of our consumption, perhaps having fewer goods and more services, or the same quantity of consumption but of higher quality and less damaging to the environment. I am against consumerism as an end in itself, but I think it's a more efficacious policy not to say it.

Hartje Reduce consumption, say the ecologists. I see it like this: environmental policies will have to be generally intensified in the near future, and if we take serious action to eliminate or neutralize all pollutants, bring down energy consumption, develop more environment-friendly forms of transport and agricultural production and so on, we are not that far away from what environmentalists want. If you think of the normal distribution of GNP, 20 per cent of that is for investment, and 80 per cent is basically consumption. It's clear that this proportion is going to change, because we shall have to invest a lot more in protecting the environmental capital, and consumption will be reduced automatically. A neoclassical economist would ask how much we have to add to the price if we want to include all the costs of environmental policies. And the result would be the same – reduced consumption. It's a different starting point but the final result is the same. You can either clean up technology or reduce the volume of consumption. Which of these two factors is more important? You seem to think perhaps the second is more important ...

I think that they are both important.

Yes, I agree. But where do we start from? If we consider the question in terms of policies that have a chance of being developed, then it's easier to begin with technology. It's something people can understand, while they don't realize that they have to give up a whole lot of unnecessary things they consume. But once you achieve the first objective, the second follows naturally, it becomes more convincing to everybody. This is politically the most practical path to follow.

Hirschman Reduce growth, yes, it could be done, and in some cases it should be done. But I have the impression that in some sectors there will be a spontaneous reduction in growth quite naturally, due to saturation. There are already signs of this kind with the automobile. There's no doubt that the traffic problem will force us to invent something new or rediscover something old, such as buses, trams, public transport ... I spent a few months in Berlin recently, and there public transport has been relaunched, and it functions much better than in American cities. But this is possible only when there is already a widespread environmental awareness, and that only happens when there is a crisis. It's very difficult to get a person to reduce his consumption if other people don't, and if there isn't a powerful set of circumstances which force him to.

Some of the criticisms of anti-consumer proposals were not limited to fears of authoritarianism, but were based on a consideration of some of the largest sociopolitical problems.

Wallerstein I think that when the environmentalists talk about waste, consumerism and the need to encourage different lifestyles they are touching on a very important problem, but in a rather simplistic way. Of course, consumerism – by which is meant expenditure on consumption which the person using the term does not deem socially necessary – affects the total problem. But the question is, who decides what is socially necessary? There is a part of the ecology movement that is trying to impose its values on the unwashed masses, whom they think are too foolish to understand their true interests. The unwashed masses want to consume more, and the environmentalists come along and say 'If you consume more you will create all sorts of problems.' This is perfectly true, but the political risk of pursuing such a line is that it is the puritanism of people who are relatively well off and who wish to reduce their standard of living, and simultaneously impose upon people who are not well off a non-improvement in their standard of living.

My favourite example of this problem is from an international conference on the problems of the ozone layer. The Chinese delegates said, 'We need to eliminate chlorofluorocarbons in refrigerator production? But this is the only production process we can reasonably engage in. If we don't, we will have a still lower standard of living. Are the richer countries ready to pay the difference for the installation of alternative modes of production?' But the bill for that was so enormous that no one was ready to agree to it. Faced with environmental problems, there are only two things you can do. One is spend a lot of money, but the question is, who is going to spend it and that opens up the whole issue of world inequality.

Since the bill is so enormous if you want to do something serious about the environment, there is no way it can be responded to without talking about the whole system of world inequality. The alternative is to get everybody to reduce their standard of living, but I don't think that's a winning ticket for the two thirds of the world that haven't gotten to the point where they have a standard of living worth reducing. Furthermore, there are very dangerous side effects: people who push that to an extreme can get onto very dangerous political ground. There is the so-called Deep Ecology movement which has made some really embarrassing statements, like when they said that, after all, AIDS wasn't such a bad thing as it was killing off a lot of people and therefore there'd be less consumption.

Yes, but statements like that have nothing whatever to do with the arguments of serious environmentalists ...

Yes, yes, but it's always interesting to note extreme positions and try to understand the logic underneath. Anyway, I don't think that reducing consumption, as a practical proposition over the next fifty years, is going to be politically very significant. It may be possible to persuade the tenth of the world population that is well off to reduce their consumption by 5 per cent. But if you're talking about big strategies over fifty or a hundred years to attack the environment problem, I don't think anti-consumerism is the fundamental tactic to follow. I do agree that consumerism has gotten out of hand, that it's become a sort of collective madness, and I don't expect that two hundred years from now people will behave in the same way. But

I don't think that focusing on that issue is the way to tackle the problem politically.

I see what you mean, but can we go on producing more and more all the time? In your book, Historical Capitalism, *you discuss the irrationality of a system founded on endless accumulation.[9] But it is this endlessly increasing accumulation and production that causes the destruction of the natural environment. Isn't this further evidence of the irrationality of the system?*

Oh, absolutely. I quite agree about the irrationality of consumerism, I've said so. But I am convinced that you can't tackle it as an isolated irrationality without considering the other irrationalities too. You can't single out the environmental problem. You can't single it out in terms of the emergency of the ozone layer, and you can't single out that other great environmental problem of the destruction of the world's forests. It can't be resolved politically in isolation from other problems.

In your book you criticize the idea of progress that has developed inside the capitalist industrial system, and that has been taken over by the left too. You support your criticism with reference to the Third World, which you say has not improved its position at all with the introduction of the industrial model, but has been worsening it steadily. Now, you said a little while back that we cannot force the peoples of the Third World to reduce a standard of living which is already very low. Agreed. But can we continue to force on these countries a pattern that has had negative effects for them, and look at them only as new possible markets to exploit, giving everyone a car, a television, rivers of Coca-Cola, mountains of plastic goods and so on?

Not only can we continue to do it, we will go on doing it. Furthermore, there is a way in which the environmental movement has actually abetted this, perhaps unwittingly, by obliging politicians to respond to the problems on the spot. One of the responses was in passing new laws concerning clean-up provisions, which increase the costs of production, which gives manufacturers one more reason to move their factories to countries where there is lower environmental pressure. Of course the environmentalists have only given an extra push to a process that had already started. The percentage of persons employed in manufacturing activities today is almost equal (and increasing) in semiperipheral countries to that in core countries, where it is diminishing. This reality also displaces the locus of problems of toxicity and waste. It's South Korea that will now have to worry about what to do with chemical waste and not Germany, which makes people in Germany a little happier, but from a world

---

9. Immanuel Wallerstein, *Historical Capitalism*, New York, 1983.

perspective doesn't solve the problem at all. So, the overall amount of production will go on increasing, because we have to support a population that is increasing, and the situation will go on getting worse.

Now you ask me, can we continue to do this? It depends what you mean by 'can'. Will we reach certain limits? Will it come to a point where people will say 'Stop'? Perhaps it could happen when Korea, Malaysia, India and twenty other countries become completely industrialized, and it becomes clear that they haven't thereby solved the income gap problem with the core countries. That will be deeply disillusioning and will put an end to the expectation of national development. This is already happening in Latin America, which was the first area of the Third World to follow this path: they invested their political and administrative energy in trying to industrialize. Now they are quite badly off, and they no longer have the illusion that state investment in industrial activities will automatically improve the standard of living. That could lead to the system breaking down. Now can it go on? This involves what we think will happen politically in the world in the next fifty years or so.

I was really referring to the constant increase in the enormous quantity of production as a physical fact: its encumbrance, its weight, its toxicity, its continuing presence as waste all inevitably contribute to environmental degradation. The development of human civilization has always been in some way at the expense of nature, all human activity has damaged the environment to a greater or lesser extent, but up to a certain point in human history nature was able to heal its wounds, which were quantitively limited. But when the harm increases to the extent it has now, up to what point can the planet resist?

So the question is, will the Earth die? I don't feel I know enough technically to take a strong position on whether we're on the edge of ecological disaster. I tend, however, to be mildly sceptical. I think we're on the edge of political rather than ecological disaster. Can we go on another hundred years or more from the point of view of ecological resistance, the capacity of the biomass to sustain itself? I suspect that we can, because we can partially solve various problems technically, and we have more space than we think. So when I read in the newspapers that we can manage another twenty years and then we'll all die … well, perhaps they're right, it's worth taking seriously as a problem, and building one's argument around biological catastrophe is a good short-term tactic. But in the long term there are more serious economic problems, which have more political weight. Once again, it's a matter of my tactical discomfort with the environmental movement. Preaching disaster is an old story. We've had a lot of religious movements prophesying the end of the world.

Yes, but this isn't prophecy: it's something that already exists. Just look at the Mediterranean with its oil spills, urban waste, agricultural waste and wars ...

Yes, I know, but if we took the money we've just spent in the Persian Gulf and used it on the Mediterranean ... that's an awful lot of money ...

Polluting and cleaning up ... repairing damage with the same means, the same logic ...

Well, any intervention in nature causes damage. If I kill off the mosquitoes that carry yellow fever I disrupt some vital cycle or other. So it means ensuring our choices are sensible and cause the minimum damage. But you began by asking me if the environment was an economic problem. I think it's more an economic problem than a biological problem. The biological doomsday is further down the line than the economic doomsday, so we will first of all have to face it as an economic issue. We could, so to speak, postpone the biological doomsday by reallocating our worldwide expenditure of money. If in the next twenty or thirty years we had a world government that could decide everything, decide to spend money on x rather than y, we could probably increase production and postpone the biological doomsday. But what we have to do first is get out of this crazy system and make some rational decisions about what to do.

What would you suggest?

No one in the West wants to give up what the modern world has to offer in comfort, speed of communication and better health; and the underdeveloped countries want these things too. Everyone wants the benefits of modernity without its negative features. Certain decisions have to be made, and we need some collective decision-making process which we don't have at the moment. These problems won't be solved by minor reforms. Yes, I've said that in print, one of the issues that will mobilize us over the next fifty years will be the environment. It's so clear, and it's hitting very close to home, it's the world in which we are living ...

Altvater The question of the environment is essentially a question of quantity. The dissipation of energy and matter in entropy is an inescapable law of nature, but today we are witnessing an acceleration of these irreversible processes of degradation.

An acceleration that is difficult to arrest ...

Exactly, because halting it would mean introducing other forms of production and consumption, because growth stems from the profit system. When there is profit there is accumulation, and accumulation means growth. But there's no such thing as capitalism without profit, and so a non-growth economy cannot be a capitalist economy. And this is one of the contradictions of mainstream environmentalist thinking, even among those who hope for zero growth. Zero growth in a capitalist economy has no meaning. On the other hand, zero growth is possible alongside enormous consumption of raw materials and energy, as happened in the socialist bloc. Only zero growth in the transformation of energy and matter would lead to an improvement in the environment, but this is unimaginable. So the idea of zero growth is a nonsense. What we must try to do is reduce the rate of acceleration of the processes of entropy, and contain entropy both nationally and globally as much as possible, and a proper use of technology is fundamental in this. It's no use being against industry or technology; what matters is knowing how to put them to good use.

From what you are saying, I imagine you regard the environmentalists' proposal to reduce consumption, waste and the superfluous as a nonsense too?

The truth is that all this would involve a radical transformation in the rules of day-to-day behaviour, and so of production and technology too. It wouldn't necessarily mean a worsening in the standard of living, but the transition to another way of living. It would be a revolution, not of the traditional socialist or communist kind, but a green revolution.

Is there any possibility of this coming true?

I really can't see any. Today we are faced with a global economy, which includes the use of energy, raw materials, technology, etcetera, and any threat to this system sets off a global reaction. Bush's idea of a new world order is very serious, it's the projection into the future of the system that is already being actualized on an economic plane. So I see no prospect of a revolution.

So there's no hope for the environment?

The environment in itself does not exist without reference to all the other economic, social and political coordinates for the possible development of humanity. Thought about the environment will get nowhere if it doesn't translate the ecological problems into political terms, so that action can be taken in relation not only to nature but instead to the whole of the environment, in all its complexity.

CHAPTER 7

QUANTITY AND/OR QUALITY

The hypothesis of the environmentalists, that it might be possible to halt or even simply to reduce the growth in production that has characterized the two centuries of industrial development, seems to terrify economists. It is flatly rejected, or rather not even taken into consideration, by the most conservative of them and those least interested in the environment, and (as we have seen) it is no more warmly received by those who are more sensitive to the problem and who have a genuine desire to face it, or even by some of the most noted environmentalists.

The possibility of reconciling growth and the protection of ecological balances, whether as a commitment or just a hope, was the most common position among the economists I spoke to, who were in effect taking over the concept of 'sustainable development' launched in 1987 by the Brundtland Report[1] and since then subject to the most diverse interpretations, sometimes analysed seriously and in depth, sometimes no more than a tautological slogan.

A significant number of them emphasized the importance of a different quality of production, as a corrective to the most destructive aspects of industrial activity. Technological innovation, integrated with various kinds of provisions and manoeuvres, is the instrument in which most of them placed their hopes.

Sylos Labini I don't accept the thesis that sees a halt to economic growth as a civilized objective.

But economic growth is the essential category for the type of development you have often criticized for its destructiveness.

But there's growth and growth. Take the case of agricultural growth. The banning of pesticides would certainly mean a growth reduction of 2.5 or 2 per cent. That doesn't worry me at all if we're

---

1. World Commission on Environment and Development, *Our Common Future*, Oxford University Press, Oxford, 1987.

talking of countries where famine doesn't exist. Where it does, we should try to maintain the same growth rate, eliminating or reducing to a minimum the use of toxic products. Difficult, you say? If it were easy there'd be no problem. Yes, it's difficult but not impossible. In this case it's a matter of encouraging research in technical innovations and alternative products, which is not only difficult but also very costly. I'm convinced we need to think seriously about forming a large permanent international organization at the United Nations with responsibilities for the environment at global level, and for sustainable growth policies, especially as far as the developing countries are concerned.

Environmentalists assert that 'sustainable growth' is a contradiction in terms. As the ecosystem is finite, unlimited growth can't be sustainable. They tend to speak in terms of 'sustainable development'.

It's a rather formal distinction. Growth is simply the quantitive aspect of development.

But that's just the point: is this quantity of indefinite growth acceptable?

Indefinite, no ...

So where are the limits then?

I'm referring to short-term or mid-term periods. Obviously infinite growth is unsustainable. But our problem is this: can we say today, 'That's enough' or not? With the Third World in mind, we can't. Nor can we if we take into account the relation between growth and employment, which can be modified but not completely eliminated. But we can pursue sustainable growth if we take action on what it is made up of: an increase in high-tech services; more highly qualified jobs which take account of an increasing average level of education; a slow but systematic modification of the production system that would give major importance to technology and research, and would be alert to the choice of non-polluting production processes. And all this, in the long run, cannot fail to have an effect on quantity as well.

Agambegian The problem is not growth or non-growth, but the structure and the quality of growth. Growth can be increased and quality improved. If we measure growth in terms of tons weight of production, it is obvious. In the United States, for example, they produce 10 million cars a year, while in the Soviet Union we produce 1.5 million. But we produce 160,000 tons of steel and the United States produces 70,000. If we modernize our industrial production sufficiently, we will be able to make five times more cars and reduce our production of steel by half, and so reduce pollution.

But don't you think that growth is in itself a cause of pollution? Ecological problems have become explosive during the boom in production of recent decades ...

Yes, I know, but energy consumption, for example, has been significantly decreasing in the West since the seventies. I remember when that famous book *The Limits to Growth* came out: the alternative seemed to be between stability and reduction, while growth was out of the question.[2] But since then production has continued to rise in the West while energy consumption has gone down. Not here, though. We have been consuming more and more energy and raw materials. One of our tasks is to reduce energy consumption in proportion to output by developing an electronic industry, using solar energy, and contracting the mining industry. In this way growth that is not destructive to the environment will be possible.

Leontief A lot depends on what we mean by economic growth. There's no unanimity about this, even among economists. Some think, and I'm one of them, that pollution and growth go hand in hand.

You have written that production always causes pollution to a greater or lesser extent, and that pollution can never be completely eliminated because the clean-up technology creates a certain amount of pollution itself.[3] And this inevitably means that if the present rate of growth continues and the Third World reaches Western levels of growth, the disruption of the environment will increase dramatically.

Absolutely. Especially if we consider the problem of population growth, which is now more or less under control in the West, but in the Third World is very serious. And we should not forget the responsibility of the Catholic Church, which has absolutely no right to talk about the environment so long as it remains opposed to birth control.

And so?

Let's just think a moment. Modern aeroplanes are much lighter than old ones, and so are many other products. Perhaps pollution increases in proportion to tonnage. If we miniaturize things we can increase production without increasing the overall volume. In the same way, if we are able to bring about other forms of technological progress, less polluting production processes that consume less energy, different forms of energy ... well, at least we will slow down the rate of environmental degradation. In any case, saying 'Stop pro-

---

2. Massachusetts Institute of Technology–Club di Roma, *I limiti dello sviluppo*, Mondatori, Milan, 1972.

3. Wassily Leontief, *The Future of the World Economy*, Oxford, 1977.

duction!' – what does it mean? Completely freeze the economy? You can't stop human beings. Fortunately there is a net tendency towards an increase in services, and they don't cause pollution.

Some do. Tourism, for example. It has destroyed some Italian cities, it's destroying some beautiful parts of the countryside, it has a very significant role in the pollution of the sea …

I agree. Florence and Venice have become unrecognizable. And some natural parks are at risk too … So perhaps we should introduce restrictions? But what kind? Can we restrict human travel? And who is to decide who has the right to enter Venice and who doesn't?

It's extremely difficult. But isn't the tourist boom, too, part of our society's characteristic tendency towards overconsumption and overproduction, production as an end in itself?

I agree absolutely. But we live in a society based on the profit motive, and the Soviet Union's attempt to create a different society has hardly produced positive results. Perhaps it's a matter of education. A higher level of education for everyone could be useful.

Simon First of all we have to ask ourselves: are we chasing a Utopia or are we talking about what can in fact be done about the environment? I think the only rational way to face the problem of growth is to observe our society as it is and to ask what a tolerable steady state would be one hundred years from now. And what do we have to know and what do we have to do to get there?

Do you have a precise idea of what a society of that kind would be like?

Not really. That depends on calculating what kinds of loads the environment can tolerate in terms of population, energy and temperature, and so on.

Many environmentalists are convinced that the planet cannot even tolerate present levels of production …

Well, you can look at that in two ways. You can say 'We just have to go back', or you can say 'We have to find ways of making it tolerable', through different and better sources of energy, for example, carrying on down the path of scientific and technological research; or by counting on people changing their patterns of behaviour, not by coercing them to do what we think they should do, but by bringing environmental costs into the decisions they make about their lives, that is, by raising prices.

Pearce No, I don't agree at all with those who want to lower levels of production and consumption. I think it's self-flagellatory: they're just giving themselves up to pessimism.

In your book you deal with the problem of sustainable development, saying that economic growth and respect for the environment may not only coexist but even be complementary.[4] But this undeniable contradiction between two quantities, one finite (the Earth), the other indefinite (economic growth) – don't you think sooner or later it will become explosive?

What you say may be true in the long run. Maybe. But before thinking in terms of a low-growth or zero-growth society, there are other things to be done. First of all, growth is not a physical concept: to the economist it is essentially the idea of adding value to resources. It's true that as you grow you tend to use up more resources, but you don't have to. A lot of environmental destruction takes place needlessly because we take development decisions without thinking about the environment at all. We haven't learned yet to 'design with nature', and that is what we need to do. And we would discover that we can have many of the benefits of development without destroying the environment. Of course, there will be environmental losses: how can you build new houses, new roads without destroying the environment? But we must get used to being fully aware of what the environmental losses are, and try to anticipate these, to compensate for them in some way. They are possible policies, which have not yet been adopted on a large enough scale. We need to do more in this direction.

But for some ecological economists it is not just a question of different modalities of growth, of a 'sustainability' to be pursued through appropriate policies and technologies. They distinguished growth from development, two concepts which, without semantic hair-splitting, some saw as absolutely antithetical. They pinned their hopes on new technology as well as on new economic rules, on a completely different approach to the relation between production and the natural environment. As can be seen, however, there was no unity of attitude among them. As we have already seen, Daly made a clear distinction between development and growth, but forecast that development would take place within a 'steady-state society', a society stable at the optimal level of growth.

Leipert Production, consumption and urban concentration have reached levels now that cannot safely be sustained much longer by the surrounding ecological system, by the limits of space and by the human race's capacity for assimilation. There can only be a lowering of standards of living.

You are quite close to Daly's views. Do you agree with his proposal?

---

4. David Pearce, Anil Markandya and Edward Barbier, *Blueprint for a Green Economy*, Earthscan, London, 1989.

No. I agree with his analysis of the problem. I agree that the level of inputs cannot be determined by the market. But I don't think we can define the right level of production and consumption on the basis of cost–benefit analysis of yesterday's production and consumption. And imagining a steady-state society in the future seems to me a bit mechanical. The ecological problem is too complicated for that, as it is connected with the complexity of ecosystems. This is going to be the biggest challenge for society and our politicians. I think we have to try to define a general project based on a relationship between society, economics and nature that can be reproduced in the future. Once this framework has been achieved, everyone involved can interact, they can use their creativity to create new technologies that use less energy and materials, new production processes that are more environment-friendly and so on, and they would have to be stimulated by strong incentives. Yes, because we must be realistic. We can't expect individuals who have grown up in a capitalist industrial society, used to considering personal interest first, suddenly to become ethical beings. Of course, we all dream of a better society, but we know that the transformation of values is a long-term process. In the meantime we must rely on incentives, we must encourage the birth of new economic activities through ecologically orientated incentives.

Passet Zero growth – I just don't believe in it. And still less in zero development.

Some time ago you expressed an extremely critical judgement about economic growth. You wrote that it was possible to identify economic growth with social well-being up to a certain point, but that beyond a certain level this relationship was overturned.[5]

That's true. But first of all we must distinguish between growth and development. Growth is only a quantitive factor: the increase in GNP. Development is something much more complex: it is an economy that isn't satisfied with growth but diversifies, through the many different channels of an increasingly complex process, in which the activities that multiply remain nevertheless closely interwoven and connected. Take the Emirates, for example: when some people make colossal fortunes out of oil, while the traditional economy is untouched and completely separate from the oil industry, that is growth not development. Development for me is three-dimensional, it's part of the natural and the social spheres as well as the economic. And if the change of material growth is accompanied by a process

---

5. René Passet, *L' économique et le vivant*, Payot, Paris, 1979.

of deculturalization, of loss of cultural identity, of deterioration in the relationship with the environment, then there is no development.

Which is what has happened not only in the Emirates but also in many Third World countries.

Yes, what I'm saying is particularly true for the Third World, but it's true for us as well. In a society like France where money is profit, means become ends, and a crisis of values, deculturalization and impoverishment of the environment are inevitable negative effects of growth. But why don't I believe in zero growth? Because movement is inseparable from life. In economics, as in life in general, and perhaps in the universe itself, everything is moving and evolving. Starting from the big bang, there has been an evolution from elementary forms of life to superior forms of life, through more and more complex forms, in a process of progressively increasing complexity. All the images of the world that come to us from modern science, such as Prigogine's dissipative structures or today's chaos theory, are images of creative destruction.

Entropy and the degradation of energy are only one aspect, the destructive one, of a more complex reality, in perpetual movement, reaching out towards creation. Entropy is simply the inevitable price of creation. That's why I think Georgescu-Roegen, for whom I have the highest admiration, is a little too defensive in his elaboration of bioeconomics. I prefer a more constructive position, one that says: the process of the universe and of the whole of nature is a process of creative destruction. Economic development is creative destruction too: on the one hand it takes materials, transforms them, throws away the waste, and this is entropy; on the other hand it produces goods and wealth, and this is creation. All development takes place by destroying old structures and creating new ones. This is the view of a great economist who is almost a contemporary of ours, Schumpeter. It's not stasis we need, then, but something dynamic, the insertion of one process of creative destruction in another. But the process of creative destruction of economic development must take place without upsetting the process of nature's creative destruction.

And we can be optimistic about this. Today we are witnessing a genuine technological mutation. Until now all the technological transitions have been based on energy, all the great economic revolutions were powered by energy. Today we are witnessing the first technological revolution with an immaterial basis: computer technology, biotechnology, new materials. It is not the material side that is important, but the combination of natural elements to produce things that nature has not produced. Yes I know, this computer society has its risks, it creates damage, but it has already produced good results too. For example, between 1974 and 1984 we have had further economic growth in the industrialized countries while using less energy, not just per unit of product but overall. So I criticize the ecologists a little for always looking on the dark side: 'technology is bad, progress is bad', and so on. A more intelligent course would be to ask how all this can be used in a way that will avoid risk to the environment and produce positive effects.

You have great faith in humanity. You won't mind me saying it, but I find it difficult to accept your point of view. I can't forget the undeniable contradiction between the physical limits of the Earth and unchecked growth, people on the one side and economic production on the other, which, even if it isn't just material production, still takes up space, produces waste, requires technical processes that are in some degree polluting, which causes temperature increases, acid rain, reduction of the ozone layer ...

Yes, if I think of all this, I answer, 'Things are going very, very badly.' I have to say, 'Objectively speaking, we're screwed.' But, if there is one possibility in a thousand of avoiding all this, we have to seek even the smallest gap we can wriggle through. If we don't try, then we have zero chances. And even when I say, 'we're screwed', at the same time something inside me says 'It's not true.' Of course, all this is very iffy, but we have to believe it. And if there is something we can do, we have to do it. Remember, the problem isn't the planet, it's the human race. Even if you damage the biosphere so much that all superior forms of life vanish, some bacteria or other will survive, and sooner or later the biosphere will manage to regain its equilibrium. We have to do what we can for the human race, not for the planet.

Bresso I don't believe in the widespread conviction that the solution lies in a shift towards 'immaterial' growth. First of all, there's no such thing as an immaterial good. Everything has a material support. Music, for example, seems very immaterial, but there's nothing immaterial about the enormous quantity of discs, cassettes, turntables, tape decks, radios, stereo systems and so on. On the contrary, there's a noticeable tendency in this type of consumption towards privatization and materialization. Music used to be something you heard in the concert hall, with an orchestra that played for a large number of people, one auditorium and so on. Today music is something you listen to mainly in private, with discs and equipment that are replaced and thrown away. Like the cinema: rather than one copy of the film and one auditorium for a large audience, which was what happened until recently, today one person on his own consumes a large number of videos, and there is a tendency to make more use of the videocassette, that is, of an object, than of television programmes, which are telematic signals. It's true that products are tending to get lighter, and there is less use of raw materials per product unit, but the numbers of units are increasing, and at the moment there is no sign of a fall in consumption of either energy (the only fall coincided with the oil crisis) or raw materials. Not at global level anyway. And so long as the reduction in energy consumption involves only a few advanced countries, it doesn't mean much. Japan, for example, has a good internal environment policy, and what seems like a production system geared to a reduced use of materials. But Japan is destroying the forests of Indonesia, from which it's taking all the wood it needs, and it has the steel it needs produced in Korea. So are we really sure that the lightening of Japanese production isn't making production heavier in other countries?

O'Connor The problem is: what kind of growth? I'm in favour of the growth of eco-cities and a rational integration of town and country; organic agriculture and small-scale farming that involves urban consumers in the production and distribution of food in an active way; self-organizing villages that generate their own economic activity; public health systems and self-help medical care; mass transport that people want to use, and so on. But these or other changes presuppose radical changes in capitalism, the capitalist state, in culture generally, that is, the birth of an eco-socialism. In particular they presuppose an end to capitalist expansion, to neo-colonialism, to economic imperialism, and to consumerism. They also presuppose the reconstruction of political life in the direction of more radical forms of democracy: on the one hand, a more direct democracy from the ground, on the other, more democracy within the state, which administers the social division of labour. None of this will come about until labour and the social movements collect their demands within an eco-socialist political movement.

As for 'sustainable development', practically everyone uses the expression, but it has many different meanings. Capital uses the term to mean sustainable profits and steady and stable capital accumulation, which presuppose (among other things) long-term planning of the exploitation and use of renewable and nonrenewable resources. Sustainability may also be defined in terms of natural systems, wildlife preservation, air quality, and so on. But these definitions have nothing necessarily to do with sustaining profitability. In many cases there will be an inverse correlation between ecological sustainability and profit. Capital is very adept at trying to appropriate the concept of sustainability for itself: for example, the 'state environmentalism' that is ravaging much of the Third World today, or the attempt on the part of certain parts of capital to define sustainable agriculture in terms of biological control of pests and weeds. Red greens of all shades should be alert to the ideological uses of the term 'sustainability', and should fight them whenever possible.

CHAPTER 8

CONSUME AND MULTIPLY

The questions raised by the world's ecological imbalance, which are difficult enough to answer in relation to the advanced industrial countries, become even more dramatically problematical when applied to the Third World.

The southern hemisphere, for all the many different situations and gradations of development to be found there, is on the whole the area where the two primary coefficients of the environmental crisis have assumed appalling dimensions. In many already highly overpopulated areas the continually rising birth rate, and poverty and famine on a scale that leaves no room for other priorities make rapid growth in production seem an essential. For three quarters of the human race it seems that the two exponential curves of productivity growth and population growth must inevitably rise and interact with each other, reciprocally multiplying the difficulties, in an ecological prospect which is terrifying.

The Third World has already appeared as a crucial environmental problem many times in these interviews. Here the question is raised explicitly.

Sylos Labini   We in the West could perhaps put our house in order, limit consumption to a certain extent, adopt a more moderate lifestyle, and, most important, as I said before, orientate growth in productivity towards quality rather than quantity. But you can't ask this of the Third World. They are hungry, they are in the most terrible state of underdevelopment, they need to grow materially, quantitively, and they haven't even started yet. If they were to follow the same path as the industrialized world then the damage to the environment would reach catastrophic levels. It's up to us, the rich countries, to do something about it. That means, first of all, supplying the Third World with suitable technology, which won't pollute, or which will pollute as little as possible, and with low energy consumption. The technology can't be too sophisticated, though, not just because it is very expensive, but also because sophisticated technology requires skilled and very expensive labour, whilst poor countries have large quantities of low-cost but unskilled labour. It is extremely difficult, but if the human race wants to be saved it must make this effort.

What you're saying in effect is that we should be reversing our current policy. It's common practice to export to the Third World the most polluting industrial processes, obsolete machinery that has been discarded because it is banned on environmental grounds in its country of origin, and even toxic waste.

That's true, and I have had first-hand experience of it. It must stop in the future, and I think it's up to the UN to take responsibility for doing this, not just by promoting action of its own, but by encouraging, coordinating and giving a proper importance to all the research centres that are studying these problems, and to the growing number of efforts of this kind all over the world. I emphasize this hope in a book of mine on development, which is coming out soon. In fact, in the last chapter there are a series of suggested courses of action which I offer for the experts to consider. I suggest the establishment of a large body at the UN, which would be divided into three sectors. The first would be delegated all the problems of the environment and regarding all countries, and would have to follow a complex strategy involving taxation, research, public and private investment, bans, incentives and international agreements, concentrating particularly on three aspects of the pollution question: cars, chemicals and agriculture. The second would oversee the choice and evolution of technologies particularly as regards sustainable development of the Third World. The third would be concerned with what is to me the most frightening problem of all, population growth, which is, in any case, directly linked with agricultural development, and so with the environment. This last problem has worsened dramatically in recent years, and here the Catholic Church has a grave responsibility. It's extremely difficult to understand their thinking in this: until a few years ago at least some forms of contraception were allowed, whilst now the hierarchy of the Vatican seems to have the sole objective of uncontrolled reproduction of the human race. And when one sees on the television masses of tiny creatures reduced to skeletons by malnutrition, one starts to wonder what this has to do with Christianity.

Action of the kind you are suggesting would involve heavy financial aid to the developing countries, which, as is well known, are already weighed down by enormous debts to the richer countries ...

Of course. The problem of the Third World's debts has had a serious effect on environmental policy. It's a problem we've been living with for fifteen years, which derives principally from the monetary policy of Ronald Reagan, a US President who had his virtues, but also many faults, particularly in the field of economics. Increase military spending and at the same time reduce taxes, especially for the rich – that was Reagan's policy. It was a bad policy ethically and socially, but also economically: it created an enormous hole in the United States budget. The only solution Reagan could find to fill up this hole – and it hasn't worked so far – was to sell government securities on the national and international markets at interest rates that in the end reached 15 per cent. The US interest rate became the world interest rate, for Third World countries too, which found themselves suffocated by debts as a result of an internal US policy. Many of us have underlined the United States's grave responsibility in this, and have asked for a reduction of interest rates for the Third World, which has been achieved in a few cases, but not in any systematic way. On the contrary it seems to have been done almost on the sly, on the initiative of a few banks that were aware of the fact that they were never going to get their money back. The United States has blocked some international proposals for the environment, and should remember the responsibility this entails, especially as it is the greatest producer, and, as a result, the greatest polluter.

The urgent necessity for production growth in the Third World is one of the greatest risks for the ecological balance of the planet, given the explosive situation of the birth rate, which is unanimously recognised as crucial. With the exception, as we have seen, of Milton Friedman, all the interviewees were conscious of and worried about this agonizing problem, and the most common solution offered was that already mentioned by Sylos Labini, the search for 'suitable' technologies, or at least the hope that technological evolution would resolve the problem. Leontief, Hirschman, Simon, Spaventa, Hahn and Gerelli were all agreed on this point, Gerelli stressing the need to respect, as well as the environment, local cultures and lifestyles where they still exist. There were also some more fully worked-out theories.

Pearce   In the Third World we have to think about the transfer of green technology and we have to assist in the conservation of their resources. If you travel in those countries you note the terrible waste of energy amd raw materials, due to the lack of real incentives. We have to change the way we think about international aid and trade and the transfer of technology, because free trade once again can prove damaging to the environment. We should look very carefully at those cases where we may wish to discriminate against a country that is imposing costs on other countries by exporting unclean technology and unclean products. So this requires quite a transformation in our thinking, and we have a long way still to go.

I'm not saying that what you are proposing is against the capitalist market, but it is something very different.

Yes, that's right. It's a kind of a soft capitalism, something we might call the 'social market', a market with a human face. This is a change in philosophy that has come. We have seen the worst of capitalism in Western Europe, and we can look forward to something more caring.

Solow   Faced with the prospect for the environment of even a production growth that would bring developing countries up to two thirds of our standard of living, some economists can think of nothing better to say than that there's no imminent danger as these countries are developing so slowly. But this isn't an acceptable argument. We have to encourage economic growth in the Third World, but not by letting them follow the same path we have taken. We must try to develop more environment-friendly scientific and technical resources, which will create less pollution – in energy, housing and transport. One concrete example: the Third World doesn't yet have the infrastructures we have in the West, which are both cause and effect of the predominance of trucks for transporting goods. Before building a highway network there like ours, which would lead to the same kind of transport, we should propose alternatives.

Passet   Up to now we in the West have been the largest producers of carbon dioxide, and that means we are the ones most responsible for the greenhouse effect. But when the Third World takes off economically there will be an enormous increase in energy consumption and also in carbon dioxide production, which means further disturbance to the temperature of the globe. So the immediate problem is to find a way for the developing countries to grow without excessive energy consumption. Some specialists have studied the problem in detail and insist that it is not impossible. There are three scenarios. The pessimistic one is this: world energy consumption is today around 10,000 billion watts; that means that in 2020, allowing for population growth and the development of the Third World, it will be around 55,000 billion, more than five times what it is today. And that means catastrophe. A less pessimistic scenario: if the French norms, which aren't that bad (or the Italian or Japanese, as these are the three countries which seem to consume least energy per product unit), were to be applied generally, in 2020 we would have a consumption of 30,000 billion rather than 55,000 billion. Even then, the situation would be very serious. The optimistic scenario is the work of Professor Goldenberg: energy consumption can be kept to a minimum, so much so that even with a significant increase in the national product of the developing countries, world consumption in 2020 will be around 11,200 billion watts. It's true, there's a lot of waste today. Transport, heating, refrigeration, in all these fields saving is possible, and we must start saving urgently. We're also learning a lot. Before long we may be able to extract energy from waste. And it may one day be possible to obtain energy from the biomass and use solar energy on a large scale. This is what we must aim for.

There are other aspects to the industrialized West's responsibility towards poorer countries, and these too were underlined. Here the lifestyles and consumption patterns that the affluent societies are setting for the rest of the world are relevant.

Galbraith So long as we go on producing along lines that have such strongly negative effects on the environment, I am much more sympathetic to production in the Third World, and much more tolerant of its effect on pollution than I would be in the developed countries. We can afford to forgo polluting products, but the poor countries cannot afford to forgo increased production of food or clothing or medicines or housing. I've had very practical experience of this, when I was ambassador in India. There was great concern in the West about the effects of DDT, but I insisted that DDT continue to be available in India because spraying houses with DDT had a great effect on malaria. Whatever the environmental effects of DDT, they were far less than the effects of illness from mosquitoes. So long as we continue making our own mistakes we're not going to be able to tell other people to do better. So long as we have a high level of consumption we can't lecture other countries to have a lower rate.

Daly Is it conceivable for another 3.5 billion people to reach Western levels of consumption? I don't think it's ecologically possible. But we certainly can't say to poor nations 'Too bad, but you're too late.' We need to redefine development in such a way that it's generalizable for everyone, which means a lower rate of resource consumption in the wealthy countries. But we have not been willing to face up to that. So far the only way we have found of helping the poor countries has been to increase our consumption, importing their products and selling them on our markets.

Malinvaud I believe the responsibility for certain decisions lies with the developed countries. If they decide that chlorofluorocarbons should no longer be used for refrigeration, then it's up to them to offer a possible substitute. But not all of the responsibility is ours. Of course, we can't forget that North Africa, for example, was colonized by the French and that our presence has left its mark on those societies. But now they can decide for themselves. If the Moroccans import toxic waste, that's their decision, their responsibility, at least as much as ours. And on the subject of consumption patterns, yes it's true, the developing countries are taking over our pattern of consumption. But if we export it to them it's because they want to import it. I just can't accept this idea that all the bad things in the Third World are the responsibility of the industrialized countries; I find it an intolerably paternalistic attitude. I think the best way to help those nations would be to modify our own nations, change our lifestyle. And that would mean making people more aware. It comes back to what we have already said. And it's something that has got nothing to do with economists.

Simon It will be very difficult to stop Third World countries following Western patterns. They often try to reproduce them completely. One of the amazing things to me, because there are a lot of things about our society, US society, that I don't care for, is the enormous popularity of the American way of life everywhere in the world. Everyone wants to wear jeans, listen to rock music and drink out of cans. How do you make them change their tastes?

Spaventa I'm not very concerned at the prospect of the Third World taking over Western models. They are countries so distant from our levels of consumption – and the inequality is growing – that the real problem seems to me very different. These nations want to become industrialized and they are not too particular about how the opportunities for development and profit can be seized, and perhaps they couldn't care less. Anyhow, they are more willing to sacrifice the environment than are prosperous societies, which can afford to consider the environment question important. On various occasions, rulers of Third World countries have described the environment question as a luxury. And there's no point being shocked by this: the environment certainly isn't a luxury for the human race as a whole, but it's easy to see how it can be considered as such by people who are dying of hunger or living at the limits of subsistence. And this is because environmental problems have a social cost, not a private cost, and a social cost that hurts the West too isn't noticed by nations that are so desperately far away from Western living conditions.

O'Connor   Independent of the question of the desirability of the South following the industrial, consumerist path of the North is the question of its possibility. To take four examples, Indian, Brazilian, Mexican and Nigerian industrial capitalism exists at the expense of the grinding poverty of the local populations, and also of ecological stability. 'Development' in the rich oil states will go on for a long time, then cease when the oil has disappeared. Most of the rest of the South is an economic, social and ecological disaster zone. East Asia is doing well economically but, with the particular exception of Japan, has not yet proved that it can be an industrial powerhouse and also pay good wages and provide good working conditions, progressive social policies, meaningful environmental protection, and, last but not least, stable forms of liberal democracy. In other words, there are many barriers to capitalist development in the Third World, independent of ecological conditions in particular, and of conditions of production in general. If I can make a large generalization: in most of the Third World non-ecological capitalism will never come about; even less likely is an ecological capitalism.

Georgescu-Roegen   Merely financial aid to countries of the Third World is useless if not harmful; often it goes into the pockets of the privileged governing class, or it is used to develop industries and products that are unnecessary and alien to the local culture. I believe that all resources should be controlled and distributed at world level: it's the only way, in my view, to prevent increasing scarcity from emphasizing the inequality that already exists between North and South and causing wars. More than ten years ago I said that if the use of resources continues to be entrusted to the whims of the market, then the struggle to take possession of the last drop of oil will be conducted with bombs. The Gulf War is a clear example of what I was talking about. But, most important, one real help to the countries of the Third World would consist in abolishing all passports. It's a bioeconomic idea, designed to help people from the poorest countries, allowing them freedom of movement towards places where they can have better opportunities to use their skills, rather than falling back on the conventional approach of exporting the tools of capitalism to their countries, something which is both difficult and harmful to the environment. I've been saying this too since the early seventies, and everybody has treated me as an incurable Utopian. But now the pressure of the poorest parts of the world on the richer countries is such that we must start rethinking the question.

Others, too, referred to the possibility of massive migration from the Third World to the industrialized countries. Some were worried at the prospect. Some regarded it calmly as something inevitable and perhaps desirable. Some doubted that it was the best solution even for those migrating.

Hartje   Apart from social tensions, it could have disruptive effects on the environment of the countries they migrate to.

Zeman   I believe it is a necessary process of integration, which is part of the present tendency towards the globalization of the complex problems of the world. It will change borders, bring down the barriers between states, and extend to the whole planet the ethnic melting pot that gave birth to the United States.

Martinez-Alier   I'm not against Georgescu-Roegen's proposal, which, apart from anything else, is extremely farsighted, but I do wonder what government would ever be prepared to accept it. In any case I think it would be possible to help the poorest people of the world in a less traumatic way. In some cases economic growth in the Third World could improve the standard of living and solve some environmental problems. For example, the recent explosion of cholera in Latin America is the result of a lack of any proper water system and an unfair social distribution of resources. In the outskirts of Lima the poor use 25 litres of water a day, and they have to buy it at a very high price from lorries, while in the richer parts of the city they use 300 litres a day, and in California they use 1,000. Obviously, the best solution would be not to live in Lima, but a proper water system would be a big step forward both hygienically and for the environment.

Another big ecological problem is deforestation in the tropics, partly caused by the export of timber, and partly by the fact that it is the only fuel available for cooking. The alternative is dung, which the people need for manure. If there were a gas supply, even in cylinders – and the quantity would not be that great – the problem could be resolved. We're not talking about cars or luxury items, but about the need to satisfy the basic needs of the 6 billion people who will be living in conditions of extreme poverty forty years from now. Astronomic sums aren't necessary, as the difference in consumption is so enormous. In the rich countries we consume about 3,000 kilocalories in food per person per day. One third of this would be enough to save the world's poor, but it is still twenty times what an Indian consumes now. So there is room to improve the living conditions of the Third World through small-scale actions – which are always preferable, if we want to avoid damaging the environment.

You seem to be saying that it would be possible in this way to recover traditional local cultures?

Yes, of course. If we look at certain countries in the Andes, such as Bolivia and Peru, we can see that agroecology, which is becoming fashionable in Europe now, goes very far back in their history. They were agroecologists before the arrival of Columbus, and they are very proud of the fact that they produce finer fruit and vegetables than the United States. These are the roots from which the environment movements of the Third World are growing, and I think they will flourish much more than in the industrialized countries. There are many people like Chico Mendez. Of course these peoples should be helped, or at any rate not be exploited, by the industrialized world. At present much of what is produced in the Third World is exploited by the West: much of the gas we use in Italy and Spain comes from Algeria and Morocco, and we pay a very low price for it, while we don't allow the people from those countries to enter ours.

Altvater Very few of the problems of the Third World can be solved without the involvement of the West. Perhaps agrarian reform is possible, a more equitable distribution and different use of the land (but not always), perhaps even some technological improvement, or depollution at a local level. But for most problems, including the most serious environmental ones, one cannot treat the countries of the Third World separately: they have to be seen in relation to the developed world. The fact that 20 per cent of the human race consumes 80 per cent of resources, most of which are supplied by the poorer countries, is a fact that concerns the capitalist industrial system of the West. The Third World is a problem for everybody. To face it we need to think in terms of a new political and economic world order. Unfortunately I see no indications of an interest of this kind. No one wants to have to decide to do without things, to reduce energy consumption, no one wants to reduce automobile production ... Yet everyone knows that it's unthinkable for the whole world, all 5 or 6 billion of them, to have the same density of cars as we have in Europe.

I'm not so sure that everyone knows that ... It seems obvious enough, but politicians and economists just don't seem to see it at all ...

Yes, they always come up with the same old solution: the market, according to which everyone who can buy a car has the right to have one, and those who can't don't. That is justice for them. They couldn't care less that the global village of the mass media shows the populations of the poorer countries what life is like in Western countries. Naturally enough, they want the same things.

Bresso Looked at through the lens of the environmental crisis, the problem of the Third World has two main aspects. The first is connected with the fact that these countries have imported cultural, economic and production models radically different from their traditional ones. This importation was often imposed with violence, especially during the colonial period, but in any case was always too rapid, leaving no time for the new models to be assimilated. And this broke the existing balances in their ecosystems, which were often fragile and achieved with difficulty, as in Africa, for example, where the soil is poor and always subject to the risk of erosion and desertification. Western intervention, which was sometimes simple robbery, sometimes well-meaning, but always unjust, had seriously destructive effects. The population explosion itself is an index of the imbalance in the ecosystem. Before, the populations of the Third World were almost all very limited in number, contained within limits suited to what the given ecosystem could bear.

But that was an ecosystem based on an extremely high death rate ...

The death rate was high in all pre-industrial societies. What I meant was that there were mechanisms that regulated the birth rate, which have not been studied, but through which the areas with scarce resources were sparsely populated, and those with greater resources had a greater density of population. It was an equilibrium like that we can find in the animal kingdom. This equilibrium has been broken, and has not been replaced with any other that could produce a fall in the death rate at the same time as a fall in the birth rate.

It has been broken most of all by the importation of hygiene measures, sanitary practices and medical knowledge ... Are you saying that artificial intervention disturbs the balance of the environment even when it has positive effects?

Yes, when it isn't accompanied by an overall economic and cultural evolution. This doesn't mean, obviously, that we should block health-directed aid, but it does mean that it must be accompanied by development aid, which leads to a fall in the birth rate. Otherwise what's the point of raising people's life expectancy if these lives can only be spent suffering the horrors of famine?

And the second aspect?

This concerns the relation between the Third World and the economies of the West, which are organized in such a way that they consume an enormous and increasing quantity of – let's just remind ourselves – nonrenewable resources. The result is that the countries of the West, which were the first to become industrialized, soon exhausted their raw materials and began to import them. The Third World's function is that of an exporter of resources, but, given that, it's difficult to see how these countries can hope to reach our standard of living, which would mean being able to add value to materials bought elsewhere.

Does that mean that the poverty of the Third World is an inevitable part of the West's prosperity?

Today, yes, unquestionably. Not just because the economic relations of the post-colonial period are very similar to those of the colonial period, but also because in the present state of things we need the resources of the Third World. The Gulf War was fought to stop Saddam occupying Saudi Arabia and turning off the petrol tap. This is less obvious for other more widespread resources, which have a lot of taps. But if these taps were turned off, if and when the countries where they are to be found were to become industrialized and started needing the resources, then it would be a big problem for the West.

Put like that, it seems a blind alley.

But there's something else to be taken into account. At this moment we don't know how great the stocks of existing raw materials are, but we do know that they are limited. Above all, we can be certain that we have already exceeded the tolerance limit for the pollution of the planet. The world's climate is already changing and we can't place any further burdens on it. It's obvious that there's no room for further development, not even for the developed countries let alone for the developing countries, which make up two thirds of the world. In short, it's obvious that the Western model cannot be exported, cannot be extended to the whole planet.

But there must be a solution. In the Third World hundreds of thousands of people are dying of hunger.

The question has to be faced here in the West: it is the specific duty of the rich countries. Even the Brundtland Report says that in its own bland way, but it has to be said much more severely: the rich countries have to create space in the ecosystem, liberate resources, reduce their consumption not relatively but absolutely, and divert the surplus towards Third World countries, but not in accordance with our paradigms, our patterns of development. What we need is a reorientation of our whole economic system to try to stabilize consumption and contain it within sustainable limits, and to propose a new model on this basis. The only way is a collective international decision, which would opt for a huge humanitarian and voluntary effort for the poorer countries. After all it's in our own interests: the masses of the Third World are knocking at our door.

CHAPTER 9

TO MOSCOW, TO MOSCOW!

Under the attack of air pollution and acid rain, medieval cities are turning black and crumbling away, whole hillsides are being deforested, harvests suffer, rivers are being transformed into open sewers, and drinking water is becoming scarce. But what is more alarming is that people are dying as a result of the pollution; in the zones most seriously hit, life expectancy is lower than in uncontaminated areas, and the incidence of tumours, reproductive problems and many other diseases is notably higher.[1]

These words come from the opening paragraph, devoted to the Soviet Union and other countries of Eastern Europe, of the 1991 Worldwatch Institute report, and what follows contains information and data of extreme gravity. One needs only to mention the figures for the emission of sulphur dioxide, which in 1988 were 31 grams per unit of GNP in East Germany, 24 in Czechoslovakia, 21 in Bulgaria, 20 in Poland, 19 in Romania, 17 in Hungary, and 10 in the Soviet Union, against 5 in Britain, 4 in the United States, and 1 in Sweden, France and West Germany. Nor has the situation improved since then.

In economic circles experts, planners and businessmen do not seem very concerned about it. The Western press devotes great space to the passage from a planned to a market economy in the former socialist countries, and display particular interest in the extraordinary prospects for highly profitable transactions that are opening up for the capitalist world. Space is given on the subject to the opinions of Harvard professors and leading European diplomats, advisers to Gorbachev and Yeltsin, governors of the central banks, industrialists with experience of this type of investment, and a motley crew of intermediaries of every political colour; and the move away from a planned economy is always presented as an enormous joint venture, which will be a fountain of new wealth for both East and West. In

---

1. Lester R. Brown et al., *State of the World 1991*, Earthscan, London, 1992.

all the pages of this sort of coverage, I have never come across a hint of the risk that the creation of this wealth will mean the further destruction of territory that has already suffered from the neglect and incompetence of the socialist bureaucracies. No one seems to be aware that the countries of Eastern Europe also, to a different extent and in different ways from the Third World, are faced with the extremely difficult question of reconciling the necessity for development with the equally urgent necessity of not exacerbating the condition of the environment, and, if possible, improving it.

I brought up the subject with many of the economists I met, but few of those from the West displayed much interest. Many avoided the question, claiming they did not wish to pronounce on the internal matters of other countries. A very different attitude was to be found in the economists from Eastern Europe, or at any rate the few I was able to question, who, as is already clear from some of their comments in previous chapters, are not in the least tempted to undervalue the risk to the environment, and recognize in its fundamentally economic nature something of immediate concern to them. This awareness is only proper, given the appalling ecological conditions of their countries, about which they are quite frank.

Agambegian The Soviet Union is an enormous country, and this gives us a certain leeway to pollute, dump waste, set up destructive activities, and then move somewhere else, distributing the pollution over vast areas, without seeming to create any problems. But this is what has encouraged the general attitude of indifference. There is no doubt at all that, on the whole, the environment in our country is in a bad state. The main reason is that the previous administration attached great importance to high production levels in heavy industries – metallurgy, mining and chemicals – with a high pollution level. And we weren't very bothered about this, and fought no battles over it. Our cars, for example, don't have catalytic converters, we don't have anti-pollution equipment or firms specialized in producing it, and so on. But, on the other hand, in the past there was no public debate about the environment because of censorship. The publishing of articles that gave information about incidents or situations that were dangerous to the environment was forbidden. The press has been free to discuss all this as a result of perestroika and the democratic process, and people have become more aware of the problem. Since then local government has started to try to take the situation in hand.

Shatalin The condition of the environment in our country is very serious indeed. A number of areas should be considered ecological disaster zones. Everyone knows about the Chernobyl catastrophe, but in the Aral Sea area pollution from mineral fertilizers and crop protection chemicals has caused irreversible changes in the water ecosystems, which in turn are a threat to all living creatures in the surrounding area. In more than a hundred cities air pollution exceeds admissible levels tenfold. For decades our country proclaimed that the socialist system, based on common ownership and a planned economy, provided the prerequisites for the rational use of resources, and the preservation and improvement of the environment. But in reality the centralized bureaucracy simply increased the exploitation of nature for short-term ends. The squandering of natural resources was not only the effect but also a precondition of the system of administrative power, and a guarantee of its vitality. Instead of giving economic incentives for the application of scientific and techno-logical advances to enhance the creativity of the workforce and increase production, it achieved economic growth by using an increasing amount of natural resources. Not only that, but the environment and natural resources have always been regarded as 'free goods'. This created a situation of utter inefficiency and a total lack of technology aimed at protecting nature and saving energy and raw materials.

Zeman Czechoslovakia is one of the most polluted countries in Europe. And for us the term 'ecology' involves not only the natural environment but our architectural heritage too. Prague is the only medieval city left in central Europe, which was never bombarded but remained intact, a miracle of inestimable value. And it is not only a question solely of Prague. During the communist regime approx-imately one third of our architectural monuments were destroyed; for example, little churches in old towns were turned into barns. Now we have two thirds of this heritage and we must try to preserve it. So it's not just a matter of environmental programmes to save forests, water, air and so on, but of defending our historical heritage.

With the change of regime I suppose measures of this kind are being taken now ...

This is a transition period in all Eastern European countries. It's a complicated period, in which the political pendulum has moved from the extreme left to the extreme right. In the post-communist world (apart from the Soviet Union, which is a separate problem), totalitarian psychology has re-emerged and is once again gaining the upper hand, so that even the miracle of the market, in the way in which it is being presented in Czechoslovakia, runs the risk of ending up like the market dictatorship of Chile; and I don't know if it's such a good thing to get rid of Brezhnev only to find yourself with Pinochet. In this situation our official economists, who are still Marxist determinists, say, 'First we must build a new market economy, and we'll think about the environment later.'

They see economics and the environment as two separate problems?

Not just separate, not even parallel, but to be considered one after the other ... The formula of our finance minister is this: first let's organize a solid economic base, and, when we have some results there, we'll start to think about the environment. For our government the environment is secondary, almost a luxury, while the opposition, of which I am a member, insists that action for the environment, like education and social reforms, must keep pace with economic transformation, that they are part of the same process of development. Massive capital investment is needed for this, of course, whilst our national budget is so weak it can hardly afford the costs of ordinary administration, let alone sustain new investment.

What does the opposition suggest?

To find sufficient funds, we have two false possibilities, so to speak: foreign debt and tax increases. Why false? Because borrowing money only postpones the problem and increasing taxes only brings down a government. There is only one reasonable solution and that is privatization. State ownership is enormous, and gradual privatization is the only way in which we shall be able to sustain long-term environmental, educational or social programmes. In any case, so far as the environment goes, we need to pass from therapy to preventive medicine. It's crazy to go on taking action only retrospectively, depolluting what has been polluted. To have clean air and water we need rational production processes. As for nuclear energy: what's the sense of repairing obsolete plants and making them safer when we should be eliminating nuclear energy? But I repeat, these are long-term programmes, and they need a lot of money.

Dealing with the environmental damage created by decades of neglect seems an even more arduous task in the Soviet Union. Various measures have been taken, however, and the most serious emergencies have been faced. As both the economists from the Soviet Union whom I interviewed reminded me, a good number of the factories with the highest levels of pollution, mainly those in the chemicals sector producing fertilizer, biological materials for medicines and so on, have been closed, as have some nuclear reactors that were considered unsafe, and some mines that were particularly destructive to the environment.

As well as this, local government in some regions has imposed precise limits on the cutting down of forests and the use of ground at risk of desertification. But the concrete results of glasnost and the current process of democratization that they regarded as most positive were a number of binding decisions taken by central government, which have blocked some extremely dangerous large-scale schemes, such as the famous 'project of the century', which would have diverted the rivers of Siberia towards central Asia, and the planned exploitation of the deposits of natural gas in the Yamal peninsula, which has been temporarily halted until safe and environment-friendly extraction and transport techniques have been perfected.

However, the economists I spoke to were by no means satisfied, even if Agambegian's judgement was less severe than Shatalin's.

Agambegian   There is still much to be done, but we cannot hope for rapid results. There is a whole series of priorities apart from that of the environment: we must develop our food industry, the pharmaceutical industry, and production of domestic appliances. And our financial situation is none too good either. But I believe that the best hope for the environment lies in a radical change in our economic structure, with the transition from heavy to high-tech industry, and a development of service industries. Our production system was based on decrees that imposed output targets. We produce, for example, 160 million tons of steel a year, which is more than the whole of Europe, and twice the production of the United States. This requires enormous quantities of raw materials, coal for the furnaces, energy for transport, wood for equipment, etcetera, and that means air and water pollution. But we don't need all this steel, and we shall need it less and less if we can create a market economy.

Shatalin   The measures taken for environmental protection in our country can hardly be considered either sufficient or efficient. In general these measures were of an *ad hoc* nature concerning specific situations with high ecological risk, taken under pressure from the greens, who are often characterized by a spirit of nationalism, and motivated more by opposition to central authority than by anything else. So far, in many respects the situation has got worse since perestroika. The dismantling of the old bureaucratic system has not always been followed by the creation of new administrative bodies, and there has been a disruption of the relations between regional organizations and businesses, and a deterioration of discipline in the workplace. All these factors, together with the economic crisis, have led to a situation in which only half the modest budget for the environment is being used. The local authorities, unable to meet ecological targets, and pressurized by public opinion which has united around the greens, try to compensate by closing down the most dangerous plants; but this has simply added an additional factor of economic destabilization.

Other recent measures have not provided more satisfactory results. In recent years the USSR instituted a state audit of all the major economic projects, an audit that included an examination of environmental effects. But as a rule a negative judgement about the environmental effects of a project had no influence on the project itself. If a ministry was determined at all costs to have a project commissioned then it managed to get finance for the project before the environmental evaluation had been completed, often backing up its claims by providing the conclusions of its own ministerially appointed experts. The logic of the ministries was very simple: if finance is promised before the results of the environmental evaluation are available, it is highly probable that the project will go ahead even if the environmental verdict is negative. The result is further damage to nature.

Privatization and the market. These two words are on the lips of the economists of Eastern Europe just as much as on those of their United States colleagues, evoking an economic policy that will save and heal the seriously damaged environment along with everything else. But are they really convinced of this?

Zeman No. I don't agree with those who think that the invisible hand of the market can solve everything. So far as I know, in the United States air and water pollution were increasing until the early seventies, that is, until the birth of the Environmental Protection Agency. I think that the market and privatization are necessary but not sufficient conditions. We need good laws, compatible with those of the EEC.

Agambegian In a market economy the manufacturer produces goods for the consumer. It's the consumer's interest, not his own, that is primary.

Don't you think that the manufacturer too has his own interest – profit?

Yes, they make profits, but only if they provide goods the consumer wants. Our hope is that this will force our economic structure to change and become more efficient, and that greater efficiency will improve the situation of the environment. A market economy also means paying – paying for pollution too. We are now fixing special environment taxes, and soon pollution will be very expensive, and it will no longer be in anyone's interest to cause it. In addition, in a market economy all resources have a price, while in a planned economy resources are the property of the state, they are owned jointly and have no value: there's no charge on wood or on water for irrigation, and waste is the rule. When resources have to be paid for, it's in everyone's interest to make the best possible use of them.

In Eastern Europe, the transition to a market economy is seen as the potential solution to many problems, including those of the environment. But in the West those economists who have given some consideration to the subject are either much less certain or decidedly sceptical.

Altvater   The market solves nothing, neither problems of development, nor ecological problems. The market works only when it has its roots in social institutions. As well as Adam Smith's invisible hand and Alfred Kendland's visible hand – that of the state and the big corporations – we need a third hand: that of institutions that express a social awareness, and through which the economic system can function to produce development and make welfare possible, and so on. Will the countries of the East be capable of creating a system of this kind, made up of state, market and social institutions? Because it is easy to introduce the market into an economy, but with the market alone the only thing created is a mafia capitalism. It is very difficult to initiate and foster institutions. It's possible to restructure a society like those that have been destroyed by socialism, but this means creating essential institutions, not just introducing the mechanisms of the market. And institutions have a cultural dimension, which cannot be created overnight: it requires a generation at least. In the immediate future the only possibility I see is a mafia economy.

Daly   I think the countries of Eastern Europe have unrealistic expectations of the transition to a market economy. Perhaps it's because of all the negative consequences of a planned economy, of the inevitable overvaluation of what they don't have. I think the myth of consumerism has a big influence too, which they idealize and dream about just at the moment when we are discovering all its damaging effects on the environment.

Then is it wise to adopt Western models of consumption uncritically and without variation in those Eastern European countries that are trying to create a new economic order?

Agambegian   We are poor and still a long way off from becoming a consumer society. We may be able to reach the Western standard of living in twenty or thirty years' time, step by step, and during this period it should be possible to acquire all the necessary know-how to reduce pollution to a minimum. We can learn from the West in this, and perhaps do better. We have a kind of advantage in our lower level of consumption. In the Soviet Union, for example, we have only 18 million cars, not 110 million like in the United States: it will be much easier for us to fit catalytic converters or any other anti-pollution device.

If you don't mind me saying this, there is an impression in the West that the people of Eastern Europe are being seduced by the Western way of life without asking any questions, as if it were absolutely perfect and without faults. In the United States, the richest country in the Western world, 12 per cent of the population, to mention the most significant fact, live below the poverty line. Your country doesn't seem to be aware of this ...

Life in the United States seems to me better than it is here. We don't have so much food, nor is it of the same quality; we don't have so many cars, nor such large houses. But this doesn't mean that we want to take over the American way of life. We have other values too, which we don't want to abandon, a deeper concept of friendship, more solid family ties, traditions of inestimable value. I don't want to live anywhere else, and I don't believe that quality of life is linked to the production figures of consumer goods.

Zeman I agree with you, the introduction of consumerism is a danger. If I look round I see people hungry for material goods, particularly if they are expensive and prestigious, flashy goods designed for display. New social classes have emerged, people who are rich but uneducated, with all the usual defects of the *nouveaux riches*. This is destroying our finest cultural traditions. For example, we had a vast and rich network of scientific, medical, theatrical, literary and cultural magazines. They have almost all disappeared, because they don't have the wherewithal to survive. Instead porno-graphic magazines are flourishing. This is what people want, and in the short and mid term I'm afraid there's little we can do about it. But I also hope that there will be a sort of immunological reaction in the social organism, a kind of rejection that will enable us to recover our traditional values. After all, between the two world wars Czechoslovakia was a cultural oasis. But for this to happen we need intelligent government programmes that will form a new, highly educated generation. And this is also the premiss for an adequate culture of environmentalism.

In any case, production and consumption are bound to increase in the former socialist countries. And this will mean more environmental degradation.

There's a risk of that if the directives of some of our official economists prevail, which I have already mentioned. Some of them think only of reaching the production levels of Western Europe, massive consumption and so on; others think of going back to the nineteenth century. But we have to prepare ourselves for the future.

Which means ... ?

Sustainable growth can only be based on the maximum exploitation of new technology. Computer technology could be the 'third way'. It would not only give us production with a significant reduction of inputs, and so of the use of energy and raw materials, but also allow a whole series of other positive solutions. Consider teleworking, which would drastically reduce the need for transport, and so partially solve the traffic problem. At the same time, teleworking would encourage the decentralization of housing, away from the big cities, towards the country and small towns, reducing the need for second homes. A video network can allow the organization of international conferences and long-distance working meetings without anyone having to move. This would reduce air traffic and the pollution deriving from that. There are endless possibilities of this kind. And we should remember that while we must save the environment and our cultural heritage, nevertheless we cannot go back to the Middle Ages. We must create a new culture, one no longer founded on *homo oeconomicus*, but not founded on *homo oecologicus* either. We need a combination of the two, a 'stereo-paradigm'.

In the economic and political evolution taking place in the territories of the former Soviet Union, some saw a risk of a different kind, involving far more than just the environment.

Shatalin The acquisition of state sovereignty by the republics of the former Soviet Union and the economic independence of Russia in the context of the economic crisis that is affecting all regions and all spheres of the economy – all these factors risk causing heavy unemployment. As a result, ecological problems are easily given second priority, and some plants that were closed down because dangerous to the environment might be allowed to resume operation. The need for economic survival, coupled as it is with an absence of reliable legal and economic regulators in this period of transition, may lead to a pronounced deterioration of the situation. As part of the process of privatization the new owners should undertake to respect the environment; economic measures to control the use of natural resources should include taxes on the producers and consumers of materials that are hazardous to the environment, but also benefits, low-interest loans, rapid amortizations and so on for enterprises producing environment-friendly equipment and using waste-free and energy-saving technology, as well as tax benefits on revenues invested in ecological activities. Additional benefits should be granted to foreign investors contributing to environmental protection, and could probably be included in the financial provisions for our country made by the West.

As well as the desire for Western investment, many in Eastern Europe worry that what has happened in many areas of the Third World might happen there: that obsolete, high-pollution technology is exported to them or, worse, that they are used as a dumping-ground for dangerous waste. This is a risk that many Western economists are aware of, and which the EEC itself is dealing with through an ad hoc code of conduct.

Shatalin   It is not acceptable that our country, or any other, should be turned into the world's dump. It is immoral to use the economic difficulties of a country to stockpile dangerous waste on its territory, or to export ecologically harmful products to it under the guise of economic aid. To prevent all this, closer international contacts are required, based on openness, trust and moral criteria.

Gerelli   One general principle should be observed: that when plants and factories are installed in other countries, only technology used in the country of origin should be employed. If this principle is abided by then it is likely that there will be an improvement in the environment in Eastern Europe, which until now has had little environmental protection and has suffered much harm. Obviously, if the transformation of the economic system brings with it a significant increase in production, we do not know what the effects on the balance of the ecosystems might be. The strategy adopted should be a gradual one capable of inducing these countries to look after the environment themselves. But I don't believe that the race to invest in Eastern Europe, of which we have heard so much, will be as rapid as has been suggested, or that there will be an explosion in production.

Bresso   There's no doubt at all, Western economies are looking on Eastern Europe merely as the site of a potential increase in consumption. A country such as the former USSR, for example, which is rich in resources of every kind, which exports raw materials and imports finished products, is seen as manna from heaven. Not only that but, unlike the Third World, the countries of Eastern Europe have high levels of technology and well-trained manpower. If they succeed in converting their production systems, reducing military expenditure and overcoming the terrible inefficiency caused by centralized control, they can certainly present themselves as the ideal sites for the transfer of the most innovative technology, for the setting up of branches of Western companies, joint ventures and so on.

No one seems at all worried about the negative effects such a development could have on the environment.

In practice, no. Even the EEC, which *is* worried about the increase in levels of emissions of greenhouse-effect gases since the establishment of the Common Market, doesn't seem to have given any consideration to the problem. And obviously it is unlikely that consideration will be given until the West changes its attitude towards growth: the West can hardly sell what it doesn't have. On the other hand, though, given the waste of resources there has been in the Eastern Bloc economies up till now, a real improvement in efficiency might increase production while at the same time reducing the consumption of raw materials in absolute terms. And if they import cleaner technology they might be able to improve the general ecological situation. But a long-term risk exists.

Altvater I really don't believe there is going to be an economic boom in the countries of Eastern Europe. Take what was East Germany: the production system has simply disintegrated. They produce 25 per cent of what they produced two years ago. The rest of what they consume is produced in Italy, France, West Germany, South Korea, Japan, etcetera. The former socialist countries today consume more but they do not produce, because now they have opened up the world market system, they have to be able to withstand the competition, and they just can't. It's in the West that we'll see an increase in production, and, as a result, a worsening of the ecological conditions of the West rather than the East. It's here in the West that we need to control the production process, and it's here that we need to begin to review and change our lifestyle. The subject can't be simplified, broken up, compartmentalized: it needs to be complicated, and we must make the effort to see the subject as a whole, in which everything hangs together.

In order to secure adequate levels of commitment on the part of the individual nations to those problems that cannot be solved locally, all my Eastern European interviewees were convinced of the need for international agreements, and were ready to collaborate to the utmost towards this end. Some had precise proposals in mind.

Shatalin   A World Foundation for the Protection of the Atmosphere could be set up. The financial contribution of each state should take into account the balance of oxygen and greenhouse-effect gases on their territory (it is well known that some states consume more oxygen than is guaranteed by their territory). This foundation could provide aid to those states that are protecting forests, especially tropical forests, which is something that concerns the whole world, it could finance the work of eliminating ocean pollution, such as the removal of oil spills, and it could support in every possible way intergovernmental cooperation in the field of environmental protection.

CHAPTER 10

A COMMERCIAL BREAK

For all their uncertainty, caution, mistrust, and open fear of a possible reduction in individual freedom, many economists seemed to feel that a change in the characteristic consumerist lifestyle is necessary in the interests of the environment.

But fashions and lifestyles don't just appear from nowhere, without cause. Immoderate consumerism obviously has its origins partly as a psychological reaction to years of austerity, and is common to many different social classes, who, as soon as they achieve prosperity after generations of poverty, seek a kind of compensation for the privations of the past in the acquisition and possession of not only far more than is necessary, but far more even than can readily be enjoyed.

But this is just one of the causes of consumerism, which also has far deeper roots, structurally connected with our economic system. Too often we tend to forget that fundamental turning point in industrial history that is marked by the celebrated phrase Henry Ford addressed to his employees, 'There's an automobile in the future for all of you,' putting up their salaries as he did so. He realized that continuing to make cars only as a bourgeois luxury, as they were considered then, would have placed an unacceptable limit on the mechanisms of accumulation, contradicting the expansionist essence of capital. Hence new markets had to be sought, of which the working class itself could be an essential part.

The transformation of the worker into a consumer was the crucial moment in the prelude to the present socioeconomic system, dominated as it is by consumerism. Like any other mass behavioural phenomenon, it was induced and encouraged by various cultural pressures working through the media, such as radio, television, the cinema and the press, in conformity with the expansionist parameters of the economic system, that is, as a function of growth. Among these, advertising is notorious for the influence it possesses. In the words of the president of J. Walter Thomson, one of the largest US advertising agencies, advertising is able 'to create needs in people's minds they didn't have the faintest idea they had before', thus 'provoking the changes in demand that we need'.[1] There is a huge sociological literature on this subject, whose most obvious arguments have filtered through to the general public.

Not to the economists, though. Is this yet another consequence of the more and more noticeable divisions between different branches of knowledge? Or is it the well-known attitude of distance that an 'exact science' like economics feels towards a discipline largely based on empirical observation, such as sociology? One thing is clear, however: my question on this subject aroused very little interest and attention from my interviewees, as if it were a subject they had never considered in relation to economic activity. There were, though, one or two important exceptions.

Friedman I think the influence of advertising is grossly exaggerated. I can quote you many cases of products launched with tremendous advertising campaigns that were a failure. Let me ask you a question: if you were a producer, would you persuade people to have tastes that they don't have or appeal to the tastes that they do have?

Yes, I know this argument. Obviously you can't make people buy what they don't want, but you can induce them to buy and consume.

Perhaps you can try to bring into the open the tastes they have.

But you can model these tastes, and thus their lifestyles.

Very little.

But if advertising is so useless, why do companies spend so much money on it?

Because it provides information.

Friedman's opinion was very close to those of the majority of his colleagues. Some were even more dismissive.

Solow Too much advertising serves no purpose. One ad cancels another.

Simon Basically I think people will consume what they can produce.

Even those who were very critical of advertising did not seem fully to understand its importance in forming consumerist models and in promotion of the market.

---

1. Quoted in André Gorz, *Metamorphoses du travail*, Paris, Galilée, 1988, p. 153.

Hartje   I'd like to see less advertising, but I don't think there's any connection with the environment, or that there's a cause-and-effect relation with consumerism ... I'm really not convinced there is.

Martinez-Alier   Perhaps the problem is not with advertising as such. There are other ways of inducing consumption. For example, today the highest consumption of meat in Europe is in Spain and Italy, two traditionally poor countries, because only now can they afford to buy it. It has prestige. While in the United States, which was prosperous much earlier, they're all afraid of cholesterol, and want to go on diets, and so on.

That too is another form of consumerism, with its own advertising campaigns ...

Yes, that's true. And there's also the trend to sponsorization. Travelling through Mexico and Peru recently, I saw advertisements everywhere for the forthcoming Olympics along these lines: 'Barcelona '92 – Coca-Cola'. What has Barcelona got to do with Coca-Cola? The truth is that Coca-Cola is very fashionable in poorer countries. There are two tendencies in human nature, one towards conspicuous consumption, and one towards renunciation. I look at my students and my colleagues ... they're not great consumers. In Berlin there are plenty of people who are happy to use a bike.

But isn't it true that, as we just said, the people who are willing to give things up are those who already have everything? Or who could at least afford to give things up? You can't throw away what you haven't got. It's very human to want things that you haven't got, but which others have. In fact, advertising tends to encourage consumption in countries and social classes that so far have had very little. They are the areas the market wants to break into ...

I try to be optimistic. The only hope is that people's mentality will change, helped by political movements. But perhaps advertising has a role to play in this, if it is used correctly, as in the battle against smoking. Focusing attention on health could be the right way ...

Earlier, I mentioned some important exceptions to the general lack of interest in advertising shown by my interviewees. The most significant is certainly James Meade, who as long ago as 1972 not only carried out an extremely lucid analysis of the relation between advertising and consumption, but also advanced a proposal designed to affect this relation and so contain consumerism. He still subscribes without reservations to both his analysis and the proposal.

Meade Much of modern competitive business seeks new openings for good business by means of commercial advertising, whose aim is to generate new wants or to make consumers desire to discard an old model of a product in order to acquire a new model of what is basically the same product. Commercial advertising stimulates in this way the continual desire for new purchases and unnecessary gadgets, creating an atmosphere of restless discontent which can be satisfied only through a higher level of consumption. I think we should try and discourage commercial advertising by means of heavy taxes, and try to return to broadcasting systems that are not basically organs for the stimulation of new wants, as they are now. Moreover, some steps could be taken to give incentives to manufacturers to produce more durable products rather than objects expressly designed to need rapid replacement. For example, if cars were taxed much more heavily when they are new, and less when they are older, consumers would demand more durable and solid cars. And, in general, similar measures could be taken as an incentive to go for durability of every kind of good.

In all the interviews I carried out after Meade's, I asked for an opinion on his ideas, and on his proposal to tax advertising. These are the most significant answers.

Gerelli It's a proposal a pupil of mine suggested some time ago. I fully agree with it. A tax on advertising could be a useful instrument for modifying certain tendencies and certain models of consumption.

Do you agree too that it would be possible to promote another type of non-commercial advertising, publicly sponsored, to encourage ecologically correct behaviour?

Undoubtedly. So long as the consumer is able to choose.

But do you think that the proposal would be easy to put into practice in a world dominated by advertising, with television channels that live on commercials, newspapers and magazines whose survival is guaranteed in the same way, activities of all kinds that are sponsored by commercial products?

I realize that it wouldn't be at all easy. Here too, though, the general rule of economics and ecology is still valid, a rule that should never be forgotten, however painful it is, that 'there's no such thing as a free lunch'. There's a cost to everything. Naturally with a provision of this kind, everything would depend on the interventions being carefully phased, so that, for example, commercial television would have to change, partly financing itself with other types of commercials, of a pro-environment kind perhaps. Or we would have fewer television stations. We are in a world where resources are scarce and everything has a cost. To the extent that certain products and a certain level of production damage the environment, it seems fair to me that whoever wants to advertise them should pay the social cost of the fact that some people are buying five refrigerators when one would do.

Sylos Labini   There's no doubt that advertising has a clear role in the explosion of consumerism. Keynes foresaw that consumption would rise at a slightly lower rate than the increase in income, but it hasn't been like that: there has not been this gap, and advertising has contributed to this. Placing a specific tax on commercials could be very useful, as part of that overall strategy I have mentioned, made up of bans, incentives, standards, technological research and so on. It's an idea that I think Nicholas Kaldor would have appreciated. He was very critical about advertising.

Bresso   I am absolutely convinced that advertising is one of the greatest promoters of consumption, and I'm in favour of every possible attempt to hold back the avalanche. But I don't know how useful fiscal measures would be. It's a bit like any environment tax: if a product causes pollution, let's put the price up by raising its advertising costs as well, and in this way we reduce its consumption.

Couldn't this mechanism have an effect on the advertising itself too — reduce it by making it more costly?

I'm rather doubtful, because commercial advertising has a decisive role in the functioning of our economy. Monopoly competition is different from genuine competition: it's a situation in which everybody produces very similar goods, they are competing among themselves, and they all have to accept the price as a given fact and sell what they produce at that price. For example, a farmer doesn't advertise: wheat is wheat and he can't advertise his own as the best.

Oh, but he can …

That's true, they can even do that now, borrowing from industrial products ways to differentiate certain agricultural products, putting a blue sticker on them, for example, like they do for the bananas, and in this way advertising products that are absolutely identical to all the others. Because one banana is the same as any other banana, whatever Chiquita says. They simply select the quality and sell bananas that are all the same size. But this is the mechanism of monopoly competition, typical of an industrial economy, which makes it possible to sell a certain product as extra-special, differentiating it with a brand name, and creating in this way a little monopoly. All clothes with a well-known brand name – Versace, Armani, Benetton and so on, which are just industrial merchandise, and not the work of tailors as they used to be – are operations of this kind. But as the differences are unreal, the monopoly can be created and imposed only through advertising. But it's a very short-lived mechanism: you have the idea of the brand name, others will have the same idea, and then you will have to invent something else ...

The same old unstoppable spiral towards 'more' ...

A spiral that leaves a manufacturer in no time with surplus production capacity, that forces him to increase advertising expenditure in the hope of being able to sell enough to reach acceptable levels of production capacity utilization. That's why a company often increases advertising rather than reducing it in moments of crisis. In short, advertising is an integral part of the mechanisms on which the functioning of industrial economies are based, it is part of the system. If they don't change the mechanisms of the economic system, eliminating or even significantly reducing advertising will be very difficult. Maybe regulations could be more effective than a tax, like forbidding newspapers and television to devote more than a certain amount of space to advertising. Perhaps even the companies, which often get into serious difficulties in the vortex of expansion, might be satisfied by that.

Altvater Advertising is certainly crucial for the spread of consumerism, but high taxation of commercials would mean the end of capitalism. Advertising is an expression of the process of production and accumulation: by creating an ever-larger demand it is a part of that process. Discussion of advertising cannot be limited to lifestyles and consumerism: it involves the Henry Ford syndrome too. The discussion needs to be complete and coherent, and not many people are interested in having it. Many even of the more radical greens are strongly against any anti-capitalist suggestions, or any anti-capitalist battle. They keep on reminding us – which is true – that planned economies haven't worked, even from an ecological point of view, and go on insisting on the need for the market. It's a line of thought that is not only weak but false.

CHAPTER II

CAN TECHNOLOGY
SAVE US?

Cleaner production processes that will use up fewer scarce resources, more and more sophisticated systems which will be better able to reuse more of the growing mass of waste, lighter and more 'immaterial' products, fertilizers that do little or no damage, cars that are small and 'clean' – technology, almost everyone seems to believe, will be the principal instrument by means of which to aim for a development less destructive to the environment, especially for the countries of the Third World and Eastern Europe, whose economic development has yet to take off.

So widespread are the number of different processes and materials with a very strong negative impact on the environment, that to develop a less ecologically destructive economy will be a huge task, one which will require an enormous programme of directed research to provide the necessary know-how long before any concrete results can be achieved.

Many times, however, several of my interviewees mentioned (in part to justify the scant attention economists have given to the environment) the lack of scientific certainty, the dramatic divergences of opinion even between experts, on questions such as global warming or the gap in the ozone layer. But it is obvious that in these cases too only a serious attempt to increase our knowledge of these subjects, which means a commitment to a wide-ranging programme of research, will be able to overcome this handicap.

So it is natural to ask if state financing of research of this kind is adequate. The almost unanimous reply was, no. Almost equally unanimous (and not only for environmental reasons) was the positive answer to the question posed by environmentalists as to whether the enormous expenditure on armaments could not be used for environmental purposes in general, and in particular for scientific research. The reply was much vaguer to the question, why on earth do the big names among economists not impose this policy line on their governments? But here are some of the opinions recorded.

Solow   One of the most efficient weapons against the destruction of the environment is certainly scientific research. We will only have machinery and production processes that create less damage, and alternative forms of energy, such as solar energy, instead of traditional forms like oil and coal, if there is serious scientific and technological research, and if governments give sufficient funds for this research. Here something *is* happening: Bush not only mentioned the importance of the environmental problem in one of his last speeches, but also referred to the need to give greater support to research. It's not very much, but it's something. I have been part of a group that has suggested assigning a part of the expenditure on military research to research into non-polluting sources of energy and materials. We spend tens of billions of dollars a year on military research, and one tenth of that sum would make a dramatic change in the effects of production on the environment.

Sylos Labini   In my proposal for the establishment of an environmental body at the UN, an Agency for the Environment, adequate financing for scientific and technological research are among the principal priorities envisaged. At the moment very little expenditure is earmarked specifically for the environment. Italy spends even less than other countries. But there is also a complete lack of proportion in what is funded. A couple of years ago, for example, I wrote an indignant article about the EEC budget, which devoted 63 per cent to farming subsidies (much of which are often sheer waste) and only 1.5 per cent for the environment. There was no immediate reply, but steps were taken later to revise such a disproportionate allocation of funds.

Simon   I don't think it's true that we spend too little on environmental research. In the United States we spend several billion dollars a year …

Yes, but how much does the United States spend on armaments and space exploration? Couldn't that money be spent on the environment?

Yes, fine, I'm all for that.

After all, we can go to the moon, we can walk in space, we have all these formidably intelligent weapons. Just to give one example, are we really incapable of inventing a material with the same characteristics of plastic but which doesn't cause such terrible pollution? Don't you think that really serious, properly financed research of this kind could produce results?

It's possible, but there's a very simple objection. It's much easier to spend money on sophisticated weapons or space exploration, because they excite people's imaginations, which serious scientific research doesn't. When certain objectives are set, and they are publicized so emphatically that they become absolute priorities, people get used to the idea. If you send a man on the moon, everybody wants him to get there, it doesn't matter how much it costs or if other things are more important.

Bresso I'm not very optimistic about the role of technology. Research today, particularly applied research, is exclusively directed towards goals related to increased productivity. It's pure chance if new products and materials can lead to environmental improvement. There is no adequate development of what Claude Raffestin calls 'the checks and balances of scientific knowledge', able to take account of all the side-effects of scientific inventions, which are many, very complex and diverse, and concern the functioning of the whole of the human environment in all its aspects. This kind of knowledge is almost never orientated in an assured way. No one wins the Nobel Prize for demonstrating that a product is highly toxic; in fact, if he does demonstrate that, he risks being driven out of the scientific community. Anyone who invents a new substance wants to get it on the market as quickly as possible, in case someone else gets in first, without developing the necessary sense of checks and balances – which means without knowing what the consequences might be.

This is because most of our science takes place in the laboratory. The unknown factor is in the transition from the laboratory to the outside world. Ecosystems are extremely complex, everything is connected to everything else, whilst the laboratory can isolate a cause and an effect; it is a place in which the knowledge developed is that which is functional to the question posed. There is no complexity. The distinction between the economics of the environment and 'ecological economics' lies precisely in this awareness of complexity, and in insistence on the need for interdisciplinary work. Science rejects this because it would mean slowing down the process of discovery, whilst the tendency in science, like everywhere else, is towards acceleration. Or it would require a God-like intelligence, in command of everything that was knowable ...

This has been possible to a certain extent. It was possible for a single individual such as Leonardo da Vinci to possess the entire field of human knowledge ...

Yes, but the universal scientist can no longer exist. To reconstruct him would mean building bridges between scientists and between the various scientific disciplines. This is one of the objectives of ecological economics – to try to create a dialogue with physicists, biologists, etcetera, along the following lines: 'We are concerned not with economics but with the effects that economic activity has in every field, and with the effect that what happens in the world, as observed by other disciplines, can have on the economy'; we are interested in the totality of things in which new processes and products will find their place.' Until science adopts an approach of this kind I don't think it can be of any real help in the improvement of the environment. But, as we know, science notoriously has always done what those in power asked it to do. In theory there are grounds for optimism: if we choose to put the right questions to science, put, though, with the force of those who have the backing of economic and political power, then scientists have the intellectual means to give answers. But at the moment science is going in exactly the opposite direction: becoming more and more specialized and sharply honed.

Samuelson   This is my credo: as science improves our potential for material living, it gives us the opportunity – if we are willing to use it – to employ some of the fruits of science in preserving and enhancing the beautiful garden mankind has inherited from the distant past. The challenge is to persuade ourselves, and persuade our neighbours everywhere, to make the gradual policy changes that will slow down the rate of ecological degeneration and that will even reverse the ecological degeneration of the historical past. The challenge is a vital one. And it calls for refinement and good will.

CHAPTER 12

AN EXACT SCIENCE?

More than one of my interviewees was at times strongly critical of traditional economic science, and not only because of the methods and instruments with which it deals – or fails to deal – with the problems of the environment. At times the argument came close to questioning the very foundations of the discipline.

The most radical attack was formulated and articulated by the adherents of ecological economics, a marginal group in comparison to the academic mainstream, as I have already mentioned, and one that likes to distinguish itself even within the world of environmental economics. The group represents a stream of thought that is still in its early stages but intellectually well-equipped, and that in recent years has expanded notably, especially among the younger researchers in the field, who see their intellectual fathers as economists such as Georgescu-Roegen, Boulding and Kneese, who, themselves disregarded for decades, have accused economics of ignoring nature and concerning itself almost exclusively with quantifiable social activities and human relations, that is, with what can be expressed through the mediation of money.

The extracts that follow are from interviews with some of the most distinguished of these ecological economists, who tried to justify their dissent from what they call 'standard economics'. Their arguments were also passed on to the other economists I spoke to for their evaluation and comment.

Bresso As far as the environment is concerned, the original sin of economics is not so much not having dealt with it – it has dealt with it a little – but having considered it a marginal question. It has not realized the real significance of the phenomenon because it has never given any attention to the physical reality of production, only its economic and monetary aspect. In economics, when we talk about products we always talk about value. Economics is based on added value. But by ignoring the physical content, the materiality of production, we have failed to recognize that externalities are not accessory but the other side of production itself. In fact, in the course of industrial transformation the mass of materials used does not decrease, but tends to increase, because there is the addition of water, oxygen and everything else that is part of the production process ...

And everything is bound to become waste in the end ...

Solid, liquid or gaseous waste, but the mass remains the same, it's the same quantity in circulation, except that in the end it has become a negative value. The other serious deficiency in economics is its failure to face the question of growth, as something that cannot continue indefinitely.

And yet it should be an obvious enough consideration ...

Perhaps the old error has been made of interpreting the historical phase in which we are living as the end of history. At the moment we are in a growth phase that has lasted two hundred years, and we believe that it will continue like this. But probably the Industrial Revolution has been a stage at which the economy must settle for a long period of stability. A first step was that of the agricultural revolution, which made life on Earth possible for a much greater number of people than in the societies based on hunting and gathering. The Industrial Revolution has been another step: today the planet can allow many more people to live on it than was the case in rural societies, and, broadly speaking, at much higher levels of prosperity. But this is no longer valid for a population that is growing without check, and still less can we think of making available to all these individuals unlimited quantities of resources. Economists need to reflect on all this. And they need to do it urgently.

Passet   The serious analysis of the environmental question has revealed how narrow traditional economics is, so much so that it has called its very logic into question. It's like this: in addition to the 'classic' forms of pollution – air, water and so on – which we have more or less learned to deal with, we are faced with what I call 'global pollution', the greenhouse effect, reduction of the ozone layer, diminution of animal species, etcetera, and here it's no longer enough to talk about the environment, it's something that concerns the biosphere. So it's no longer a matter of devising an economics of the environment, but of completely rethinking our economic policy. It's something that happens in every science: when you come up against a phenomenon that resists or can't be reconciled with the theory, it's obviously not the phenomenon that doesn't work, it's the theory that doesn't take it into account; in that case you have to find a new theory that does take it into account, that can do what the old theory couldn't. Economics is in this situation when it's faced with ecological problems.

How many economists share your conviction?

Very few. It seems impossible to explain certain things to the representatives of what some people would call 'normal' economics, that which corresponds to the dominant paradigm of the age, that is, neoclassical economics. They are used to reasoning in monetary terms, that is, within the clearly defined closed system of production and exchange, and they cannot deal with the problem of the reproduction of the natural environment except in monetary terms. It's impossible to make them understand that the economy embraces not only monetary flows but also physical and energy flows. For example, a business extracts raw materials and turns them into products, gets rid of the waste, and this is one dimension; then it tries to obtain from the operation a certain profit superior to the cost, and this is another dimension. Economists interpret the activity of companies only through this second dimension, the monetary side, as if money and the flow of goods were just counterparts of each other. But money is only a means, and it doesn't represent real economic activities. Take another example. When a species disappears, then, yes, there is a loss which is calculable in economic terms. Suppose, for example, that there's a diminution in the production of mussels, and that has an economic cost which can be evaluated in monetary terms. This is a real dimension, but is insufficient as an expression of the problem. Because mussels are a species that, like any other, has a precise function within a certain ecosystem, and if a species disappears or becomes scarce then that given function will no longer be performed. Calculating the economic costs at this stage of development isn't much use. What we need to know is if we are irretrievably upsetting the biological mechanisms of the planet, including any possibility of life on the planet. We are in the field of physics and biology, a dimension completely separate from the monetary one. Not that the monetary dimension doesn't exist, obviously, but we have to take account of both these dimensions, which exist and coexist, but do not obey the same logic, and are irreducibly separate.

What possible solution is there?

I believe economic science stands in need of a fundamental change. I believe economists should act on the economic variables to modify the behaviour of economic agents, and bring them into line with the physical requirements for the reproduction of the biosphere. But official economics, especially in the universities, is totally deaf to these arguments. It's no coincidence that men like Georgescu-Roegen or Boulding, who have raised fundamental questions on this subject, have been completely neglected. They are not following the official line, and they will never get the Nobel Prize. It's not just the height of the absurd, but symbolic in its absurdity, that this year, while the debate has been going on about the survival of the planet, the Nobel was awarded to people who are interested only in pocketbook economics.

Leipert   Economics, as it was conceived in the eighteenth century, was deeply rooted in nature. The first economic school, the physiocrats, regarded nature as the only source of wealth and value. But as economics evolved, this thought got lost. The neoclassical school that prevails today follows a model based on purely economic relations, without seeing that in reality the economic process works in nature. The very concept in business and politics of economic growth as it developed between the thirties and the fifties was something measured in goods and income, based on GNP, and not taking into consideration the effects of growth on the natural environment and on people. For a long time the environment wasn't even recognized as a problem that concerned economists, and that was possible so long as production levels were relatively constrained. But today, after two hundred years of industrialization and high growth, this economic model seems more and more obsolete: the levels of transformation of energy and raw materials and the emissions of toxic substances and waste into the natural environment, and the resulting disturbance to the balance of ecosystems, have reached such a point today that we can no longer ignore the relation between economics and ecology.

You also talk about the inadequacy of the present economic model for future generations.[1]

Current economic theory, which essentially deals only with market activity, is not only mechanical but static, extremely impoverished compared to the thought of the great founders of economics such as Smith, Ricardo and Mill. All three of them had a vision of long-term economic development, a historical vision, which has been lost and which today we need to recover. Today we cannot afford to go on ignoring the fact that every production process is irreversible, that it destroys energy and produces energy. The concept of economic growth, which disregards these facts completely, and is based

---

1. Christian Leipert, 'Social Costs of Economic Growth', *Journal of Economic Issues*, vol. xx, no. 1, March 1986.

on the premiss of the unlimited availability of natural capital, has no historical dimension whatsoever, and completely ignores the consequences of production on social and human evolution. We need to elaborate a new economic model, a more complex one, which takes account of the many relations between production, society and nature, and as such reflected both in economic theory and in evaluation and accounting.

Can you describe this model to me?

It's not an easy process, obviously, and will need a long time. It can only be defined in detail through testing and practice. But first of all we must abandon the simple model of the market and devise forms of economic behaviour that take account of the needs of nature and of people. The institutional relations that determine the type of economic relations in a particular culture at a particular historical moment will naturally be very important in this. We need to reconstruct our concept of production and income, bearing in mind that the natural basis of economic activity is natural capital. But very probably this will meet with strong opposition not only from the business world but also from politicians and trade unionists, all of whom are absolutely in thrall to the fetish of growth and GNP, which, in any case, is not only quite improperly identified with social welfare, but also far from being a faithful mirror of the real wealth of a country.

Daly In the Environment Department of the World Bank, where I work, there are many economists who are trying with good will to apply to environmental problems the economic theories they learned at university, but who realize that these theories are flawed and practically useless. I think that many environmental problems have to be dealt with at the level of economic theory, and this requires a radical reformulation of economic thinking. This should be the job of the university departments, and they have failed miserably in this. The only people who have come up with new and challenging ways of thinking about economics are Boulding and Georgescu-Roegen, but they are not taken seriously, and have been more or less written out of the profession. Now some people are starting to think again, trying to make use of their economic thought, but it's amazing how conservative our discipline is.

What are the most serious errors of traditional economic thought?

The basic error is that of a mechanistic epistemology, by which the economic process is represented as a circular movement, closed and reversible, moving between production and consumption, without taking into account the physical and biological aspects of economic activity, which operates on natural elements subject to exhaustion on the one hand, and deterioration through entropy on the other. Traditional economics behaves as if nature were a free good, immutable and unlimited. This means that the fear that the macroeconomy might grow too much with respect to the planet's ecosystem is completely absent from economic theory. It was taken for granted that the macroeconomy must grow forever. This premiss is mistaken in itself, but absolutely unsustainable today, when we have an enormous level of overall production and growing ecological imbalance.

The classical definition of income is the maximum you can consume over a given period and still be as well off at the end as you were at the beginning; it means the most you can consume without consuming capital, without running down your capacity to produce in the future. So the idea of sustainability is built into the very definition of income. But we don't respect it; indeed, the consumption of our capital is increasing, we are using more and more natural goods. I have a thesis on the subject, which I'm playing with at the moment: we are moving from an era in which the limiting factor on economic development was manmade capital into an era in which the limiting factor is the remaining natural capital. It's not the fishing boat that limits the fish catch but the amount of fish left in the sea and its reproductive capacity. It's not the capacity of refineries that limits gasoline production but the amount of petroleum in the ground. It's natural capital that is the limiting factor now.

That's not at all the normal way of considering production.

It's an attempt to ground economics in the biophysical world and give it the tools needed for that. But we should also ground economics in ethical values. We can't go on pretending that economic growth is the only valid treatment for combating poverty, when the opposite has been proved beyond any doubt. We should think in terms of redistributing and dividing wealth with the poorer countries.

Georgescu-Roegen Economics should be the science of the whole of society, in all its manifestations and fields of action. This includes production, but the environment too, and it should take into account that what we do cannot go against the laws of physics, chemistry and biology. If I put my arm on a stove it's my arm that gets burnt, not the stove. But mainstream economics, anchored as it is to a scientific paradigm borrowed from mechanics, is unable to understand the concrete facts of life. It is absurd to think we can solve all our problems with the aid of numbers alone, to believe we can foresee the future through econometric models. Jevons and Pareto were the founders of this form of economics. Their followers have been imprisoned by their concern with a series of problems dominated by money. And new problems don't interest them; if they were to take an interest in them they would have to say, 'We've been wrong.'

Altvater   The economists who dominate the scene today argue in terms of the rationality of the market, prices and monetary equilibria. They fail to understand that economics is also the transformation of nature: their perfectly balanced models are fundamentally mistaken.

Are you close to the group of ecological economists?

Yes, I agree with their basic ideas. Unlike some of them, however, I believe that our theories need to combine what happens in the world of use values with what happens in the world of exchange values. Economics cannnot be reduced to ecology.

Many ecological economists see the need to balance economic needs with those of the environment.

But this is just on the level of norms. What we need is a proper theory, and we must define its analytical tools, categories and concepts in order fully to understand the complex ways in which the economic system and the environment are interwoven. There is still no theory of this kind; we can only just begin to glimpse the beginnings of one.

Martinez-Alier   Traditional economics has many faults, in particular its lack of interest in the unequal distribution between rich and poor, and its kidding itself it can solve social injustices through the market. This is an old accusation, which Sraffa made very strongly. But from the point of view of the environment, this kind of economics cannot evaluate nonrenewable resources, consider the problem of waste or take any interest in future generations. How can you give a monetary value to biodiversity, or to the greenhouse effect, or to the plutonium we're producing in nuclear plants, which has a life of 24,000 years? And how can purely economic models based on the market understand and deal with phenomena such as the enormous pressure of the population of the Third World, which is tending to migrate towards the First, and which is certainly going to increase in the near future? The worst of it is that these extremely serious limitations to economics are reflected in the most negative way on politicians, who give great weight to the pronouncements of economists.

You are one of the most famous spokesmen for ecological economics. Could you briefly describe the general ideas of this new school, which is opposed to the dominant form of economics?

Politically we are a group of people with very different positions. We are united by the conviction that the economy is an open system, a flow of energy and materials that are transformed ultimately into waste. We see the economy as a huge ecosystem, of which human beings are a part and within which the values of the market are a minor part. Our discussions focus on those values that the market does not recognize, on the unknown factors in technological innovation and on the need to introduce ecological economics into teaching and all public discussion. In the long term all this would result in new ways of thinking and concrete policies. I believe that ecological economics is going to become very important in the coming decades, and will force conventional economics to change, if not disappear.

Your group has strongly criticized the market economy, but a planned economy can hardly be said to have given better results, either for the environment or for general prosperity and civil rights. What proposals do you have?

I think an alternative could be an extremely open political system, with representation for all minorities, which could allow the people themselves to determine what is best for them.

But it has to be admitted that, historically, the left has not been particularly sensitive towards the environment ...

Marx said some interesting things on the subject, but didn't give much attention to it. Engels, who had read everything on the fundamental studies on thermodynamics, said some very silly things on the subject, which unfortunately became part of Marxist dogma. But if we look at the left in the twentieth century overall, we find some interesting strands of thought on the environment, especially among the anarchosyndicalists. But, for the most part, those factions of the left which were most influential, the Leninists and the social-democrats, were completely deaf to the question: they had embraced the idea of progress as material growth, prey to an uncontrolled optimism in technology. And this continued throughout the 1960s and 1970s in the communist parties of Europe, Cuba and the Soviet Union: they believed in a technological and scientific revolution, encouraged nuclear energy, and accused capitalism of holding back technological invention ... And when the German greens appeared on the scene, many people on the left dismissed them as romantic reactionary nationalists. It's true, there is an element of this among the greens, but for the most part they are people of the left ... The left just didn't understand what these new political groups were talking about.

The environmental economists and the ecologists are not the only ones to criticize economic science. An awareness that traditional economics is inadequate in the face of a reality that is more and more complex and changing more and more rapidly can be heard in other voices. But economic science in its present state still has its defenders.

Sylos Labini For me, most of the prevailing economic theory is static, not dynamic. I've been convinced of this and of its limitations for a long time now. I've sometimes said that economics works with photographs, not with films, which is what it should do. It can't see movement. And this is why it excludes all the problems of development, or sees them as marginal. Consequently it can't be expected to deal with the negative consequences of development. It's no accident that the problem of the environment is so little present in the world of economics: the economists who deal with the subject of development are a minority, and many of them either give no weight to the environmental question or consider it a specialist subject that doesn't concern them. Others, like me, for example, regard it as a very serious problem, but don't feel sufficiently qualified. Then there are some very important economists like Baumaul, Sachs and a few others, who have dealt seriously with this negative aspect of development. But there are very few of them.

Spaventa It's undeniable that economics has ignored the interaction between production processes and the natural environment. But it should be added that, as economics can only say anything precise if it proceeds through formal models, constructing one with this point of view is extremely difficult. Some attempts are being made. There's a centre at Santa Fe, in the United States, where complex systems are studied, with the participation of biologists, chemists and so on, and with incredible mathematical backup. There they are doing things fairly close to what Georgescu-Roegen proposed. Unfortunately, the complexity of these problems from the biological, climatic, etcetera, point of view is enormous. And there seems to be no scientific certainty on the phenomena of environmental imbalance, especially on the largest, those with international dimensions. In the newspapers you can read everything and the opposite of everything on this subject.

But don't you think that the reason we know so little is that we study it so little?

I don't know. It seems to me that it is objectively difficult to understand what the real effects are of the hole in the ozone layer.

But if we don't try studying them we may never understand it ...

Well, there's now a great deal of energy being devoted to these subjects.

Apart from the accusation of a total lack of interest in the natural environment, the ecologists make a more radical criticism of economics, which is connected to the first objection. They say that economic theory is abstract, absolutely detached from social reality, because it excludes from its field of observation all activities that can't be translated into financial relations. Among other things it excludes family and domestic work as a producer of use values rather than exchange values, that is, it excludes the main activity of half of mankind, the female half.

That's true; in recent years, especially, economics has been developing in this direction. There has been an excess of utilitarianism, the assumption that every conclusion can be drawn from the hypothesis of the maximization of the function of utility. I quite admit that these are the normal tools of economists today, particularly after the turning point of the 1970s, with the neoclassical Chicago school. On the other hand it must be said that this allows a certain precision in results which otherwise would risk being lost in generalities. But yes, of course, I could make a long list of the failings of economics ...

Hahn Economic theory too abstract? Too tied to figures and models? Whereas in the past the economist's attention took in the whole of society? Possibly. Perhaps his attention was more wide-ranging, but it may not have been better. I think people underestimate the very humane influence of economics, because putting numbers on things is the beginning to thinking clearly about things. I'm sure of that. My view is that many of the ills of the world's history have been due not to wickedness, although there has been some, but to sheer intellectual laziness and not thinking carefully enough. If we have enough numbers we can really have a good argument. If I say, it's terrible that these children are not properly educated, well, that's one thing. But if I produce some numbers to show what they could be contributing to society if they were educated, the argument becomes clear. Generalized good will gets us nowhere; everything has to be sufficiently precise, whatever the subject. The greatest poetry too is very precise. It translates emotions into something disciplined, precise, comprehensible, from which you can get the feeling of an experience.

If you are right, that would be another reason for economists to be interested in the environment: putting some numbers on the problem, making it clear and precise ...

But you didn't ask me that. There are lots of economists putting numbers on the environment, who are doing research on it ...

Yes, but they are 'small' numbers. I'm not thinking about those who are trying to put a price on the various elements of environmental damage, fixing the cost of 'pollution permits', or proposing to make machines that give you five minutes of oxygenated air for a nickel. I'm thinking of the momentous numbers you were talking about, those of the poets who bring clarity to ideas and sensations ...

My friend Ken Arrow tackled some questions about the damage produced by supersonic aeroplanes, what would be the increase in skin cancer and so on. Well, he and his collaborators got some very good numbers, they calculated probabilities, and concluded that they should prohibit the development of supersonic civil aircraft. But you can't ask an economist questions like, what is the probability of catastrophe? I don't think we have the slightest idea. Of course, we do know certain things – the need for huge transfers to the Third World, population control, etcetera. We know what should be done, but I don't think it will be done, because people still don't perceive the danger. It isn't sufficiently based on facts.

Because very few people want to know the facts. The facts are known.

But I recently read a most interesting account that apparently, using some sort of technology, you could replant the Brazilian forest in twenty years.

So let's hope in technology?

We have to.

Gerelli I've been dealing with the environment since the late sixties, and time and again I keep hearing this radical thesis, by which economics is unable to deal with the environment. Then, when you get to the nitty-gritty, no alternative proposals are offered, while traditional economics has a whole series of instruments which everyone finds useful.

Ecological economists don't exactly reject these instruments. They maintain that they should be integrated with others as part of a more complex horizon of ideas.

Sometimes these criticisms come close to the absurd. It's like the situation in which, I can't remember if it was Harlequin or Pulcinella, one of them in a duel says to his enemy, 'Stand still or I can't run you through'. I'd really like to know what idea these critics have of economics to be able to run it through. But in the end, their positions seem to me much less radical than is thought. And I suppose every contribution can be useful.

Hartje I don't agree with the environmentalists' criticisms of economics. Most social sciences necessarily have a limited perspective. Psychologists are interested in individuals, not social organization. Political science is interested in governments and parties ...

But it has been suggested, for example, that economics with its interest in production should not exclude from its investigations those forms of production that don't pass through the market ...

I don't think it's like that. Behind economic analysis of the market there is the concept of utility. If one looks at the political process in this way, then economics embraces a large part of it. If one looks at family relations as an exchange process, I think one gains considerable insights ... But in any case I think that like any other discipline economics should be aware of its limits.

One of the environmentalists' most insistent criticisms of official economic theory is the way in which the GNP is calculated, this datum which, especially since the fifties, has been taken as the unquestioned indicator of the wealth of a country and of the social well-being of its population.

But GNP, according to the ecological economists, is anything but a faithful instrument for measuring economic and social reality, because it is tainted by the constituent 'sins' of economic science mentioned above. Thus GNP is quantified without any account being taken of either those human activities that escape monetary definition or the subtraction of natural goods, which have traditionally been considered unlimited and free.

In this way there is no trace in GNP of the progressive exhaustion of raw materials, the deterioration of the environment and so on, or of the immense work carried out, almost always by women, in the home to guarantee the reproduction of the human race and the vital continuity of society. The paradoxical consequence of this is that looking after a child, for example, is calculated as contributing to the national income if performed by a babysitter, but is absolutely disregarded if performed by the mother; the work of cleaning up a lake is a positive factor in the calculations, without any consideration of the undeniable loss of value to the lake (in terms of beauty, tourism or fishing, etcetera) caused by the pollution; and overtime work by doctors following road accidents is counted positively as an increase in wealth and welfare. And so on.

This false image of the wealth of a country produced by the conventional measuring of the GNP, the environmentalists say, gives false signals to the politicians in charge, reinforces the dichotomy between politics and the environment, and offers governments an alibi for continuing to destroy our natural capital in the name of economic growth and progress. For some time, on the basis of this analysis, various representatives of ecological economics have been elaborating proposals for a different and more complex system of measurement of the national product, which would also include the negative effects of economic activity (damage to the environment and the population, diminution of natural capital, degradation of buildings, countryside, works of art, etcetera) and, generally, all those things that have never been considered by traditional theory as having either positive or negative value. One of the most well-known representatives of this line of environmentalist thinking is Christian Leipert, who has already made several contributions to this book.

Leipert I am trying to organize a new system of national accounting, integrated with a whole series of indicators relating to social costs, such as those of the environment, which have so far been ignored: they are the hidden cost of progress, the social damage deriving from industrial production, on which the prevailing economic paradigm has so far blocked detailed research.

Does that mean your work will be of interest mainly to economists and politicians?

Not only them. In addition to providing a more accurate evaluation of income on which environmentally aware policies can be based, I would like to raise the consciousness of everyone: the business world, the mass media, and ordinary people. We need a public debate that would force people to look at the economic facts in a new way, reconsider the concept of economic development in the light of ecological requirements, and start asking questions about normally unquestioned traditional economic concepts such as economic growth, efficiency, prosperity, income, profit, and costs. I would like us to get used to thinking in terms of the Ecological National Product, which would measure income in real terms, rather than the Gross National Product.

But is it easy to put a price on things that have never had one so far?

No, it's not at all easy. No one has done the sums in nature's terms yet, even though there are some attempts to do so now, in the Netherlands, in Germany, and, I believe, at the UN. It has to be admitted that fixing a price for environmental well-being is very often arbitrary, but in some cases it is possible. My proposal is to evaluate the loss of environmental well-being through the hypothetical cost of its conservation. Here opinion polls are useful that give us an idea of how much people are prepared to pay for the cleaning of a lake, for example. In this way we measure the loss not through the market but through public opinion. The result is not a price but a value, which can be set against the clean-up cost.

But wait a minute, aren't you afraid that this kind of approach is too close to the logic of standard economics, which thinks a price can be put on

*everything? The very kind of economics that you are so critical of, and which
we can see to be so terribly inadequate to the environmental problem?*

But my proposal is very different ...

*Can I play devil's advocate for a moment? Don't you think your proposal
can be interpreted in this way? Because there is the fact, as you probably
know, that many 'orthodox' economists accept the idea that we should
review the method of calculating GNP. Of all the proposals from environmentalists, this would seem to be the only one to get a good press. That
doesn't make you suspicious?*

They probably haven't thought hard enough about what I've
said, or they've misunderstood it. Because if we were really to put
a price on environmental damage, this would mean a serious decrease
in net product. Reaching a sustainable product means investing a
great deal in protecting nature and in the expense of looking at
other social costs; and this would ensure a reduction in our normal
consumption and customary standard of living. I don't know if the
economists you refer to have really taken this in.

*Perhaps they haven't. But don't you think it's difficult to avoid being
misunderstood like this in a world like ours, where money is everything,
where a price can be put on everything, and where everything can be bought
or sold?*

No, for me it's a matter of a completely new vision, a new way
of evaluating the development of the past and its meaning for the
future. This new way of calculating the national product cannot be
put on the same level as the old way. It's an approach that seeks to
integrate the interaction between the economy and nature within
economic thought. We can't go on saying 'The economy is here,
and ecology is there.' We must enlarge our idea of the subject of
economics and start rewriting the textbooks – not just to add a new
chapter on housework and the family or on the environment, but
to review the basic models.

Capital and labour in the marketplace are not the only factors in
production; there is also nature, and there is the work of reproduction, in which the presence of women is fundamental; and this
isn't separate, but intertwined with the traditionally recognized
production factors. The result is a broader and more complex picture
of the economic reality of our society, which also allows us to
understand more fully the production system in the Third World –
much better than the narrow approach we use now.

*As emerged in the preceding conversation, the great majority of economists,
even those completely in line with traditional economics, accept the need to
review the present system of national accounting. Any reservations tended to*

turn on the difficulties rather than the opportunities of such an operation. There were few absolutely contrary views.

Friedman   The proposal to calculate the national product in a different way is just the result of bad economics and bad statistics.

But ecological disruption, depletion of natural assets, water, air and soil pollution, the spoiling of landscapes and ancient monuments, all these things that don't figure in the GNP as it's calculated now, are they a loss for the country or not?

Not at all.

If you have a polluted lake ...

But how did it get polluted?

Because there was a source of pollution nearby, I suppose.

Because people live around the lake. The first person to build a house there caused pollution, the second person even more. The real pollution is the existence of human beings. And if human beings exist and use resources you have to be careful of what you call pollution.

Yes, I follow you. In calculating GNP you regard the construction of houses round the lake as positive, but you should also take the damage to the lake into account, and that's negative ...

Of course. But how can I judge that the net effect is negative? Perhaps it's positive.

Isn't the pollution negative? And shouldn't we take that into account?

To an extent we do take it into account. The costs are calculated.

The costs of depollution yes, but not those of pollution.

But the resources used and the costs are calculated.

But they are added, not subtracted.

It depends on the circumstances and on what you mean by GNP. If you measure output, not input, then the ability to produce more output with fewer natural resources increases GNP. The GNP is correctly measured ...

Malinvaud   Yes, I think it's right to review and amplify the way in which national wealth is evaluated. But we shouldn't make the mistake of thinking that this in itself can resolve in any way the major problems of the environment. Redefining GNP won't solve anything, won't change anything.

Changing the measurement of the national product is proposed mainly as a way of enlarging our understanding. The French are at work now on a detailed inventory of all their ecological assets, and this too is basically a fact-finding operation to establish a correct policy for the environment. Don't you think that the new method of calculating GNP could incorporate the French statistical method?

Yes, OK, but it wouldn't add much in itself. I agree, the inventory is very important. We need a better understanding especially of the various forms of pollution on the planet, such as acid rain, the greenhouse effect, the reduction in the ozone layer. But I don't see what use it will be to synthesize all this in a figure, which would inevitably have a conventional value, given that we would have to decide what weight to give to this or that fact. The result will be a calculation slightly different from the present one, we'll all get used to it, and nobody will change their behaviour at all as a result. The idea that the synthesis expressed in GNP is what rules the world is completely false.

Spaventa I don't know. They're such arbitrary things that they don't interest me very much. Of course we should have fixed principles that are the same for all countries ... But in Italy we can't do the sums even with traditional methods.

Solow The environmentalists' critique of the present system of calculating GNP is very important. If we reform our accounting system, calculating environmental damage, we will accomplish two things: we'll keep the problem in the public eye and force it on the attention of those who have so far taken no interest in it, and also reinforce the notion that the environment is an economic problem. The UN should do something, and then individual countries would follow. But the UN has already taken an interest in the question, and is trying to define new standards for national accounting.

Sylos Labini There's no doubt at all. As it's calculated at present, GNP is a fraud, for a whole series of reasons. The plain truth is that GNP registers only those activities that pass through the market, but those activities outside it are no less important. Why does economics focus only on what passes through the market? Because in the market everything is quantifiable, everything has a price, everything is clear. And what isn't quantifiable ... well, out of sight, out of mind. But we shouldn't generalize, and reduce everything to black and white. It's true that there is a dominant form of economics, but we shouldn't forget that within it there are all sorts of different positions, on the environment like everything else. And there is a growing awareness of the environment.

Galbraith I've long felt that the standard calculations of GNP conceal some very important things. They conceal, for example, the enormous contribution of unpaid women's work. And, undoubtedly, to include the value of steel produced and not the negative value of polluting emissions coming from the steelworks is a deceptive way of accounting.

Simon That's true; in the traditional way of calculating GNP, not only environmental damage but many social activities are not taken into account. And one of the reasons the standard of living in the Third World seems so much lower than ours is because of the method of social accounting.

Hirschman Yes, I agree, many things are excluded from economic calculations and we should correct that. There has been, for example, a notable reduction in our forests, which should be registered in the statistics, and it isn't. But there are undeniable technical difficulties. It's hard to put a price on things like air, or the beauty of a lake. Perhaps the loss in value of a lake that stinks because it is polluted could be set at the cost of eliminating that stink. But I repeat, it's difficult.

Hahn The problem of giving a monetary value to things that have traditionally been outside the market doesn't seem to me to be an obstacle. Many people who are not economists find it difficult to understand the influence of prices. They ask, for example, how can you put a price on human life? The answer is, we do it implicitly all the time. For example, if instead of four-lane highways we had six-lane highways we'd probably save lives, and we're implicitly calculating the cost of lives all the time. So why not do it explicitly? I agree that we should revise the system of calculating GNP, and so do most other economists.

Becker In the present way of calculating GNP we're only interested in what people pay for, not the value of what they pay for. Yes, I think environmentalists are right on this, it would be good to measure net costs and bring them into the calculations. And not just for the environment.

Wallerstein It's an old debate, whether there's some way of quantifying what some people call quality-of-life factors. Many people have tried over the last fifty years, and it's rather tricky and has many arbitrary elements in it: how do I quantify the absence of trees, how do I quantify the trees I don't see? But I'm in agreement all the same. And it's a proposal that attacks one of the worst vices of economists. It's like the old joke of the drunk who is looking for his wallet under the lamp post, and the policeman asks him, 'What are you doing?' 'I'm looking for my wallet.' 'Where did you lose it?' 'In the park.' 'Then why are you looking for it here?' 'Because here there's light.' Economists as a group tend to go where there is hard data, on the grounds that if you don't have hard data you can't be serious. The fact that they lost the wallet in the park doesn't concern them.

Surprisingly, serious reservations about the possibility of a different form of national accounting came from the environmentalists, both from those who consider it no more than an instrument and a starting point, and from those who disagreed with the very modality of the proposal.

Pearce   I'd say that the argument about national accounting is now out of date. All economists are more or less agreed that change is needed. Even the UN is trying to measure in the GNP the value of housework, of time that is not paid on farms and so on, social costs and environmental damage, and not just expenditure on the protection of natural capital. The only debate now is between those who consider measures of this kind just tinkering with the system, and those, like me, who find the others unnecessarily pessimistic, and not imaginative enough in applying the tools we have available at the moment.

Daly   There's no doubt about it, the traditional method is just bad accounting, and we have to change it. It's important, because the present system of measuring the wealth of a country is absolutely unreliable. If you subtract the exploitation of nature in its various forms, then the result might well be negative growth. Obviously it's not a solution, it's not even a policy, it's just a measure that corresponds to reality. Then, you need the courage to make the policies that are indicated by that measure.

Passet   There's no doubt that we should correct this absurdity by which certain costs concerning the degradation of the natural environment emerge as wealth-producing. What's more, just as when we withdraw a sum of money for a particular reason we redeem the capital, in the same way where human resources are concerned, all earnings below the bare minimum should be considered as a redemption that allows the renewal of the resources, and not as a net income. In short there is a great deal that needs correcting. Many people now, at the World Bank and elsewhere, people I admire a lot, are working hard on the attempt to define what they call the

Green National Product, starting from the normal product and subtracting the degradation of the environment, expenditure for its protection, deterioration of natural capital, and so on.

I have to admit that I haven't thought about this enough to have a definite opinion, but I'm sure that all this is a very positive development. First of all, there's an aspect of this reduction of everything to a monetary level that seems to me inadequate, in relation to the depletion of a resource for example: when a natural resource is depleted, this cannot be expressed in monetary terms. Or again, take the case of the production of use values. In the industrialized countries, production for use is only a minimal part of the national product, and it is absolutely legitimate to evaluate this starting from market values, since the market price is based on 80–90 per cent of the flow of goods. But in the underdeveloped countries the proportions are reversed: 3 per cent of the product passes through the market, while 97 per cent is consumed directly. And in this way we end up with data which are completely unrealistic.

I remember a case in which the nearest market to a certain town was 300 kilometres away: since transport enters into the calculations of market value, the result was a balance of production for use that was actually negative. There are very many analagous examples in the environmental field. It's like when you want to evaluate a large volume from a small flow: it doesn't work. So my question is this: must nature be incorporated in the form of a correction of the national product? Aren't they two completely different realities? Shouldn't we distingish between on the one hand the need to improve the calculation of the national product, as we said, bearing in mind certain elements that are not included at present, and on the other hand the description of the flow and evolution of natural assets, which is part of another system of accounting and shouldn't be linked so simply to the national accounting. I think this idea of correcting GNP can improve the description of an economic reality, but if it's mixed up with questions of nature the risk is that it won't express anything, neither nature nor the economy. I think nature's accounts are best kept separate. And in any case there are accounts of nature that have been calculated so fully and carefully, like the great French inventory, that, once done, no further action was taken. It was impossible to bring them up to date. Probably the scheme followed by the compilers of the inventory, which was so complex and perfect, should be simplified to make it more practical and easy to use.

Gerelli I recently took part in a meeting of the Italian Bureau of Statistics where there was a discussion of this proposal, whose application has already produced interesting results in some countries, such as Norway. I'm broadly in favour of it, as are almost all economists. One of the partially negative characteristics of the Western systems is, I admit, excessive monetarization. This makes it difficult to evaluate a loss that has no equivalent in monetary terms. I think a good environmental education should also encourage us to realize that money is a useful instrument but not the only one, and teach us to analyse activities in physical terms too. So I think it would be a good idea for GNP, which should be an indicator of social welfare, to give a macroeconomic view, and not just of what is measurable in monetary terms; because I believe that, all things being equal, the more material goods there are the better, so long as this doesn't bring about damage of other kinds, which unfortunately happens, especially in the environmental field.

Does that mean Italy too is considering the possibility of reforming its national accounting?

Yes, but there are many disagreements on technical matters. I think the solution will be to present different national products, each having equal weight, one calculated in monetary terms, others calculated in physical terms. In this way we'll know that production has increased by, say, 2 per cent, and that, for example, the quantity of woodland has decreased or increased by so much, and that that is the object of political evaluation.

Won't there be the risk that the monetary indicator, by force of habit, will go on being considered the only important one, or at least the one that is crucial in economic decisions?

I believe that there is a real heterogeneity here. Cars have a value. The pollution they cause is not immediately calculable in monetary terms; it's a fact and it's pointless pretending not to see it. When we are faced with quantities that are not comparable, any attempt to reckon them up within homogeneous indicators would have little credibility. What we can do is correct the monetary calculation, by subtracting, for example, clean-up expenditure from GNP, rather than adding it on as we do today. But alongside this indicator we need others, which measure variations in physical terms.

Bresso Of all the attempts to recalculate the national product, the most interesting in my view is that carried out in France by the National Statistics Bureau, which the EEC is now studying. It proposed a way of reckoning natural assets, involving all resources, evaluated in detail in their initial and final quantities, and in the variation in quantity they had undergone. It was an extremely ambitious project, for which so far we have only the main outlines, with experimental data for only small parts of it. So we are still a long way from having a working tool. But what matters is the decision, first of all, to start from a knowledge of natural assets, rather than using money as a measure, and, second, to begin from a definition of the general picture, to which information can be added as it becomes available.

Altvater There's no doubt that this proposal is a more rational and honest way of calculating the social product. All the same it has serious limitations. First of all, it's impossible to put a price on all sorts of elements in our lives. Doing it is very arbitrary and even a little dangerous.

Perhaps because it remains inside the traditional logic, which tends to evaluate everything in monetary terms and reduce everything to the 'universal equivalent'?

Yes, because the precondition for putting a price on something is reducing it to a good. And making it a good means dismembering and destroying ecological systems. But it is a necessary step, to give people a more precise idea of the national wealth, a necessary act of clarification.

O'Connor Ecological economic planning is impossible without green budgets. But these must also be red budgets! Not only the amount of resources used, the amount of soil decline, hectares of wetlands lost to development, cubic metres of clean air gone, and so on, but also the amount of labour utilized, the amount of labour wasted as a result of the 'sales effort', the costs of production of GNP in terms of homelessness, stress-induced disease, drug addiction, family violence and so on, must also be included. So must the costs of urban congestion and traffic fatalities occurring during commuting to work, among other factors. Not only the degradation of nature but also the exploitation of labour must be revealed in these budgets. Green–green budgets alone reveal the costs of development, meanwhile concealing problems of inequality, social injustice, and economic and social irrationality generally. Red–green budgets reveal the entire range of issues pertaining to nature *and* social labour. I don't know whether or not anyone has begun to make up or even try to develop a method by which one could construct a red–green budget.

CHAPTER 13

CAPITALISM AGAINST ITSELF

In his most recent book *Making Peace with the Planet*,[1] Barry Commoner returns to the theory he worked out twenty years ago in the book that brought him world fame, *Closing the Circle*,[2] the possibility of reconciling development with the protection of the natural environment, on condition that the 'technosphere' – all the different means of production and production processes now in use – is profoundly modified to reduce ecological damage as much as possible and forestall pollution.

The proposal seems harmless enough and something that more or less everyone could agree on, but it takes on more radical significance when his analysis brings pollution prevention up against the free market:

> Forestalling pollution means regulating the planning of production processes in harmony with society's interest in preserving the quality of the environment. In the United States and elsewhere, the free market is founded on the principle that production processes are chosen and run by private groups, and so are planned with the sole purpose of giving to market forces, businessmen and investors, one single result – maximum profit.

The question that logically follows is to what extent the choice of production technologies made by the private sector, and as such having the aim of maximum short-term profit, can be responsive to far-reaching long-term social interests such as the quality of the environment.

'A society's technological structure clearly reflects the fundamental characteristics of the economic system it originates from,' Commoner says. 'The motor of a car is not a neutral piece of technology without immaterial values, but the instrument of an economic policy.' The

---

1. Barry Commoner, *Making Peace with the Planet*, Gollancz, London, 1990.
2. Barry Commoner, *Closing the Circle: confronting the environmental crisis*, Jonathan Cape, London, 1972.

petrochemical industry is planned for the conquest of new markets and greater profits, without worrying about the consequences for the environment. And so on. Nor does the objection that pollution in the Soviet Union and other Eastern European countries has reached higher levels than in the West cut much ice as 'most of the production systems adopted in the countries of the socialist bloc derive from capitalist countries'. The fact is, Commoner concludes, that 'the interests of the dominant ideology, that of capitalism, clash with the reality of the environmental crisis'. In short, dealing seriously with the environmental question means changing the political system: 'institutional means must be found to achieve "social" guidelines for the decisions which concern production'.

Barry Commoner is one of the very few environmentalists known, if not by everyone, by a fair number of the economists I spoke to. Those who know him know he is neither a fellow-traveller, nor a Marxist, nor a follower of extremist ideologies. I thought it would be useful to ask for opinions on his views.

Becker I don't know his book, but I don't see how these problems can be resolved outside the democratic system.

I don't think Commoner is at all thinking of abandoning democracy. He talks about institutions able to defend social needs, something that in his view capitalism is unable to do.

No. However imperfect the system is, the combination of democracy and capitalism seems to me to function better than any other system in the world. And I don't think it's at all wise to propose radical changes for dealing with the environment.

Hirschman I believe that it's possible, even without modifying our system, to give weight to interests that concern the overall wellbeing of society as a whole as well as those of private profit. We need to mobilize public opinion and make people more aware of the problem.

Simon I totally disagree. I'm very sceptical about proposals of this kind.

Samuelson *Laissez-faire* markets cannot optimize the environment. However, abandonment of capitalism and the mixed economy in favour of socialism's command economies would probably worsen environmental problems. There is no 'third way' in the wings that we can use instead of the market and the socialist way.

Hartje Commoner's sounds like a strange, apodictic statement.

He is saying that protecting the environment is a social interest. Of course it is. But is this in contradiction with individual rights? I believe that individualism is one of the ethical prerequisites of capitalism, it imposes respect for all human and civic values, it is the motor of the economic system, and guarantees the diversity of opinions that make democracies representative. We cannot give up individual values, they are the most important thing ... And as far as the environment goes, I don't see how a dictatorship could do any better.

But Commoner isn't thinking in terms of a dictatorship at all ...

So long as there is freedom, individuals can change their behaviour, and, if it is bad for the environment, make different choices. Individuals can orientate the economic and political system. And the capitalist industrial system imposes all sorts of restrictions: punctuality, performance levels, ability to separate work from emotions and personal questions. It is a discipline that could work in favour of environmental protection.

Gerelli   I frankly find the position one big oversimplification. A purely capitalist system doesn't exist, any more than a purely socialist system. They are always mixed systems. It's true that the protection of the environment depends fundamentally on public intervention, but to say that this type of intervention is not possible in the West is unacceptable. Look at the United States, where there have been many significant interventions.

But Commoner has analysed a whole series of these interventions that have had results that have been very modest if not actually negative, and in which private interests have prevailed over that of the environment, which is a social interest. The need for political change derives from these premises.

What needs changing is people's attitudes. I really don't believe that a change in the political system would help the ecological situation. Let's not forget that the economies of 'real socialism' have performed much worse than the economies of the West, in the environment as in everything else. It's a question not of ideology but of awareness, of value choices, of moral positions towards future generations. These are difficult to achieve in any system, but maybe less so in the mixed systems of the West, where we have two big trump cards: the market, which can be modified for ecological ends, and freedom of speech, which is the fundamental instrument for the defence of the environment. Where protest has no voice the environment is damaged disastrously.

Pearce   I would make two observations. One is that since we have to choose between two systems, the Western one seems to me to offer a better chance of looking after the environment. The second is, that it's true that the capitalist system is based on self-interest, but I would use self-interest to improve the environment. Some environmentalists – maybe Commoner is amongst them – think that you have to change human nature to improve the environment. I don't think this is possible, and it would mean losses in human freedom, which is just as important as the conservation of the natural environment. I don't know what proposals like this mean, and as someone who every day has to advise politicians and civil servants it offers me no policy statement that I could make. You can't say to a politician, 'You must change the system.' Fortunately not all environmentalists are like this.

Sylos Labini Commoner is good and full of passion, but passion isn't always a virtue. People like that have the best intentions, but they can sometimes do harm. Obviously, the environmental risk is a social question and should be faced with adequate means – I said as much just now. But Commoner says that capitalism cannot deal with it. First of all, what does capitalism mean? Is the present economic system the same as that of a hundred years ago? It's meaningless talking in these terms. Let's talk instead of the market. The market, whatever its faults, offers all sorts of opportunities for positive effects. You can modify it, creating limits through national budgetary policy apart from anything else, which a business has to take into consideration: costs rise, and this too is the market. You can modify it, even drastically, but always monitoring financial policy on the basis of cost–benefit calculations. When the harm is greater than the benefits, you have to stop. You can't forget a whole social reality that would suffer the effects, the working class above all.

Malinvaud Obviously the environmental problem is one that goes far beyond what any private citizen can do individually and what the market can handle. Perhaps I agree with him.

Passet Basically I agree with Commoner. The common interest isn't the sum of individual interests, and those who maintain that it's enough to defend individual interests and the market, and everything will sort itself out, are really deeply wrong. But we need to make some distinctions, because capitalism has gone on modifying itself from its origins down to the present day while remaining essentially the same system. And its great strength is in this, in its capacity to adapt itself to change, in its flexibility, and most of all in the total freedom for individual initiative that characterizes it, that creates an extraordinary dynamism, that is obvious, especially if we compare it with the Eastern European systems. So there is something in capitalism that we must try not to lose, this flexibility linked to the multiplicity of the people and decisions involved, and that source of creativity which is individual initiative. In my view we need a mixture of individual initiative, regulations and decentralization of decision-making through all the different organizational levels, always remembering that there are some tasks that only the state can perform. But perhaps we need to distinguish between a 'market economy' and an 'economy with the market'. In the first the market is everything, it regulates everything, and *laissez-faire* is the only norm. As a result making money is easy – all you have to do is keep all the profits for yourself and dump all the costs on everyone else. In the second the market is only an instrument.

Spaventa   Commoner indicates a real contradiction, but I don't think he indicates a solution. And then, I don't know how useful it is to talk about capitalism as responsible for environmental problems when pollution in the socialist bloc is much more serious.

But Commoner is aware of this; he even explains why: the production systems of Eastern Europe are practically indistinguishable from those in the West.

That's true: from the point of view of industrial production we can't really distinguish between the two systems in the way we can with education, housing, etcetera. But to a certain extent the situation seems to me even more alarming than Commoner's description. If the destruction of the environment was the exclusive reponsibility of the maximization of individual profit and the total lack of concern about negative consequences, then it would perhaps be easier to deal with.

Daly   Historically neither capitalism nor socialism has succeeded in dealing with the problem of the environment satisfactorily, so we do need a kind of third way, which would be able to take what is best in capitalism and socialism. What's best about capitalism is the market, within the limits of the allocation problem, so let's take that. What's best about socialism is its ability to deal with the distribution of income, and the social character of the decisions taken about the scale of the overall economic system. Making use of what is good in both would mean dividing decisions into two groups: those that can be entrusted to individuals and those that require collective action. Which is exactly what I hope for.

Bresso I'm largely in agreement with Commoner. With the proviso that, faced with the failure of socialism, the only starting point is capitalism, or at least one particular aspect of capitalism: its capacity to use what is worth using in the market. We cannot consider eliminating the market from the horizon of human economics. We can, however, consider changing capitalism profoundly. Because the end of socialism is also the end of capitalism as we know it, as an alternative to socialism. Perhaps – we all hope so – capitalism will end in a less traumatic way than socialism, but the very fact that historically they have been sworn foes, means that the collapse of the one must perforce bring with it the collapse of the other.

But the evidence today seems to indicate only the triumph of capitalism.

That's true, but the right and duty to criticize, which continues to exist, is now confined within capitalism. And a healthy exercise of the critical spirit shows us that capitalism is not compatible with a sustainable society. The essence of capitalism is accumulation, its great capacity to produce and accumulate capital. This has been very useful, determining that great leap forward from agricultural societies to industrial societies I mentioned, which undoubtedly had many positive aspects. But it also had seriously negative consequences, which are manifest in the world ecological disaster, a disaster that capitalism cannot face and overcome, because capitalism without accumulation is unimaginable. An economy without accumulation is something different. And a sustainable society, that we are all trying to define but which none of us has a clear idea of, cannot be a capitalist society, in the sense in which we understand capitalism today. It will certainly be a society which uses the market, and it won't be a society where the state is omnipresent, though the state will have a serious role. Most of all (and if we can't for the moment see how, we must try, and try hard) it will be a society that tends towards stability in the production of goods. Another consequence of this would be a relaxation in the process of acquiring knowledge, a science less anxiously projected towards the discovery of the new and more able to use to the full the knowledge it already has, and to reflect on it. It's a question of less hurried tempi and rhythms, of a slowing down in the production not only of goods, but of knowledge too.

You're talking about a complete change of outlook ...

Yes indeed. It means reviewing the very idea of innovation. Today, in the name of what is new, which is automatically taken as being positive, we are not even able to enjoy what is produced, even in terms of art, culture or knowledge: it is a continuous vortex of change, whose logic is the destruction of what has just been done.

This is the weak point of capitalism, which hasn't been beaten by socialism and communism, at least in the forms realized so far, but which could well end up being beaten by itself, by the negative consequences of the mechanisms of accumulation, both in the countries where it has found full actualization, and in those where it has gone to take away resources and to offload its worst defects.

Altvater I think Commoner is right. We must get it into our heads that certain products that we use all the time, such as the car, are no longer just goods, which can be bought at a certain price, resold, etcetera. When we use the car we are also using space on the planet, the atmosphere of the planet, gasoline, which is a non-renewable resource, all the raw materials necessary for making the car, iron, water and energy. And to break it down into waste when we throw it away, we use still more energy, more space. In short, when we buy a car we are not only buying that beautiful object that the automobile manufacturers present in such seductive ways in their advertising, we are buying a piece of the planet Earth, a planet that, let's say it once again, is a finite entity. That is why we have to find another way of measuring environmental compatibility, another rationality, which would make us really understand what we are doing when we buy a car. So I think Commoner is right: we have to learn to think in terms of commonly held goods at a planetary level, and not just in terms of individual needs, in the way that the market defines them, as if they were the one and only model we had.

Do you think that people are beginning to think along these lines or elaborate a theory of this kind?

No, unfortunately – partly because since the collapse of the communist bloc all the coordinates have changed, and it's no longer clear what position the traditional left has. In my view there is only one idea worth developing: let's call it a green–red project: green in terms of protecting the environment, red in terms of the production of society. We must take account of existing social problems in our thinking about the environment, serious problems which, if nothing is done about them, worsen the condition of the environment, apart from anything else. The trouble is that many greens have no interest in social problems, but are effectively conservatives. So a green–red project hasn't even been begun yet. But we must have one.

Wallerstein Being active in something such as the environmental movement leads you to realize after a while exactly what the obstacles are, and forces some people to understand things that they didn't before. Obviously this has happened to Commoner: his work in analysing the environmental crisis has made him conscious of an obstacle of which he was not conscious ten years ago. He still doesn't know what to do about it, but at least he's aware of it.

What Commoner says recalls a little what you wrote about capitalism as an historical phenomenon, destined sooner or later to disappear. Don't you think the disruption to the environment might accelerate this process?

It could be a factor. There are many causes of this process: overpopulation and the physical–biological collapse of the planet are two of them. And the political disillusionment which derives from it is certainly able to affect the collapse of capitalism.

O'Connor Commoner says something that in some ways comes close to what I think and have already said. I believe that the solution of the environmental problem can emerge only through political struggles against capital and the capitalist state. The most important political phenomena of today, the demands coming from the work-force, social movements, and especially from the environmental movement, must be collected into a single movement capable of gaining and exercising political power. Everything else depends on it. I think of all the groups of the red–green kind that are growing worldwide, that are many and varied, taking different forms in different countries and regions: Indian women struggling against ecological disequilibrium and against gender oppression, the fight against ecological racism and for environmental justice in the US, certain tendencies in the German greens, namely those who are to the left of the Social Democratic Party on economic and social issues, the Workers' Park in Brazil, which takes up issues of urban and rural ecology along with standard issues of the left such as wages and unemployment, and the green politics of the New Democratic Party in Canada, the green communists in Kerala in India, and the red–greens of Tasmania in Australia. In sum, the hopeful sign is that environmental organizations seem to be taking up economic and social issues that they were not interested in a decade ago. This I believe must be the right course for the entire left.

CHAPTER 14

NOT A CONCLUSION

Is it possible both to satisfy the needs of advanced modern societies and to reduce to a minimum the deterioration of that ecological equilibrium that has made human life on earth possible until now? Is it possible to devise, organize and make functional a system of production, exchange and use, without altering the environment beyond its biological capacity for self-regeneration? In short, is it possible to create an economic system different from the present one, which seems less and less responsive to these requirements?

This is the question at the heart of the environmental debate. This book originated from the impression that mainstream economic science is not giving this question the consideration required, but is tending to ignore its importance and urgency. A false impression? After having met a considerable number of the most eminent representatives of the discipline and compared their opinions with those of a substantial number of environmental and ecological economists, I think I can say no.

Perhaps, though, this silence on the part of the majority of the most celebrated economists, which astonished and intrigued me before beginning this research, does not mean they are indifferent to the problem. With a few distinguished exceptions, often the message I received was not so much indifference as a kind of will not to know. The activation of defence mechanisms that allowed them to substantially underestimate the phenomenon, to evade the facts, paradoxically, was in several cases combined with genuine concern.

As we have seen, there are very different positions, but most of the traditional economists I interviewed seemed to consider the instability of the environment as a malfunctioning of the system, an incidental mishap, a drawback which minor corrections could overcome. Indeed, as I mentioned in the Introduction, when they did not change the subject to demographic, political or ethical questions (all of them of undoubted importance, especially the first) they went no further than proposals for taxes, standards, technologies and so on, the inadequacy of which they themselves seemed to be aware of, giving sometimes the impression of an impotence they could not admit.

But to what extent can the negative consequences of the economic system be amended using its own instruments and logic? No one would deny the usefulness and still less the necessity of immediate interventions, which, like those referred to above, must be to some extent consonant with the existing system of production if their introduction is not to create serious traumas in it. But how effective can policies of this kind be? Perhaps simple empirical observation of the kind of attention the business world gives to the ecological question can provide an answer.

One has only to think of the explosion of so-called 'ecobusiness'. Purifiers, incinerators, simulators, installations for breaking down and recycling waste, systems for monitoring and measuring pollution, and much more: a massive production of equipment for dealing with the damage to the environment after the event, which industry – usually so resistant towards any norms that try to deal with it beforehand – has thrown itself into with enthusiasm, to the point of creating two mutually sustaining parallel markets, one in goods that create pollution, and another in goods that clean up the pollution. Why reduce the production of plastic if it can be recycled? No one cares if the recycling concerns only 3 per cent of the total. Why try to limit waste if treating it can produce wealth? No one worries if only a minute portion of the enormous quantities of waste scattered around the land and water of the globe can be treated.

In this way the defence of the environment often becomes a further assault on it, and the very process of salvage, reuse, and recycling that should oppose the normal rule of overconsumption, use-and-throw-away, and waste, ends up assimilated to this very logic, sucked into the meaningless spiral of production as an end in itself, its initial aim completely lost. In the same way, and likewise in the name of ecology, we can see the environment being made more and more artificial, with natural processes and products being gradually substituted with mechanical, chemical and industrial ones, while the world races towards a kind of 'air-conditioned utopia', to use the prophetic title of an old novel.

The most evident symptom, one almost symbolic of industry's progressive appropriation of the environment problem, is advertising. Undaunted, advertising continues to stimulate demand for goods which are offered as good in themselves; it shamelessly uses the ecological risk as a selling point, selling automobiles incongruously photographed against green fields, selling methane in the name of a clear sky, selling 'back to nature' processed foods, and exploiting in the most misleading way imaginable the now widespread anxiety about the environment, in order to increase sales, and thus increase production, and with it pollution.

In short, the huge belly of the consumer society, notorious for its capacity to devour, digest and give back anything in the form of goods, is managing to do just that with the ecological peril. And this is bound to happen more and more often in the future, so long as environmental policy is limited to minor adjustments, out of conviction that the problem is capable of resolution with the very means and rules of the system which has produced it; so long as the decline of the environment goes on being considered as incidental and marginal compared to the overall benignity of the economic system; and so long as the many conspicuous concrete indications of pollution go on being ignored in favour of the worship of abstract figures, of the formalism of econometric models, and of an economic logic that acknowledges only those human activities which can be represented in financial transactions. This commodification of the environment problem will continue, indeed so long as the prevalent approach of economics towards environmental (and non-environmental) subjects is that of the majority of my interviewees, who made me reflect more than once that the perception of reality has very little to do with their subject.

Reflections along these lines are not new to me. For a long time now the predominance of the economic dimension (and in particular the idea of quantity-as-value) over the multidimensional nature of society as a whole has seemed to me (and I have dealt with this in a book[1]) an unacceptable distortion of the truth, an unworthy betrayal of other relations which should be given at least equal prominence, as well as a drastic impoverishment of the expressive possibilities of human beings, reducing to merely economic or, worse, monetary transactions their natural propensity for exchange, their natural inclination to communicate, share, give and receive not only material goods, but also the nonmarketable goods of words, thoughts and affections.

This has always seemed to me to be a serious limitation of economics, one that jeopardizes the complexity of reality. I have already commented on this in relation to the condition of women, a subject that has interested me for a long time. The limitation can be seen in the way that all those activities connected with human

---

1. Carla Ravaioli, *Il quanto e il quale. La cultura del mutamento*, Laterza, Bari, 1982.

reproduction, performed mainly by women outside the market, which are the necessary antecedent to the market in that they guarantee the day-to-day survival of society, and are thus an essential part of the mechanisms of accumulation even if they do not produce surplus value, are systematically excluded from the calculations of economists and from the economic dimension itself. (And on this too I have written much on various occasions.[2])

Consequently, it was natural for me to identify with the ecological economists' criticisms of traditional economic doctrine, and in particular of the strongly accentuated monetarist evolution of the last few decades. It was equally natural for me, listening to several of these distinguished economists, to feel confirmed in my long-standing impression of the narrowness of a science which is presented in our day as the interpreter and guide of the totality of our society. This was particularly the case at times when, even in those who were sensitive to the ecological crisis and worried about it, I would become aware of a sudden refusal to see the negative relation between accumulation and the environment, which is now as clear as day. It was a refusal to overcome the conceptual constraints imposed by a theory based on a self-referential process like accumulation, which begins and ends with money, abstracted from the concrete reality of the transformative process of production, from the material laws of physics and biology that govern it, from a logic completely different from that of value. It was a refusal to recognize the responsibility of a theory embodied at every level in the parameters and dynamics of the world economy and in the uninterrupted drive towards competitive expansion that is its essence and form.

But in the end, some of these traditional economists asked me, have these ecological economists who criticize their own discipline so fiercely any concrete proposals to make? What alternative model do they advance?

It is a legitimate question. Not only does no one have any alternative ready-made proposal (it would be strange if they did), but there is not even any more or less organic theory to set against that which prevails in economics. Among environmentalists, there are many different positions as regards the economic process like everything else, and these positions are often far removed from each

---

2. Carla Ravaioli, *Tempo da vendere tempo da usare. Lavoro produttivo e lavoro riproduttivo nella società microelettronica*, Franco Angeli, Milan, 1986; 'Un orario di cittadinanza', *Politica ed economia*, no. 5, 1989; 'Il salario di cittadinanza, *IRES*, Materiali, 1988; various articles in newspapers and periodicals.

other (which is normal in the internal debate of any discipline) and there is no immediate prospect of producing ideas that are of plausible practical application.

Yet one cannot fail to recognize that ecological economists are both tenaciously trying to provide an answer to the key question of if and how a non-destructive modern economic system is possible (which most mainstream economists do not even ask) and in their analysis of the situation laying the foundations for a serious approach to the environmental question.

They have made clear that an economic rationale that sees money as the only variable by which to measure the efficiency of processes is no longer acceptable.

They have insisted on the need for a multidisciplinary approach which takes account of the material, physical and biological aspects of economic processes, which no longer considers them as a circular relation between production and consumption, but as a flow which starts with the withdrawal of natural resources (raw materials and energy) and proceeds through productive transformation, exchange and use, ending in waste, an increase in entropy and ecological degradation.

This means that economics can no longer be considered as an exact science, as a dogmatic paradigm with inflexible rules, but must be structured as a historical discipline, a flexible instrument concerned with society, sensitive to change and open to contributions from all branches of knowledge that make contact with its problems.

The ecological economists have rejected unlimited expansion, unlimited growth and accumulation, as a basic category of an economic model that now seems unsustainable. It is worth underlining that, in spite of their different intellectual standpoints, agreement on this comes both from those who emphasize the importance of the physical and biological nature of production processes, and those interested in the complexity of the world's sociopolitical system, of which the economy remains an essential part, though now given an excessive importance.

The ecological economists have reminded us that the choice of a useful ecological strategy inevitably corresponds to an economic logic which includes and sustains it, and is in its turn determined by it. The forms and ends of technologies and production processes, at present envisaged solely with a view to short-term profit, abstracted from the values and needs of the environment, must then be redefined. What is more, as the anticipated uses of applied technology are choices already embodied in theory, the theory itself is brought into question. More than one of the ecological economists told me that the time has now come to start rewriting the textbooks.

Clear premises, a wealth of ideas, a shared awareness of the deep-rooted risk in the present-day economic model, and a firmly argued critique of the productionist and consumerist paradigms have nevertheless not been sufficient to produce an organic proposal, a 'strong' theory. The reasons for this are not just the obvious, though genuine, ones, of the relative youth of environmental economics as a discipline and the extreme difficulty of the task.

If the influential academic economists paid more attention to the problem of the environment and were less supercilious about environmentalists, if they did not insist on identifying the whole ecological argument with the green-fundamentalist idiocies of indiscriminate anti-industrialism, if they did not conflate a courageous facing of reality with doom-mongering, if, instead of defending the most conventional nostrums of economics, they brought their knowledge and intelligence to bear on elaborating an answer to this increasingly urgent and menacing problem, then perhaps the transition from a critical analysis to the focusing of lines of action would not prove so impossible, and ecologists too would draw help and support from their work.

If famous professors, Nobel prizewinners and government advisers, were to raise their voices against a form of production and consumption that makes the very idea of a future for humanity seem precarious, perhaps world leaders too would be forced to reconsider their policies and consider the possibility that exchangeable pollution rights alone will not be enough to save us.

Obviously, a radical re-examination of the guiding principles of the current economic system might seem an unthinkable gamble to those who have always considered those principles to be irreplaceable pillars of progress and prosperity. And obviously a hypothesis of this kind can seem absurd and untimely at the very moment in which the fall of the communist regimes has opened the doors to the worldwide spread of capitalism, ratifying the unconditional and, seemingly, definitive victory of the market economy.

Yet the very disappearance of communism from the political and institutional horizon, the end of the paranoid attribution of all our ills to the 'evil empire', the ending of the terror of its possible spread to the West, all this can perhaps allow a critique of capitalism that will not immediately be regarded as 'fellow-travelling', as a total misunderstanding of all the positive features of an industrial society and as a desire to destroy it entirely – a critique that can be offered without any suspicion of bad faith and to the advantage of the world as a whole.

Capitalism has focused attention on certain types of activity and interests, substantially identifiable with those of production, while it has devalued and treated as of secondary importance others, those concerning reproduction and the living continuity of individuals and society. Everyone, even the critics and enemies of capitalism, even the political left, has been forced in one way or another to conform to this norm, given the enormous effect on society of the establishment and spread of industrial capitalism. A capitalist culture has been imposed and diffused which has to a certain extent moulded our very mental categories and forms of theorizing. And this is particularly true for economics, which, as Claudio Napoleoni observed, first gained autonomous life as the study of capital, and has remained that ever since.

Now that the 'red peril' is over, this may be the ideal moment to correct the imbalance of a society completely centred on production, and which subordinates every other dimension to production. Perhaps the failure of the planned economy in the countries of the socialist bloc makes it possible now to think of reforming the market rather than treat it as a miraculous panacea for every social evil. Perhaps we can not only see the market as a form of freedom we cannot forgo, but also bear in mind that this freedom can turn into its opposite when it is imposed as the unique and supreme social synthesis, the unquestioned source of values, to which all our decisions must conform or remain subordinate, to the point of identifying the sum total of good with marketable goods.

So far, the celebrated 'end of ideologies' has produced only a void and a refusal to think. However, it could be a guarantee of freedom in our attempts to formulate a way of saving ourselves from the decline of the natural environment, and with it the human race. As many of my interviewees have stressed, from Wallerstein to Passet, from Altvater to Daly, from Bresso to Leipert, and from Martinez-Alier to O'Connor, any given economic paradigm is not only a producer of goods and a regulator of markets, but also a centre of values, knowledge, institutions, and human relations both personal and social – of 'order' in the widest sense of the term.

Passet mentioned an idea he has been thinking about for some time: overcoming the market economy to establish an 'economy *with* the market'. Perhaps there could be food for thought for everyone here.

PART TWO

CHAPTER 15

ECONOMICS AND
SUSTAINABILITY

Environmental unsustainability: a consensus

In the 20 years 1972–92, between the UN Conference on the Environment in Stockholm and that on Environment and Development (UNCED) in Rio de Janeiro, the scientific consensus has gradually hardened that the damage being inflicted by human activities on the natural environment render those activities unsustainable. It has become clear that the activities cannot be projected to continue into the future, either because they will have destroyed the environmental conditions necessary for that continuation, or because their environmental effects will cause massive, unacceptable damage to human health and disruption of human ways of life.

This is not the place for a detailed review of the evidence that has led to the scientific consensus, but the now perceived seriousness of the problem can be illustrated by a number of quotations of the conclusions of reputable bodies which have conducted such a review. Thus the Business Council for Sustainable Development stated bluntly in its report to UNCED: 'We cannot continue in our present methods of using energy, managing forests, farming, protecting plant and animal species, managing urban growth and producing industrial goods' (Schmidheiny 1992: 5). The Brundtland Report, which initiated the process which led to UNCED, had formulated its perception of unsustainability in terms of a threat to survival: 'There are thresholds which cannot be crossed without endangering the basic integrity of the system. Today we are close to many of these thresholds; we must be ever mindful of the risk of endangering the survival of life on earth' (WCED 1987: 32–3).

The World Resources Institute (WRI), in collaboration with both the Development and the Environment Programmes of the United Nations, concludes on the basis of one of the world's most extensive environmental databases that 'The world is not now headed toward a sustainable future, but rather toward a variety of potential human and environmental disasters' (WRI 1992: 2). The World Bank, envisaging a 3.5 times increase in world economic output by 2030, acknowledged that 'If environmental pollution and degradation were to rise in step with such a rise in output, the result would be appalling environmental pollution and damage' (World Bank 1992: 9). The Fifth Action Programme of the European Community states that 'many current forms of activity and development are not environmentally sustainable' (CEC 1992a: 4), as indicated by 'a slow but relentless deterioration of the environment of the Community, notwithstanding the measures taken over the last two decades' (CEC 1992b: 3).

In its annual *State of the World* reports, the Worldwatch Institute has documented current environmental damage, concluding in 1993:

> The environmentally destructive activities of recent decades are now showing up in reduced productivity of croplands, forests, grasslands and fisheries; in the mounting cleanup costs of toxic waste sites; in rising health care costs for cancer, birth defects, allergies, emphysema, asthma and other respiratory diseases; and in the spread of hunger (Brown et al. 1993: 4–5).

These trends mean: 'If we fail to convert our self-destructing economy into one that is environmentally sustainable, future generations will be overwhelmed by environmental degradation and social disintegration' (ibid.: 21).

Little wonder, therefore, that in 1992 two of the world's most prestigious scientific institutions, the Royal Society and the National Academy of Sciences, saw fit to issue a joint statement of warning:

> Unrestrained resource consumption for energy production and other uses ... could lead to catastrophic outcomes for the global environment. Some of the environmental changes may produce irreversible damage to the earth's capacity to sustain life. ... The future of our planet is in the balance (RS and NAS 1992: 2, 4).

The symptoms of unsustainability

The concept of sustainability will be discussed and amplified further on pages 187–94. For the present, an environmentally unsustainable activity is simply taken to be one which cannot be projected to continue into the future, because of its negative effect either on the environment or on the human condition of which it is a part. The main symptoms of unsustainability, with their principal causative agents and the geographical level to which they mainly apply, can be grouped as in Table 1.

Table 1 Symptoms of environmental unsustainability

	Problem	Principal agents
1	**Pollution**	
1.1	Greenhouse effect/ climate change (global)	Emissions of CO_2, N_2O, CH_4 CFCs (and HFCs), O_3 (low level); deforestation 2.2
1.2	Ozone depletion (global)	Emissions of CFCs
1.3	Acidification (continental)	Emissions of SO_2, NO_x, NH_3, O_3 (low level)
1.4	Toxic pollution (continental)	SO_2, NO_x, O_3, particulates; heavy metals; hydrocarbons, carbon monoxide; agrochemicals, organochlorides; eutrophiers; radiation; noise
2	**Renewable resource depletion**	
2.1	Species extinction (global)	Land-use changes (e.g. development, deforestation 2.2); population pressure; unsustainable harvest (e.g. over-grazing, poaching); climate change 1.1 possible; ozone depletion 1.2 in future
2.2	Deforestation (global, regional)	Land use changes; population pressure; unsustainable harvest (e.g. hardwoods); climate change 1.1 (possible in future)
2.3	Land degradation/loss of soil fertility ((bio)regional, national)	Population pressure; deforestation, over-grazing; unsustainable agriculture; urbanisation, 'development'; climate change 1.1 (possible in future)
2.4	Water depletion ((bio) regional, national)	Unsustainable use; climate change 1.1 (possible in future)
2.5	Fisheries depletion (national, local)	Over-fishing, pollution; habitat destruction
3	**Non-renewable resource depletion**	
3.1	Depletion of various resources, e.g. fossil fuels, minerals (global, national)	High levels of consumption
4	**Other environmental problems**	
4.1	Congestion (national)	Waste disposal; traffic

Three immediate observations can be made about the symptoms of unsustainability. The first is the extent to which the problems are interlinked. The second is the fact that the most important problems are those of pollution and depletion of renewable resources. The third is that the problems derive without exception from the ways that human societies are currently carrying out their activities of production and consumption, with the ensuing impacts being much amplified by the great growth in human numbers. The analysis of production and consumption is the domain, in Western societies at least, of economics. How economics treats the environment, and economists' perceptions of environmental problems, are therefore of prime importance in any attempt to understand environmental unsustainability and to formulate solutions for it.

Resource and environmental economics: a brief overview

Early history

The obvious importance of natural resources and the environment to economic activity and to human life in general has caused economists to be concerned about these issues since the dawn of economics as a mode of analysis. Two of the earliest classical economists – Thomas Malthus and David Ricardo – were much exercised by the prospect of a growing human population in the context of a fixed quantity of agricultural land of differing fertility.

Malthus's theory of population, for which Ricardo expressed his admiration (Ricardo 1973: 272) contended that:

> The power of population is indefinitely greater than the power in the earth to produce substance for man. Population, when unchecked, increases in a geometrical ratio. Subsistence increases only in an arithmetical ratio ... This implies a strong and constantly operating check on population from subsistence (Malthus 1970: 71).

Should somehow more food become available, then 'population does invariably increase' (Malthus 1970: 79), maintaining the mass of the population at the basic level of subsistence.

While there were differences between Ricardo's and Malthus's analyses of the economic consequences of these tendencies, both perceived that population could only grow by taking more land into production which, assuming that the most fertile land had been used first, would be of diminishing fertility.

In Figure 1, the line AA' shows the cost of production of food

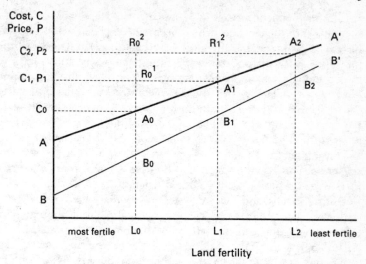

Figure 1 Returns to factors of production on land of varying fertility

per unit of land employed, as a function of the land's fertility. In situation 1, the demand for food is such that land of fertility L_1 is required to be in production, the marginal cost of producing on which is C_1, which in turn determines the minimum price of food as P_1. This is divided between wages, profits and rents. At L_1, the marginal land rent is zero, because it requires all the revenue from sale of the food at price P_1 to defray the production costs C_1. On land of fertility L_0, however, the cost of production is only C_0, so that rent on this land will be $A_0R_0^1$ (= $C_1 - C_0$). At L_1 the total agricultural rent will be the triangular area between AA_1 and C_1A_1. At L_0 wages and profits together will amount to C_0.

The line BB' divides the cost of production between wages and profits. At L_0 wages get B_0L_0, whereas profits get A_0B_0. At L_1 wages get B_1L_1, while profits get A_1B_1. It can be seen that the profit share is lower on the less fertile land. This can be understood because less fertile land demands more labour and more capital (at constant technology) per unit of product than more fertile land. But this labour requires at least the minimum quantity of food for subsistence. Once wages are at subsistence level, where population growth will tend to keep them, they can fall no further. The lower marginal product must result in a lower return to capital, so profits fall.

To support a higher population, more land of even lower fertility is required for production, say L_2. The cost of production on this land is C_2, and the associated higher price of food is P_2. On all land already in production, such as L_0 and L_1, this price increase simply translates into higher rents, which become $A_0R_0{}^2$ and $A_1R_1{}^2$ respectively. The profit on the marginal land falls to A_2B_2. Moreover, the increasing price of food raises the subsistence wage, which reduces the profitability of the manufacturing sector as well. The continuing erosion of profitability in both manufacturing and industry reduces the incentive to invest, with profits 'sinking to the lowest state required to maintain the actual capital' (Malthus 1974: 282), resulting at length in a 'stationary state' of the economy with stagnant profits and investment and population growth constantly kept in check by starvation. This was the vision that later led Thomas Carlyle to refer to political economy as the 'Dismal Science'.

Both Malthus and Ricardo recognised that the onset of the stationary state could be postponed by technological progress or a halt in population growth before the stationary state was reached. Technological progress could result in either an increase in the productivity of land or in the substitution of capital for labour, thereby increasing labour productivity. Both effects would counteract the tendency for profits to fall and maintain the incentive to invest. Contrary to his 'dismal' image, Malthus even perceived that improvements in agriculture 'may certainly be such as, for a considerable period not only to prevent profits falling, but to allow for a rise' (Malthus 1974: 282).

In retrospect, Malthus's hopes for technological progress have proved justified. Technological advance has permitted more people to live at higher material standards than Malthus ever conceived. His perception of the overwhelming power of population growth has been contradicted by those industrial countries which combine high living standards with more or less zero population growth. Future population growth, of course, may yet engender Malthus's dismal scenario, though such a scenario is more likely to come to pass through social and political upheaval due to overpopulation, rather than through a quietistic submission to natural forces. What the years since Malthus have shown incontrovertibly is that high living standards do not engender population growth; that population growth can be reduced and halted; and that the productive power of technology is enormous. It is clear today that the stationary state is not an inevitability.

Resource economics

With the exception of solar radiation, which enters the biosphere in a quantity and with a geographic distribution that is beyond human influence, all environmental resources that are used for economic activity are exhaustible. Some resources, such as concentrated mineral ores and fossil fuels, are non-renewable and are necessarily depleted with extraction. Others are conditionally renewable, dependent on rates of harvest and ambient environmental quality.

The conventional analysis of the use of environmental resources seeks to determine the 'optimal' path of such use, where optimality here involves the maximisation of the present value of the profits or consumption from the use of the resource. For both non-renewable and renewable resources it is easy to derive plausible models whereby it is optimal to exhaust non-renewable resources and to drive renewable resources to extinction.

For non-renewables, from the point of view of the resource owner, the core theoretical result was that of Hotelling (1931), who showed that in a competitive market the depletion of the resource would be such that the resource's net price, or rent, would increase at the rate of interest. The intuition behind 'Hotelling's Rule' is easily seen. Were the resource's rent to be rising more slowly than the rate of interest, its price would fall, as owners sought to acquire alternative assets instead. This would tend to restore the resource's rate of rent increase to parity with the interest rate. Were the rent to be rising faster than the rate of interest, the opposite would happen: people would seek to buy stocks of the resource, the net price of which would rise, slowing its rate of rent increase, again until it was equal to the interest rate.

Theoretical results for perfect markets have been modified to try to take into account market imperfections such as non-exclusive ownership (e.g. an oil-field that extends under differently owned plots and is tapped into by differently owned wells) or varying degrees of monopoly. As would be expected, the former condition leads to more rapid depletion than the optimal rate, as each owner tries to maximise their private return; the latter condition leads to slower depletion than the optimal rate, due to the restriction of output that the concentration of ownership brings about. Dasgupta and Heal (1979) is the classic work that reviews and derives such results, the mathematics of which can be formidably complex.

An empirical evaluation of Hotelling's Rule (Smith 1981) does not support its practical validity. Smith examined the price movements of twelve non-renewable resources: four fossil fuels and eight metals, through the use of five different economic models, including the simple Hotelling model. For four of the metals, none of the models used had any explanatory power. Hotelling's Rule was only accepted by the data for two of the resources. While the best-performing model, that of Heal and Barrow (1980), was accepted by eight of the resources, in all but three cases even it was outperformed by a simple autoregressive model that related the resource's current price to that in the previous time period. Smith's conclusion is that variables not entering the models, such as extraction costs, new discoveries, and changes in market structure and their institutional environment, for which data are not generally available in a suitable form, must also be important in explaining price movements.

Where privately optimal depletion seeks to maximise the present value of profits from a resource over its lifetime, socially optimal depletion is concerned with maximising the social utility to be derived from it. Utility is normally identified with consumption, so the problem then becomes one of maximising the present value of the consumption of the resource through time. Several conditions affect the optimal depletion path: whether the resource is essential to the production of the consumption good; whether, and to what extent, forms of produced capital can be substituted for the resource; whether technological change either economises on the use of the resource or develops a substitute that renders it inessential; whether a new resource will be discovered that serves the same purpose; and the size of the discount rate, the relative value that is given to present and future consumption.

The core theoretical result in this area (Dasgupta and Heal 1974: 17, Figure 3) is that if the discount rate is positive (i.e. if future consumption is worth less than present consumption), if the resource is essential to consumption, and no technological breakthrough, discovery of substitutable resources or substitutability with produced capital stop it from being so, then it can be optimal to drive future consumption towards zero through the exhaustion of the resource. Improvements in the efficiency of resource use (the yield of more consumption goods per unit of resource use), or a reduction in the discount rate, will prolong consumption but will not prevent its eventual decline. This can only be achieved by rendering the resource inessential for consumption by the development or discovery of substitutes. In this case, the resource may still be fully depleted but, as far as the maintenance of consumption is concerned, it will not matter.

The difference between a renewable and non-renewable resource is the capacity of the former for self-regeneration. Provided the harvest rate does not exceed the rate of regeneration, the stock of the resource will be undepleted. In Figure 2, $Q_0 Q_{max}$ shows a curve relating the stock of a renewable resource to its growth rate, G. Below Q_0 and above Q_{max} no net regeneration takes place. The

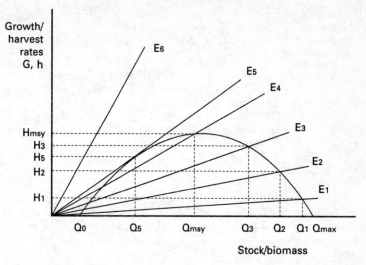

Figure 2 Growth, harvest, effort and the stock of biomass

regeneration rate rises to a maximum at Q_{msy} and then falls. The vertical axis also gives the harvest, h. The curve then also represents the equilibrium sustainable harvest, H, at any stock level. Inside the area bounded by the curve and the horizontal axis, h < G, and the stock will increase. Outside this area h > G and the stock will decrease. H_{msy} represents the maximum sustainable yield.

The lines E_1 to E_6 show increasing levels, or effectiveness, of harvesting effort. It may be that the harvesting technology is improving, so that with the same effort the harvest at a given stock level is increased; or it may be that more effort (more labour, more capital equipment) is being applied such that $E_6 > E_5 > E_4 > E_3 > E_2 > E_1$. For efforts E_1 to E_4, and for stock levels above the points where each line first cuts $Q_0 Q_{max}$, an equilibrium at the maximum sustainable harvest corresponding to that effort (e.g. H_1 for E_1) will tend to result. Thus, if for effort E_1 the stock is initially above Q_1, then harvest above the growth rate will reduce it to Q_1; if the initial stock level is below Q_1, the harvest below the growth rate will allow the stock to grow to Q_1.

Effort E_5 yields a knife-edge equilibrium. If the stock is initially above Q_5, the excess harvest rate over the growth rate will reduce it to Q_5, with equilibrium harvest H_5. However, if a natural or anthropogenic disturbance reduces the stock level below Q_5, then continuing effort E_5 will deplete the stock to extinction. At effort E_6 extinction at any stock level will occur. Where E_1 to E_6 simply

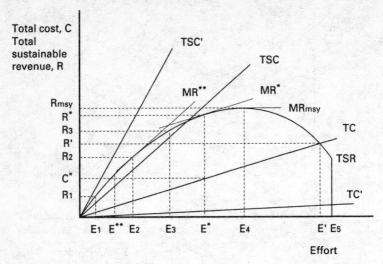

Figure 3 Sustainable harvests under different conditions

represent changes in technology, it can be seen how such changes by themselves can extinguish a resource. To arrive at the optimum stock level and harvesting rate, the effort (E) needs to be transferred to the horizontal axis as in Figure 3.

The TSR curve represents the total sustainable revenue from different harvesting efforts. It is derived from the points on Figure 2, where the E lines cut the maximum sustainable harvest curve. Thus effort E_1 in Figure 3 corresponds to line E_1 in Figure 2, yielding a maximum sustainable harvest of H_1. This is multiplied by the price of the harvested good, P, to get a total sustainable revenue of R_1. The maximum sustainable revenue, R_{msy}, corresponds to harvest H_{msy} at effort level E_4. E_5 is the maximum effort that can yield a sustainable harvest, H_5, and sustainable revenue R_5. There is an inverse relationship between efforts and stock levels in Figures 2 and 3. Maximum sustainable harvest at effort E_1 (H_1) is associated with a stock level Q_1, which is higher than stock level Q_2 associated with H_2 at the higher effort level E_2 etc.

Increasing effort incurs increasing costs, shown in Figure 3 as a linear total cost curve TC, where TC = W.E, and W is the wage associated with the effort. The optimal utilization of the resource from the point of view of its owner will be where their profit, Π, is maximised, which occurs where TSR>TC and the distance between the TSR and TC curves is greatest. Algebraically:

$$\text{TSR} \quad = \text{P.H} \; ; \; \text{TC} = \text{W.E}$$
$$\Pi \quad = \text{TSR} - \text{TC} = \text{P.H} - \text{W.E}$$
$$d\Pi/dE \quad = \delta\text{TSR}/\delta E - W = 0 \text{ for } \Pi_{max}$$
$$\Rightarrow \quad d\text{TSR}/dE = W$$

This indicates that Π_{max} will occur at the point where the TSR curve ($d\text{TSR}/dE$) is the same as the slope of the TC curve, a constant W. As shown in Figure 3, this is where MR^* is parallel to TC, at effort E^*, when

$$\Pi_{max} = R^* - C^* .$$

An important conclusion of this analysis is that, for a privately-owned renewable resource, the optimum economic use of the resource will be below the maximum sustainable yield (H_{msy}) with a correspondingly higher stock level than Q_{msy}. H_{msy}, Q_{msy} will only be the economically optimal harvest and stock when TC is horizontal, i.e. when harvesting costs are unrelated to stock size. The MR tangent to TSR, shown as MR_{msy}, is also horizontal at E_4, corresponding to Q_{msy}.

Where ownership is either not well defined or not enforced, so that an open access situation pertains, new harvesters will be attracted by the profits to be made and overall effort levels will increase to E', at which point TC = TSR and any further harvest can only be taken at a loss (TC > TSR). Unless a sustainable harvest can be enforced, and it is extremely difficult both to define and enforce a sustainable harvest in a situation of open access, effort levels may expand beyond both E' and E_5 to increase short-term revenues at the expense of sustainability and the eventual collapse of the resource. It can also be seen that this situation becomes more likely should technical progress reduce the cost of harvesting the resource, say from TC to TC'. In Figure 3 the maximum effort that is consistent with a sustainable harvest is E_5, when it yields harvest H_5, with revenue R_5. But with open access, low harvesting costs and, perhaps, social pressures from poverty of unemployment, there will be a strong tendency to expand effort beyond this into unsustainability. Such a situation prevails today in the exploitation of many of the world's forests, fisheries, soils and water resources.

In Figure 3 TC is the total private cost of resource exploitation. It takes no account of damaging externalities associated with such exploitation (e.g. the contribution of deforestation to global warming), or of people's possible preferences for conservation, as opposed to exploitation, of the resource. If these externalities and option and existence values are taken into account, the total social cost (TSC) of exploiting the resource will be higher than TC and will result in an optimal exploitation effort of E^{**}, where MR^{**} is parallel to TSC, such that $E^{**} < E^*$, the privately optimal exploitation effort. If the conservation values are high enough, they could push the TSC curve out to TSC', where no exploitation of the resource at all would take place. Such conservation values are implicit in the designation of national parks or biosphere reserves, from which all economic development is excluded.

The analysis so far assumes that the resource owner is indifferent with regard to present and future profits, i.e. the implicit discount rate is zero. Where a non-zero discount rate is used, the analysis becomes very much more complex mathematically (see Pearce and Turner 1990: 256ff.), and only its conclusions will be summarily rehearsed here:

A. Clearly defined property rights and profit maximisation, with a zero discount rate, will tend to result in a yield that is lower and a stock that is higher than that at maximum sustainable yield.
B. Open access conditions will reduce the stock from the level in A, but will not result in extinction provided that the sustainable yield is not exceeded.
C. A positive discount rate will tend to result in a stock level between that of A and B. The higher the discount rate the closer will the stock level be to B.
D. If the discount rate exceeds the net rate of return from the resource as an asset, the resource will be liquidated, perhaps to extinction.
E. Increasing the price of the resource, or reducing the cost of harvesting it, will reduce the stock level. If the price is above the cost at low population levels, then extinction becomes likely.
F. The calculated costs of harvesting the resource should include the externalities of both attendant environmental damage costs and foregone option and existence values. They frequently do not do so, increasing harvesting beyond the social optimum.

It is clear from the above that, in conditions of open access, if the price of the resource received by the harvester is high, if the cost of harvesting is low, or if the discount rate is high, then it can be optimal to drive the resource to extinction. The same result can occur non-optimally due to uncertainty about stocks or sustainable yields.

It must be stressed, therefore, that for both renewable and non-renewable resources, optimal use or depletion can be environmentally unsustainable. This was made explicit by Smith (1977), who concluded from four control theory models of natural and environmental resource use, involving renewable, nonrenewable and amenity resources, that: 'Just as exhaustion can be optimal, extinction can be optimal' (Smith 1977: 1). Optimality and unsustainability are very much compatible in the mainstream resource economics literature.

Exhaustion and extinction: the evidence Malthus and Ricardo were concerned that population levels would outstrip either the available quantity or the fertility of agricultural land, but the first economist who worried about the actual depletion of resources was W.S. Jevons, whose book *The Coal Question* (Jevons 1909) warned of the dire consequences for British industry of, in his view, the inevitable exhaustion of British coal stocks and consequent increases in coal prices:

> The exhaustion of our mines will be marked *pari passu* by a rising cost or value of coal; and when the price has risen to a certain amount comparatively to other countries, our main branches of trade will be doomed (Jevons 1965: 79).

In the event, Jevons has been proved to have underestimated, as have many conservationists since, the ability of human ingenuity under the influence of market forces to discover new reserves, develop substitutes and increase the efficiency of use of potentially scarce resources. However, this does not guarantee that human ingenuity will always overcome scarcity, the evaluation of which remains an empirical matter, over which expert opinion is divided.

Part of the reason for this division is the use of different definitions and indicators of scarcity. Barnett and Morse's classic 1963 investigation, later updated by Barnett (1979), using a unit cost indicator, found no increase in scarcity since the late nineteenth century over a wide range of resources, with the exception of forest products. Hall and Hall (1984) conversely found that coal increased in scarcity on a unit cost test, but on a relative price test oil, gas, electricity and timber all exhibited scarcity increases through the 1970s.

Most economists have followed Barnett and Morse's conclusion that natural resources, at least those that are priced inputs into production, are unlikely to become scarce enough in the foreseeable future to act as a constraint on production. The best known expression of the opposite view, *Limits to Growth* (Meadows et al. 1972), recently updated (Meadows et al. 1992) warns of a significant danger of industrial collapse on current trends, due to the combined effects of population growth, resource depletion and pollution, by the middle of the twenty-first century. The two opposing views derive entirely from the different assumptions they make about new technological developments that promote substitution, resource efficiency and structural economic change.

There is far less controversy over the empirical evidence for extinction, which, despite uncertainty over overall numbers, is generally agreed to be proceeding at a rate unprecedented since the extinction of the dinosaurs 65 million years ago. Some estimates suggest that 10–20 per cent of a possible 10 million species (though the number could be as high as 30 million) will have disappeared by the year 2000.

There are several reasons why this matters economically even if no intrinsic value is given to other species. Many people enjoy watching wildlife, or even just knowing that it exists. Plants have been the source of valuable medicinal drugs and as yet undiscovered species which may be extinguished could doubtless yield more. Genetic diversity is important in agricultural breeding programmes. Perhaps most importantly, complex ecosystems, such as rainforests, provide natural services, such as climate regulation, on which many people are dependent. Ignorance about the functions of such ecosystems is still very great. Their destruction, which is irreversible, could prove catastrophic.

Environmental economics

With the increasing scale of industrial activity in the nineteenth century, the effects in terms of environmental degradation soon became obvious. John Stuart Mill was one of the first economists to recognise that the growth of production might be at the expense of environmental enjoyments:

> It is not good for man to be kept perforce at all times in the presence of his species. A world from which solitude is extirpated is a very poor ideal. ... Nor is there much satisfaction in contemplating the world with nothing left to the spontaneous activity of nature. ... If the earth must lose that great portion of its pleasantness which it owes to things that the unlimited increase of wealth and population would extirpate from it, for the mere purpose of enabling it to support a larger, but not a better or happier population, I sincerely hope, for the sake of posterity, that they will be content to be stationary, long before necessity compels them to it (Mill 1904: 454).

The unintended and uncompensated loss to one person of natural beauty, pleasantness and solitude in nature due to the economic activity of another is an example of what, following the analysis of A.C. Pigou, has come to be called an 'externality'. Another, more often quoted, example is pollution through the discharge of wastes from production or from the disposal of the products themselves.

The idea of an 'externality' has become the central organising concept of environmental economics. Although Pigou never used the term, his description of the effect remains definitive to this day:

> The essence of the matter is that one person A, in the course of rendering some service, for which payment is made, to a second person B, incidentally also renders services or disservices to other persons (not producers of like services), of such a sort that payment cannot be exacted from the benefited parties or compensation enforced on behalf of the injured parties (Pigou 1932: 183).

Environmental externalities arise because property rights to the use of environmental resources are either non-existent − the resources are treated as 'free goods' − or ill-defined. In principle, as suggested in a celebrated paper by Ronald Coase (1960), the externality problem may be solved by the clear legal delineation of these rights, so that environmental conflicts may be resolved through private negotiation. In practice, it may not be feasible for political or other reasons to give strict definition to property rights over natural resources. It is not clear, for instance, what system of private ownership could realistically encompass the atmosphere or the stratospheric ozone layer. Alternatively, it may be that, even if such resources could be privately owned, their degradation would affect so many people that the transaction costs involved in negotiations would be so great as to prohibit the negotiations taking place. Consequently the property rights approach to the resolution of the problem of externalities, while theoretically appealing, is often practically infeasible.

Another theoretically attractive approach to resolving the externality problem is to seek to 'internalise' the cost by levying a charge or tax on the activity concerned. This approach is illustrated in Figure 4. Private producers gain benefits from an activity which causes pollution, as shown by the marginal net private benefit (MNPB) curve. Left to themselves, they will produce until the MNPB falls to zero, when the level of emissions is Q. Associated with this pollution is a cost, external to the producers, shown by the marginal external cost (MEC) curve, which rises with the pollution level. At Q the external cost is C.

Now it can be seen that at all levels of production that cause

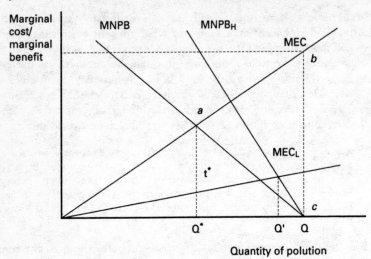

Figure 4 External costs of pollution and a Pigouvian tax

emissions higher than Q^*, at which MNPB = MEC, the marginal external cost is greater than the marginal net private benefit. In other words, although production causing emissions greater than Q^* makes the producers better off, society as a whole is worse off. At Q the total excess cost to society of the externality-induced over-production is the area abc.

The policy problem is to persuade producers to reduce their production such that their emissions fall to Q^*. This can be achieved by levying a tax, called a Pigouvian tax, equal to t^* per unit of emissions, which will cause the producer either to cut production or to abate emissions so that they fall to the efficient level Q^*. This efficient level is unlikely to be a zero level of pollution. Its position will be determined exclusively by the interaction between the MNPB and MEC curves.

The MNPB curve will be unproblematic to derive if, as is often the case, the benefit derives from economic activity which is marketed and therefore priced. The MEC curve, however, will often be representing or including unpriced, external effects, the value of which must be derived from techniques of environmental valuation, which are discussed in more detail in the next section. Here it may be simply noted that, where no surrogate markets exist to assist with this valuation, contingent valuation, usually based on willingness-to-pay (WTP) surveys, is the technique commonly employed. Because WTP survey replies are supposed to be based on existing budget constraints, the use of this method ensures that poor people's valuation of external effects is lower than rich people's.

Looking again at Figure 4, consider an economic activity with a high MNPB ($MNPB_H$) but involving serious external environmental effects, which primarily or exclusively affect poor people. Contingent valuation surveys may well reveal that these people have a low willingness to pay to avoid these effects, because they have a low ability to pay to do so. The MEC curve will be correspondingly low (MEC_L), so that the optimal level of environmental damage, where the curves intersect (Q'), could be relatively high. There is certainly no guarantee that such optimality will be environmentally sustainable.

Environmental valuation   As has been noted, the environmental effects caused by economic activity often occur outside of market exchanges and are unpriced. One result of this is that they have often been excluded from economic consideration. However, now that environmental issues have risen in perceived importance, there are intensive efforts to give money values to environmental effects and resources.

The valuation of unpriced environmental resources uses techniques of two kinds: indirect market methods, which seek to infer environmental values from market choices for other goods; and direct methods, which survey people's willingness to pay for the environment.

The indirect methods can be divided into three kinds (Cropper and Oates 1992: 703ff.): those which derive from behaviour which seeks to avert or mitigate the damage caused; those which exploit the complementarity of a purchased good with the relevant environmental good; and 'hedonic market' methods. An example of the first kind is the purchase of a medicament against the effects of air pollution; an example of the second is the cost of travel to a site of environmental quality; an example of the third is the increase (or decrease) in the price of a house which benefits (or suffers) from an environmental amenity, such as a beautiful view (or disamenity, such as aircraft noise). In each case the environmental good or bad is valued at the cost of purchase of all or part of some other good.

Direct methods, sometimes called contingent valuation methods (CVM) use the direct questioning of people to establish their willingness to pay for environmental goods, or to avoid environmental bads, or to accept compensation to forgo the former or suffer the latter. The outcome of such surveys is obviously greatly influenced by the design of the questions and the amount of information about the relevant issue which the respondent either possesses or is given.

Even with careful attention to these and other issues, however, the method has been criticised on such grounds as that: there is a difference between professing a willingness to pay and actually paying; people may resent being asked to pay for certain environmental goods and this may influence their answers; or they may seek to 'free ride' on others' professed payments. It is also clear that elicited values are likely to differ depending on the number of issues that are included in any single survey. All these considerations cast doubt on the appropriateness of comparing values derived from CVM with actual market values.

The problem is that CVM is the only method that has yet been devised of making any kind of estimate of certain crucial environmental values. Pearce (1993: 16ff.) has divided such values into use, option and existence values, where the first is the value of use now, the second is the value of preserving the option for use in the future, and the third is the value of simply knowing that something exists. Only CVM can attempt to estimate existence values and those option values for which no well-functioning futures market exists. Such values are of obvious importance with regard to the environment. CVM has been used to value such diverse environmental goods as: improvements in water quality to allow fishing or swimming; improvements in visibility from the reduction in air pollution; endangered species; and days free of respiratory ailments. CVM has become an established technique, but its results must be interpreted and used with care.

Cost-benefit analysis

The efficiency and optimality calculations of resource and environmental economics, using techniques of environmental valuation where necessary, are brought together in cost-benefit analysis in order to compare the discounted streams of costs and benefits through time. To do so, all the costs and benefits of resource use and environmental impact must be expressed in monetary terms. This is a formidable task for those complex environmental issues that have multiple moral, spiritual, cultural and survival dimensions. Two examples from global warming economics illustrate the kinds of problems that can arise.

The first concerns the valuation of the lives that are likely to be lost as a result of climate change due to global warming. Fankhauser (1992: 39, Table 11) estimates these to number 229,545 annually, of which 38,205 are in OECD countries, 12,870 in the former USSR, and the rest in the so-called developing world. In the literature of valuations of statistical lives (VOSLs) in industrial countries, values range from $200,000 to $10 million, with an average of $3 million; Fankhauser chooses a 'fairly conservative' figure of $1.5 million (Fankhauser 1992: 14). He chooses $150,000, one-tenth of the industrial country valuation, as the VOSL in low-income developing countries, such as China, which is envisaged to lose 48,690 lives per year, more than in all the OECD countries together.

Economists are quick to point out, as Fankhauser does, that VOSLs do not measure what human lives are 'worth'. Rather they are derived either from considerations of lifetime production, or from willingness to accept risk as shown in differential wages. Either way it is 'right' that poor people's lives are valued at less than rich people's. Fankhauser explains: '[the different valuation] merely reflects the fact that the willingness to pay for increased safety (a lower mortality risk) is higher in developed countries' (ibid.: 14, note 22).

This may be true, but the fact remains that the purpose of the calculation is to ascertain whether investments should be made to save the lives in question by, in this case, abating emissions of greenhouse gases. Moreover, if it were possible to discriminate over which lives were saved (as, with global warming, it is not) the valuation method ensures that it is the lives of the rich which should be saved first. Whatever the *a priori* theoretical motivation, the practical result of such valuation is to make the lives of poor people worth less than those of rich people and so more easily traded off against the benefits from economic activity. The situation is rendered even more problematic morally when, as with global warming, the benefits from the causal activity (on the whole the combustion of fossil fuels) accrue mainly to rich people, while the costs fall disproportionately on the poor. This situation, in which rich people benefit from activities which kill poor people, can be deemed 'efficient' in cost-benefit analysis by ascribing very low values to poor people's lives.

Such a procedure is controversial even within economics. For example, Lockwood (1992: 70, note 3) considers that 'in the interests of intercountry equity, it is desirable to cost statistical lives in different countries equally, but it is not sensible to use valuation of statistical life for a high-income country such as the U.K.' Instead he divides the valuation for the UK by the ratio of UK GDP to world GDP, arriving at a uniform valuation of statistical life of £540,000 in both industrial and developing countries. But this seriously undervalues industrial country lives according to VOSL techniques which are routinely used when effects in developing countries are not involved. It seems a strange logic to infer that the loss of an industrial country life is worth less when people in developing countries are to be killed as well.

The figure used for the VOSL in a global cost-benefit analysis of global warming is of crucial importance to the final result obtained. Using Fankhauser's figures for the loss of life, and his valuations of the loss, yields a figure of $89.3 billion, which contributes to an overall cost of global warming of 1.5 per cent of GWP (gross world product) (Fankhauser 1992: 43, Table 15). Valuing all the lives at Fankhauser's 'fairly conservative' industrial country value increases the value of the lost lives to $344 billion and the overall cost of warming to 2.8 per cent of GWP. Depending on the MNPB schedule, this could make an enormous difference to the amount of abatement that is 'efficient' and, therefore, to the number of lives that are saved.

The use of cost-benefit analysis for such problems as global warming would therefore seem dubious on at least four counts. It is morally questionable; many would call it simply immoral (see, for example, Adams 1993: 257). It is scientifically flawed in that the premises and methodology that generate the numbers do not sanction the uses to which they are then put. It is of very doubtful practical value, in that an enormous range of values can be generated, which can be used to justify a very large range of actions; Fankhauser has himself admitted that, in global warming economics: '(T)hrough the choice of appropriate parameter values almost any abatement policy can be justified' (Fankhauser 1993: 22). And it is politically unhelpful. Developing countries are not likely to respond positively to the suggestion that their citizens are worth one tenth of those in industrial countries, so that it will positively hinder the development of the global consensus on global warming and emission abatement that is necessary if the issue is to be adequately addressed.

The valuation of human life illustrates one kind of problem in seeking to derive monetary estimates of the non-monetary costs of seriously destructive environmental effects, namely the difficulty in justifying monetary valuation in general and an adequately narrow range of figures in particular. Another kind of problem, where market goods are involved but where their current price may not be an accurate reflection of the value of their loss, is illustrated by the treatment of agriculture in global warming damage estimates.

Nordhaus, in one of the first and most influential cost-benefit analyses of global warming (Nordhaus 1991) based his cost analysis of agricultural damage on the assumption that in 2050 the structure of the world economy would be the same as the structure of the US economy in 1990, when agriculture comprised less that 3 per cent of US output. He then estimated the net damage to US agriculture in 2050 from global warming as 6.7 per cent (central figure) and used the structural assumption to apply this figure, as a percentage of GWP, to the whole world.

Such a procedure is at best only valid for very small changes in agricultural output. If carried beyond this it implies that the total loss of the world's agriculture would involve a cost of only 3 per cent of GWP, leaving 97 per cent to be enjoyed, whereas, as Cline has noted: 'If world agricultural production fell to zero, so would world population. The economic loss would equal the entirety of GDP, not just the ex ante share attributable to agriculture' (Cline 1992: 87, note 9).

Food is a basic human need, with a consumer surplus that rises very fast once supply falls below a basic level of sufficiency. At present there is enough food for the human population, but its distribution is such that in 1988–90 20 per cent of people in developing countries, 786 million people, were 'chronically undernourished' (WRI 1994: 108, Table 6.1), with many of these actually starving. Moreover, by 2050 on current trends population is likely to have doubled and there are some doubts whether, even without global warming, the global food supply will be able to expand enough to meet this new level of need (see, for example, Brown et al. 1993: 11–14). Furthermore, to avoid disruption it is not enough for average supply levels to be broadly maintained. Extreme weather events that destroy particular crops in particular places in particular periods could have an impact quite out of proportion to their effect on such averages.

In short, it is clear that the world's food supply is currently precarious as far as millions of people are concerned, that this situation may well not improve and could deteriorate further, and that even a relatively small (in percentage terms) contribution to such deterioration could result in chaos, misery and starvation beyond all human experience. Even Nordhaus's 6.7 per cent damage could have a disproportionate effect, but some other estimates of damage are much higher. Cline's estimate of damage from long-term warming puts agricultural losses at 35 per cent of agricultural output (\$212 billion out of \$603 billion, Cline 1992: 99, 101). Rosenzweig et al. (1993) put Egypt's aggregate yield losses at 25–50 per cent for only one doubling of atmospheric CO_2 concentrations. Hohmeyer and Gärtner (1992) calculate that an extra 900 million deaths from hunger could be caused in the period 2010–30, due to global warming damage to agriculture. Such an estimate for hunger-related deaths alone is an order of magnitude higher than the

Fankhauser figures for all global warming induced fatality, and makes the overall result of the cost-benefit analysis even more dependent on how these lives should be valued.

Cost-benefit analysis is intended to facilitate decision-making by giving values to different effects using a common metric (money) so that the values may be more easily compared and the aggregate outcome more easily appreciated. According to a standard text on the subject, cost-benefit analysis has 'a fundamental attraction of reducing a complex problem to something less complex and more manageable' (Pearce 1983: 21). But it can only fulfil this function if the basis of valuation commands a wide consensus.

Where this is not the case, and the methodology of valuation itself becomes disputed ground, especially if the dispute centres on concerns with justice or morality, then the use of cost-benefit analysis is likely to enflame an issue rather than illuminate it. This can be easily seen by referring again to Fankhauser's numbers of deaths from global warming. His first-stage calculation, that the number of deaths in OECD countries and the rest of the world could be 38,205 and 191,340 respectively is informative and meaningful. It gives clear insight into the scale and distribution of the problem. His second-stage calculation that, on the basis of values differing by a factor of ten, these lives are 'worth' $57.3 billion and $32 billion respectively, cannot but cause rage and a deep sense of injustice in those who believe developing country lives to be as valuable as industrial country lives. Certainly such calculations do not make global warming 'more manageable'. They arouse passions, and will make it very difficult, as remarked earlier, to forge the global consensus that will be required if global warming is to be controlled and some at least of the lives in question are to be saved.

In summary, then, it seems that conventional resource and environmental economics can classify as 'optimal' patterns of resource use that are unsustainable; and that the central decision-making aid of welfare economics, cost-benefit analysis, can, when applied to the environment, intensify controversy rather than diminish it. There is an evident need, if environmental sustainability is the objective, to adopt modes of analysis that amend the traditional derivation of optimality, and assign values (not necessarily monetary values) to environmental resources and services that ensure their sustainable provision and use. First, however, it is necessary to understand how the environment contributes to the process of wealth-creation.

The environment and wealth creation

Following Hueting (1980), the contribution of the environment to human life is here perceived to be through the operation of a wide range of 'environmental functions'. This concept has been extensively developed by de Groot (1992), who defines environmental functions as 'the capacity of natural processes and components to provide goods and services that satisfy human needs' (de Groot 1992: 7). These 'natural processes and components' can in turn be identified as 'natural capital' (though de Groot does not use the term), which features in various definitions of sustainability and sustainable development (see for example Pearce et al. 1989: 34ff.). De Groot identifies thirty-seven environmental functions, which he classifies under four headings: regulation, carrier, production and information (ibid.: 15).

Pearce and Turner (1990: 35ff.) and Ekins (1992: 147–8) have used another method of grouping these functions, under three headings:

a. Provision of resources for human activity
b. Absorption of wastes from human activity
c. Provision of environmental services independently of or inter-dependently with human activity.

These two classifications are not contradictory. The resource functions in the second typology correspond broadly to the production functions of the first, but also include some carrier functions. The waste absorption functions are included among the regulation functions; and the provision of services includes the information functions and some regulation and carrier functions.

With the increase of the human population and the scale of its activities, the environmental functions are increasingly in competition with each other. Choices have to made between them and some functions are lost. Lost functions represent costs to be ascribed to the chosen functions. It is in this sense that the environment has become an economic factor: it is increasingly scarce; the uses to which it is put are increasingly competing; and it is an important ingredient of human welfare. The choices between environmental functions are therefore precisely analogous to other economic choices.

The concept of natural, or ecological, capital performing environmental functions can be integrated into an understanding of wealth-creation whereby economic activity creates wealth by combining different factors of production in order to produce goods and

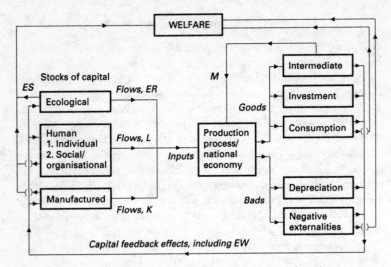

Figure 5 Stocks, flows and welfare in the process of production

services. The means of combination of a particular production process is that process's technology. Production can increase either when the quantities of the factor increase, or when they are combined more effectively so that the same factors produce more output. The latter condition is called technical change.

There are three distinct factors of production, which may be thought of as three types of capital, as portrayed in Figure 5: ecological (or natural) capital, human (individual and social) capital, and manufactured capital. Each of these stocks produces a flow of 'services' – environmental, E, labour, L, and capital, K, services. ER, L and K serve as inputs into the productive process, along with 'intermediate inputs', M, which are previous outputs from the economy which are used as inputs in a subsequent process.

Manufactured capital comprises material goods – tools, machines, buildings, infrastructure – which contribute to the production process but do not become embodied in the output and, usually, are 'consumed' in a period of time longer than a year. Intermediate goods, in contrast, either are embodied in produced goods (e.g. metals, plastics, components) or are immediately consumed in the production process (e.g. fuels). Human capital comprises all individuals' capacities for work (skills, knowledge, health, strength, motivation) and the networks and organisations through which they are mobilised.

Figure 5 shows the three distinct types of environmental function performed by the complex category of ecological capital, as mentioned earlier. Two of the types are directly relevant to the production process. The first is the provision of resources for production (ER), the raw materials that become food, fuels, metals, timber, etc. The second is the absorption of wastes (EW) from production, both from the production process and from the disposal of consumption goods. Where these wastes add to or improve the stock of ecological capital (e.g. through recycling or fertilisation of soil by livestock), they can be regarded as investment in such capital. More frequently, where they destroy, pollute or erode, with consequent negative impacts on the ecological, human or manufactured capital stocks, they can be regarded as agents of negative investment, depreciation or capital consumption.

The third type of environmental function does not contribute directly to production, but in many ways it is the most important type because it provides the basic context and conditions within which production is possible at all. It comprises basic 'survival services' such as those producing climate and ecosystem stability, shielding of ultraviolet radiation by the ozone layer and 'amenity services' such as the beauty of wilderness and other natural areas. These services are produced directly by ecological capital independently of human activity (ES), but human activity can certainly have an (often negative) effect on the responsible capital and therefore on the services produced by it.

The outputs of the economic process can, in the first instance, be categorised as 'Goods' and 'Bads'. The Goods are the desired outputs of the process, as well as any positive externalities (incidental effects) that may be associated with it. These Goods can be divided in turn into consumption, investment and intermediate goods and services. The Bads are the negative effects of the production process, including capital depreciation and negative externalities, such as those contributing to environmental destruction, negative effects on human health etc. In so far as they have an effect on the capital stocks, the Bads can be regarded as negative investment.

To some extent, one form of capital can substitute for another. It is possible to view the process of industrialisation as the application of human and social capital to natural capital to transform it into human-made capital. But it is now clear that such substitutability is not complete. If our current development is unsustainable, it is because it is depleting some critical, non-substitutable components of the capital base on which it depends.

The goods and services which comprise or, equivalently, can be purchased with, a person's or a nation's income contribute to that person's or nation's welfare. Welfare is seen in Figure 5 to be affected by many factors apart from the consumption of produced goods and services, including the process of production (working conditions), the institutions of production (family, community, political/legal system), people's state of health (part of human capital) and environmental quality (negative externalities and the stock of ecological capital).

Western industrial societies are often called 'consumer societies', presumably because it is perceived that in these societies consumption is the most important contributor to human welfare. Certainly the principal objective of public policy in these societies is the growth of the gross national product (GNP). There is little doubt that in the past and at present such growth has been and is the cause of much environmental destruction. One of the principal questions raised by such destruction is whether and on what terms continuing growth in consumption can be considered environmentally sustainable, i.e. can be sustained by the environment in the long term.

There is no mystery about the causes of current environmental degradation, which can be squarely ascribed to the patterns of production and consumption of six economic sectors: energy, some industrial processes, agriculture, transport, tourism and waste disposal from both production and consumption activities. There is similarly no mystery about the reasons why these sectors have operated in an environmentally destructive fashion. It is partly due to the fact that environmental effects frequently remain external to the price mechanism that registers costs and allocates resources in a market economy; and it is partly due to ignorance, complacency and short-termism in the political process. Moving towards sustainability will require the remedying of both the market failures, on the one hand, and the political shortcomings, which are as prevalent in the electorate as they are in all levels of the political system, on the other.

Environmental sustainability

Defining the concept

The basic meaning of sustainability is the capacity for continuance more or less indefinitely into the future. As illustrated earlier, it is now clear that, in aggregate, current human ways of life do not possess that capacity, either because they are destroying the environmental conditions necessary for their continuance, or because their environmental effects will cause unacceptable social disruption and damage to human health.

A way of life is a complex bundle of values, objectives, institutions and activities, with ethical, environmental, economic and social dimensions. While current concern about unsustainability largely has an ecological basis, it is clear that human situations or ways of life can be unsustainable for social and economic reasons as well. The pertinent questions are: for the environment, can its contribution to human welfare and to the human economy be sustained? for the economy, can today's level of wealth creation be sustained? and for society, can social cohesion and important social institutions be sustained?

Provided that the interrelatedness of the different dimensions is borne in mind, it can be useful to distinguish between the implications for sustainability of human mores, relationships and institutions (the social dimension); of the allocation and distribution of scarce resources (the economic dimension); and of the contribution to both of these from, and their effects on, the environment and its resources (the ecological dimension). Clearly human relationships may be socially unsustainable (for example, those leading to civil war) independently of economic or ecological factors; and a particular allocation of resources may be economically unsustainable (leading, for example, to growing budget deficits) independently of social or ecological factors. Similarly, a given level of economic growth may be unsustainable for purely economic reasons, insofar as it is leading to increased inflation or balance of payments deficits; on the other hand, it may be socially unsustainable in so far as it is increasing income inequalities or undermining structures of social cohesion such as the family or community; or it may be environmentally unsustainable in so far as it is depleting resources on which the economic growth itself depends.

One way of illustrating the complexities involved is through the matrix shown in Figure 6, where the rows show the types of sustainability, and the columns the influences on those types, across the same dimensions. In the example above, the sustainability of economic growth would be considered across the second row, with environmental influences (e.g. resource depletion) in box A, economic influences (e.g. inflation, balance of payments) in box B, and social influences (e.g. social cohesion) in box C. A fourth column has been added to the matrix to indicate the importance for sustainability of ethical influences. Relevant influences in box E, for example, would be concern for future generations or non-human forms of life; in box F they could be attitudes to poverty and income distribution.

Environmental sustainability may always be considered a desirable

Types of sustainability	Influences on sustainability			
	Ethical	Environ-mental	Economic	Social
Environmental	E		D	
Economic		A	B	C
Social	F			

Figure 6 Types of sustainability and their interactions

characteristic of a human situation, though some states of such sustainability may be better than others. In contrast, economic and social sustainability have no such happy connotation. As Hardoy et al. stress: 'When judged by the length of time for which they (were) sustained, some of the most successful societies were also among the most exploitative, where the abuse of human rights was greatest' (Hardoy et al. 1993: 180–1). Also, poverty and the evils which go with it may be all too sustainable. Similarly, in many countries structural unemployment is showing worrying signs of long-term sustainability. This chapter's principal focus is the environment-economy relationship (i.e. Boxes A, D in Figure 6). But such a focus necessarily includes all the above dimensions.

The ethics of sustainability   At a fundamental level, sustainability is inescapably an ethical issue, as the Brundtland Report and the UK government's 1990 Environment White Paper made clear:

> Even the narrow notion of physical sustainability implies a concern for social equity between generations, a concern that must logically be extended to equity within each generation. ... Our inability to promote the common interest in sustainable development is often a product of the relative neglect of economic and social justice within and amongst nations (WCED 1987: 43, 49).

and: 'The ethical imperative of stewardship ... must underlie all environmental policies ... We have a moral duty to look after our planet and hand it on in good order to future generations' (HMG 1990: 10).

How a society uses its environment, then, depends first and foremost on its worldview, its perception of the nature of the world and the status of human beings and other life forms within it. It is likely, for example, that a secular, anthropocentric worldview will sanction different uses of the environment, and permit more environmental destruction, than a worldview in which the earth and all life within it is perceived as sacred.

From its world view a society will derive its concept of environmental justice: the relative rights of non-human forms of life, of future human generations, and of current human generations to benefit from, share or just exist in 'the environment'. Environmental sustainability gains in strength as an imperative the more it is perceived that the well-being and opportunities of future humans and non-human beings should not be sacrificed for present human advantage.

From its world view, too, a society will derive its means for valuing and taking decisions about the environment. If the environment is viewed primarily as an economic resource, then techniques of environmental economic valuation will be perceived as the most important environmental inputs into decision-making processes.

It is likely that a society's norms of environmental justice will be related to its norms of economic and social justice. If basic personal and civil rights are denied, then environmental rights are unlikely to be respected, or even recognised. Thus sustainability and democracy are related. Further, if non-environmental economic wealth is unequally distributed, access to environmental goods is also likely to be inegalitarian. This has an obvious and direct importance for sustainability, if indeed it is true that poverty is a great destroyer of the environment, as is often asserted.

The ethics of sustainability will also determine to a considerable extent where the responsibility for promoting environmental sustainability is perceived to lie, and the degree of coercion in its enforcement that is considered justified. The Polluter Pays Principle, acceded to by OECD countries as early as 1972, but as much or more honoured in the breach as in the observance, is not only a maxim of economic efficiency; it is also a statement of moral responsibility. If polluters under prevailing economic and social arrangements do not pay, and governments are invoked to make them do so, how governments proceed with this task will depend on the political and social contract between governors and governed, on balances of rights and responsibilities and the institutions that express and enforce them. This leads naturally to consideration of sustainability's social dimension.

The social dimension of sustainability Social sustainability refers to a society's ability to maintain, on the one hand, the necessary means of wealth creation to reproduce itself and, on the other, a shared sense of social purpose to foster social integration and cohesion. Partly this is a question of having a sustainable economy, as discussed below. Partly it is a question of culture and values. Social sustainability is likely to be a necessary condition for the widespread commitment and involvement which *Agenda 21* sees as necessary to the achievement of sustainable development: 'Critical to the effective implementation of the objectives, policies and mechanisms ... of *Agenda 21* will be the commitment and genuine involvement of all social groups' (*Agenda 21*, Chapter 23, Preamble, *Earth Summit '92*: 191).

The importance that Western 'consumer' societies attach to consumption is not only problematic environmentally, because of the level of consumption and consequent environmental impacts to which such an emphasis leads. It is also problematic socially. A dominant social goal of increasing individualistic consumption does not seem likely to foster social cohesion, especially in an economic system that is subject to cyclical recession and increasing inequality. Poverty is always an economic problem in the sense that it denotes chronic scarcity at an individual level. It is an ethical problem because this scarcity often induces acute suffering. In some industrialised countries, relative (and sometimes absolute) poverty is also a growing social problem, in terms of its impacts on the social fabric and on the social sense of security, which act to reduce the well-being of the non-poor.

The sense of identity and social purpose of very many people, as well as their income, derives in large part from their employment. Extended unemployment, therefore, not only leads to poverty, but also to the loss of these other characteristics, which is probably more to blame than poverty for unemployment's high correlation with ill-health, mental stress and family breakdown. Unemployment is not just a waste of economic resources, in terms of the unemployed's lost production. It is socially destructive as well, and, at levels not much higher than those presently pertaining in Europe, may be expected to be socially unsustainable. Welfare states were established, both to give practical expression to a sense of social justice and to maintain social cohesion, at far lower levels of unemployment. At current levels they find it difficult to sustain the necessary transfer payments to accomplish these objectives, especially in a climate of growing international competition and taxpayer resistance.

Another contributor to people's sense of identity is their membership of and involvement in their local community. In an era of globalisation, the economic life of local communities tends to become increasingly extended. The concept of a local economy that contributes to local livelihoods and responds to local priorities is increasingly unrealistic. To a lesser extent, even national economic options are becoming externally determined. Yet the principal political institutions, that are expected to promote wealth-creation and foster wider well-being, operate at the national and sub-national level. Globalisation damages a sense of social connectedness, of community, while the mismatch between economic and political realities undermines confidence in political processes. Neither phenomenon is helpful for social sustainability. It is possible that local environmental action – both political and practical – will help to maintain or regenerate local social purpose and identity.

Such considerations demand that policies and initiatives for promoting an environmentally sustainable economy – by which, as earlier defined, is meant a system and processes of wealth-creation that can be projected to continue well into the future – be located securely within a context that recognises and seeks to address other social priorities and concerns. Policy integration for environmental sustainability does not only mean assessing and improving environmental outcomes over the whole range of policy-making. It also means implementing environmental policy in a way that, as far as possible, is consistent with and contributes to the achievement of society's non-environmental objectives. A trajectory towards environmental sustainability that unnecessarily violates other social priorities is unlikely itself to be sustainable. Attempts to promote such a trajectory may bring the whole project of environmental sustainability into disrepute.

Making the concept operational

The essence of environmental sustainability is the maintenance of environmental functions. Ekins (1994: 45–6) posited that maintaining environmental functions implies the following:

1. Destabilisation of global environmental features such as climate patterns or the ozone layer must be prevented;
2. Important ecosystems and ecological features must be absolutely protected to maintain biological diversity;
3. Renewable resources must be renewed through the maintenance of soil fertility, hydrobiological cycles and necessary vegetative cover. Sustainable harvesting must be rigorously enforced;
4. Depletion of non-renewable resources should seek to balance the maintenance of a minimum life-expectancy of the resource with the development of substitutes for it. Once the minimum life-

expectancy was reached, consumption of the resource would have to be matched by new discoveries of it. To help finance research for alternatives and the eventual transition to renewal substitutes, all depletion of non-renewable resources should entail a contribution to a capital fund. The need to minimise the depletion of all but the most abundant non-renewable resources implies that these resources should be used as intensively as possible by designing for resource-efficiency, durability and the maximum feasible practice of repair, reconditioning, re-use and recycling (the 'four R's');

5. Emissions into air, soil and water must not exceed their critical load, that is the capability of the receiving media to disperse, absorb, neutralise and recycle them, nor may they lead to life-damaging concentrations of toxins.

6. Risks of life-damaging events from human activity must be kept at very low levels. Technologies, such as nuclear power, which threaten long-lasting ecosystem damage at whatever level of risk, should be foregone.

These six fundamental sustainability conditions relate to today's principal perceived environmental problems. They may need to be supplemented as new environmental problems become apparent. They are also reflected in a number of international treaties, conventions and principles, including the Montreal Protocol to phase out ozone-depleting substances (1 above), the Convention on International Trade in Endangered Species and the establishment of World Biosphere Reserves to maintain biodiversity (3 above) and the Precautionary Principle, endorsed by the United Nations Conference on Environment and Development in *Agenda 21*, to limit environmental risk-taking (6 above). None of these international agreements was the outcome of cost-benefit analysis. They rest on a simple recognition that they represent the humane, moral and intelligent way for humans to proceed in order to maintain their conditions for life, and are argued for on that basis.

The actual physical standards which are consistent with these conditions will derive largely from the natural sciences, with application of the Precautionary Principle in situations of uncertainty (see O'Riordan 1993). These standards could serve as a framework of indicators of sustainability, comprising a set of physical criteria that offer as far as possible a guarantee of ecosystem diversity, health, stability and resilience, from the local to the global level. Much detailed research on these indicators is ongoing (see, for example, ECG 1994).

Humans today are part of most ecosystems in the biosphere. Through their quest for welfare and development, they exert an influence on all of them. Their activities proceed from complex motivations in pursuit of diverse goals and are promoted, mediated and constrained by a dense web of institutions and cultural relations at a variety of levels, all of which must be understood if policies directed towards the achievement of sustainability, as defined by the indicator framework, are to be effectively implemented.

The extent to which societies are and will be prepared to move towards sustainability depends not only on the value they place on the concept *per se*, but also on their situation – their ambitions, perceived realities, opportunities and constraints. If analysis and policy formulation are to help or persuade societies to become more sustainable, they will need to be located in a multi-dimensional understanding of this situation, so that ambitions and perceived realities can be appropriately changed, constraints lifted and opportunities taken.

Moving systematically towards environmental sustainability as set out in the above conditions will, of course, not be easy. Targets will have to be set, over specific timescales and with defined budgets, which will demand sacrifices in some areas. New institutions will be needed, old institutions will need to be imaginatively used, social structures and expectations will have to be changed. It should be stressed again, too, that because the use and experience of the environment are inextricably linked to the deepest social and cultural processes, the pursuit of environmental sustainability will, if it is to be successful, have to be accompanied by a concern for economic, social and cultural sustainability: the maintenance of the fundamental means of wealth creation, the social cohesion and the cultural integrity that will themselves be necessary if the environmental challenges are to be effectively addressed.

It has to be admitted that the present human situation is not particularly propitious for such a programme. Durning (1991: 153–61) has characterised the world's population as divided into broadly three groups: 20 per cent of 'overconsumers', who 'live in unprecedented luxury'; 20 per cent living in poverty, whose desperation to survive often leads them to degrade or destroy the resources on which they depend; and 60 per cent currently living nearest to a sustainable lifestyle. However, not only do the 80 per cent of non-overconsumers possess a powerful aspiration to enter into that category; but the overconsumers themselves show no sign of achieving sufficiency and are driven equally powerfully to seek to consume more, despite the fact that, as Durning says: 'Overconsumption by the world's fortunate is an environmental problem unmatched in severity by anything but perhaps population growth' (Durning 1991: 153). In such a world unsustainability does indeed present a formidable challenge: to governments, to business, to other social institutions and, particularly for overconsumers, to lifestyles.

Towards a sustainable economy

The Brundtland Report was clear that the policies needed to move towards environmental sustainability were not purely environmental in nature: 'The ability to anticipate and prevent environmental damage requires that the ecological dimensions of policy be considered at the same time as the economic, trade, energy, agricultural and other dimensions' (WCED 1987: 10).

No country has yet achieved the integration of environmental policy and priorities with other relevant policy areas that is widely recognised to be required if the challenge of environmental sustainability is to be effectively addressed. The range of issues that need to be covered and included in this integration is wide:

Macroeconomic management: narrow economic sustainability, in the sense of broadly balanced budgets and trade flows, is an essential prerequisite of moves towards environmental sustainability. Neither inflation nor indebtedness – public, private or foreign – will be conducive to the implementation of necessary environmental policies. Such policies must never lose sight of the need for macroeconomic stability.

Growth and environment: both the sign (plus or minus) and scale of the relationship between the growth of national income and environmental sustainability are variable. There are many opportunities for improving the environment that will also have positive economic impacts. There are also many environmentally destructive activities that will have to be transformed or reduced. The imperative for environmental policy is to realise the win-win opportunities; and to transform or reduce destructive activities in ways that minimise adjustment costs and create new competitive advantages. The available evidence indicates that giving priority to environmental sustainability need not reduce incomes from current levels; it may not even reduce growth. But there is no doubt that it will require economically acute and politically sensitive handling of radical change.

Trade and environment: in Europe national environmental policy-making is constrained by treaty commitments to both the European Union and the General Agreement on Tariffs and Trade, now the World Trade Organisation. The extent to which these constraints need to be modified or removed if countries are to be able to promote environmental sustainability is now a major issue of current debate. So is the extent to which current trading rules' emphasis on non-discrimination and multilateralism can or should be modified to take more account of human rights, labour standards or the specific welfare and development of low income countries. Striking the right balance between these objectives is of crucial importance to sustainability.

Ecological footprints: quite apart from the way trading rules constrain national environmental policy-making, trade often involves the import and export of sustainability. When the production processes of imported goods cause environmental impacts, then the importing country may be said to have left its ecological footprint in the goods' country of origin. Policies to move a country towards sustainability must address its ecological footprints abroad.

Sustainability and development: environmental unsustainability is a planetary phenomenon and is likely to continue for as long as large numbers of people live in absolute poverty and try to extricate themselves from this situation by following the Western model of industrial development through the exploitation and consequent destruction of natural resources. Perhaps the most important role of the West in moving towards sustainability is to embark on a new path of development that does not entail environmental destruction. But the West will also need to help lower income countries embark on such a path in a way that is appropriate for them. Environmentally sustainable trade and foreign direct investment will play their role in this, but there will also be a need for aid for sustainable development, and for the foreign indebtedness of many countries to be reduced. The environmental record of aid is not generally good and any alleviation of debt will have to ensure that further unsustainable indebtedness is not contracted. Renewed North–South cooperation will be necessary to address these issues.

Environmental accounting and valuation: it is generally accepted that the first priority for effective environmental policy is a comprehensive system of environmental accounts across all the environment's relevant dimensions, which gives a clear picture of the state of the environment and changes in this state over time. As has been seen, there is little consensus over how this state and these changes should be valued. In an economistic society it will be easier to incorporate non-market environmental effects into decision-making processes if they can be given a monetary value. The techniques of such valuation therefore have an important role, but must be appropriately used. One such technique, calculating the restoration cost of environmental damage or depletion incurred in a particular period of time, allows the national accounts to be adjusted for environmental factors. Both the United Nations Statistical Office and the European Commission's Fifth Environmental Action Programme now recommend that this should be done. Where monetary valuation of environmental effects is either not possible or not perceived as appropriate, the relative effects should still be considered in decisions.

Ecological tax reform: current taxes bear most heavily on labour. Profits are also taxed. Environmental factors of production, whether resources or waste-absorption services, are hardly taxed at all. Such a taxation system increases the economy's use of the environment, decreases its use of labour and discourages entrepreneurial initiative relative to an untaxed economy. It is hard to justify such a system in a society with worrying levels of both unemployment and environmental damage and which wishes to stimulate enterprise. A shift of taxation away from labour and profits onto the use of environmental resources could be expected to increase investment and employment and reduce environmental damage. Such a shift is probably the largest single source of win-win opportunity in the search for sustainability with prosperity.

Environment and employment: ecological tax reform will promote employment both by making labour less expensive relative to other factors of production and by increasing the demand of labour-intensive economic sectors. There is little prospect, however, that it will 'solve' the present unemployment problem. Social sustainability demands that this problem, especially with regard to long-term unemployment and unemployment concentrated in particular age-groups, ethnic minorities or areas, be addressed by a range of other measures, including the redeployment of benefit payments, training, the enhancement of competitiveness, local economic initiatives and environmental works. The formulation and implementation of a successful combination of these measures will not be easy.

Instruments of environmental policy: it is imperative for sustainability that environmental policy objectives are achieved at least cost. It is well-established that market-based incentives are most likely to achieve this. Allied to the Polluter Pays Principle, these will normally take the form of environmental taxes or charges. Such an approach meshes well with the broader objective of ecological tax reform, as discussed above. It will also be the case, however, that environmental policy objectives will sometimes be best achieved by combining market-based instruments with more traditional environmental regulations; and sometimes regulations by themselves will be appropriate. Prior ideological preference has little role to play in choosing the best mix of instruments. Careful analysis of appropriateness on a case-by-case basis is the only way that least-cost sustainability will be approached.

Environment and planning: because markets for many economically important environmental functions are either missing or imperfect, planning has a crucial role to play in policy for sustainability. This applies not only to land-use planning but also to policies for pollution emissions and resource depletion. It remains generally true, however, that least-cost moves towards sustainability will be achieved when planning works with rather than against the grain of the market. Sometimes market pressures will need to be resisted; but environmental policy will be most easily and cost-effectively implemented when market forces can be guided and redirected rather than simply thwarted. Planning will also generally be most effectively achieved when it proceeds through a process of in-depth consultation and partnership-in-implementation with those parties affected by planning proposals, especially local communities.

Subsidies and environmental investment: it is a fundamental insight of environmental economics that ecological costs are as real as any other category of economic costs. Many such costs are increased by the financial subsidising of environmentally damaging activities, such as energy use or agriculture. Because subsidies also introduce economic inefficiency, removing those that are linked to environmental destruction provides another means of securing both economic and environmental gain. Similarly, environmental benefits are as real as any other economic benefits, and the cost of securing them should therefore be regarded as investment rather than consumption. There is a need for methodologies to be developed and deployed that will permit the rate of return on such environmental investments to be quantified, in monetary terms if possible, so that the full benefits of environmental expenditures may be apparent.

Environment and technology: technical change is the driving force of an economy. In the past much of such change has been damaging to the environment. These technologies will have to be transformed or abandoned. In the future technology has the potential to produce humanity's goods and services at a small fraction of their current environmental cost. The development and widespread diffusion of such technologies, in both North and South, is one of the priorities and prerequisites of sustainable development.

Environment and competitiveness: in an increasingly competitive global market economy, there is a limit to the extent to which a country can unilaterally impose environmental costs on its businesses. There are three ways in which environmental policy can be implemented without either running counter to the imperatives of competitiveness or involving unilaterally conceived and imposed protectionism: through global environmental agreements that impose the same (or acceptably differing) constraints on all parties; through agreements brokered, for example, by the World Trade Organisation, that countries can compensate their firms for expensive environmental regulations; and through the use of environmental policy to foster new sources of competitiveness. Each of these ways will be appropriate in different situations. One of them always needs to be politically feasible if the need to compete is not to become the enemy of sustainability.

Environment and consumption: greatly increased levels of consumption are an undisputed cause of global environmental damage. To remedy this situation, either the same goods will have to be produced, used and disposed of differently (with greatly reduced environmental damage); or different goods, which inherently involve less environmental damage, will have to be consumed; or fewer goods will have to be consumed. Sustainable development is likely to require all three remedies in some combination. The first is the least problematic politically, but requires the necessary technical fix; the second depends on changing preferences, through a change in either values or relative prices; the third would become politically less daunting if there were general public recognition of what private survey data reveal: that most people do not regard increasing their consumption as the principal objective or source of satisfaction in their lives. With such recognition, the need on occasion to sacrifice material consumption for socio-environmental benefits would be a politically less problematic message. It will also be important to foster and harness consumer awareness and commitment through appropriate labelling schemes that allow the environmentally preferable products in their field to be identified. Life-cycle analysis will play an important role in providing the scientific foundations of such schemes.

Environment and cities: by the end of the century about half of the world's population will live in large urban settlements, with the proportion still growing. Cities can promote economic dynamism. They can also offer important opportunities for environmental economies of scale. But they can also constitute a major source of environmental problems. Achieving compatibility of cities and sustainability is an important requirement of sustainable development.

Environment, community and the local economy: in the global market place the very concept of a local economy may appear, and to some extent is, anomalous. But 'environment' will always to a large extent be experienced locally and, as a major contributor to economic welfare, it is important to the local community and part of a local economy. Local initiative is essential to local environmental conservation and enhancement. However, in areas on the periphery of, or otherwise badly served by, the global economy, it will not be easy to mobilise this initiative unless it is linked to efforts at economic regeneration. The creation of environmentally sustainable local economic activity is a key component of sustainable development in such areas. Whether through fostering public-private-voluntary sector partnerships, or taking their own initiatives where appropriate, local government has an important role to play in the promotion of such activity, in the development of more sustainable ways to deliver local services, in the stimulation of local environmental awareness and commitment, and in building the institutions to undertake the transition to sustainability.

Environment and the welfare state: it is widely acknowledged that the welfare state in the UK and in other industrialised countries faces formidable challenges from a combination of taxpayer resistance and the need for competitiveness, on the one hand, and, on the other, from growing demands from an ageing population, high expectations for health care, expanding education and training needs and persistently high levels of unemployment. Together with growing job insecurity, the pressures on the welfare state increase a sense of social anxiety and insecurity overall, making more difficult the achievement of settled, long-term environmental commitment that is necessary for progress towards sustainability. Resolving the crisis of the welfare state – finding affordable means to enable all people to secure satisfying work, health for all and dignified retirement – is therefore an important objective for environmental as well as social sustainability. However, the extent to which moves towards environmental sustainability alone can mitigate the welfare state's problem of financial unsustainability should not be over-emphasised. But there are relevant connections. Unemployment coexists with large amounts of environmental work that needs to be done. Pollution causes ill-health at the same time as health budgets are under stress. A cleaner, safer environment would save substantial costs which currently fall upon the public sector. Major programmes of public environmental works could reduce unemployment. Where, as with energy conservation, they contribute to more efficient resource use, they may involve small, or even negative, costs. Where they can be organised through community service programmes, they may be similarly inexpensive, and foster community spirit and social commitment. Creative thinking and imagination is needed for new schemes at the local and national level.

Conclusion

In all the above areas it is very largely known what needs to be done and how to do it in order to move decisively towards sustainability. It is clear that sustainability cannot be achieved overnight; it will be a process of decades, but the process needs to be started with determination now. However, as in 1989 with the end of the Cold War, transformations can happen quickly, which calls for preparedness to take opportunities as they arise. Vested interests or power structures that have thrived on unsustainability will need to be transformed or overcome. This will involve establishing new vested interests and building up the power of those who will benefit from sustainability; tackling issues one by one where winners from sustainability can overcome the beneficiaries from unsustainability; putting together coalitions for sustainability and building momentum towards it.

What role will economists have in this politico-ethico-socio-economics of sustainability? First, they will not have the responsibility of deciding whether it is economically efficient or optimal for people, individually or collectively, to live or die. For some economists this will come as something of a relief. Second, they will move beyond models of optimality that generate unsustainability, and, where issues of sustainability are concerned, will give up using discount rates that render insignificant any impacts more than a few decades away. Third, they will work with natural and other social scientists, philosophers, politicians, lawyers and business people to generate understanding and prescription appropriate for environmental sustainability in a complex reality. Fourth, and perhaps most particularly, they will use their concern with efficiency to advise on least-cost approaches to sustainability. The crucial message from economists must be that sustainability does not come with a fixed price tag. How fast societies decide to move towards sustainability, especially before the idea really catches on, depends to a large extent on how much it is perceived to cost. It is the economists' task not to define the goal of sustainability, but to advise on ways of minimising the cost of achieving it.

This will require economists to be what Keynes, at any rate, wanted them to be, 'humble, competent people – on a level with dentists' (Keynes 1972: 332). Dentists prevent and relieve excruciating pain in the human body, often with simple and inexpensive means. It is to be hoped that economists can do the same for the body economic, by developing an analytic and practical economics of environmental sustainability effectively to address current unsustainability, which is probably the most pressing and intractable problem of the present time.

References

Adams, J. 1993 'The Emperor's Old Clothes: the Curious Comeback of Cost-Benefit Analysis', *Environmental Values*, 2: 247–60.

Barnett, H. 1979 'Scarcity and Growth Revisited' in V. Smith (ed.) 1979 *Scarcity and Growth Reconsidered*, Johns Hopkins University Press, Baltimore.

Barnett, H. and Morse, C. 1963 *Scarcity and Economic Growth: the Economics of Natural Resource Availability*, Johns Hopkins University Press, Baltimore.

Brown, L.R. et al. 1993 *State of the World 1993*, Earthscan, London.

CEC (Commission of the European Communities), 1992a Proposal for a Resolution of the Council of the European Communities, *Towards Sustainability: a European Community Programme of Policy and Action in Relation to the Environment and Sustainable Development*, Volume 1, Commission of the European Communities, Brussels.

CEC, 1992b Executive Summary, *Towards Sustainability: a European Community Programme of Policy and Action in Relation to the Environment and Sustainable Development*, Volume 2, Commission of the European Communities, Brussels.

Cline, W. 1992 *The Economics of Global Warming*, Institute for International Economics, Washington DC.

Coase, R.H. 1960 'The problem of social cost', *Journal of Law and Economics*, 3: 1–44.

Cropper, M. and Oates, W. 1992 'Environmental economics: a survey', *Journal of Economic Literature*, 30: 673–740.

Dasgupta, P. and Heal, G. 1974 'The optimal depletion of exhaustible resources', *Review of Economic Studies*, Symposium on the Economics of Exhaustible Resources: 3–28.

Dasgupta, P. and Heal, G. 1979 *Economic Theory and Exhaustible Resources*, Cambridge University Press, Cambridge.

De Groot, R. 1992 *Functions of Nature*, Wolters-Noordhoff, Groningen.

Durning, A. 1991 'Asking How Much is Enough' in Brown, L.R. et al., *State of the World 1991*, Earthscan, London.

Earth Summit '92, Regency Press, London.

ECG (Environment Challenge Group) 1994 *Environmental Measures: Indicators for the UK Environment*, ECG, London (also available from New Economics Foundation, London).

Ekins, P. 1992 'A four-capital model of wealth creation', in Ekins, P. and Max-Neef, M. (eds) 1992 *Real-Life Economics: Understanding Wealth Creation*, Routledge, London.

Ekins, P. 1994 'The environmental sustainability of economic processes: a framework for analysis' in Van den Bergh, J. and Van der Straaten, J. 1994 *Toward Sustainable Development: Concepts, Methods, and Policy*, Island Press, Washington DC.

Fankhauser, S. 1992 'Global Warming Damage Costs: Some Monetary Estimates', CSERGE Working Paper GEC 92–29, CSERGE, University College London.

Fankhauser, S. 1993 'Global Warming Economics: Issues and State of the Art', CSERGE Working Paper GEC 93–28, CSERGE, University College London.

Hall, D. and Hall, J. 1984 'Concepts and measures of natural resource scarcity, with a summary of recent trends', *Journal of Environmental Economics and Management*, December: 363–79.

Hardoy, J., Mitlin, D., and Satterthwaite, D. 1993 *Environmental Problems in Third World Cities*, Earthscan, London.

Heal, G. and Barrow, M. 1980 'The relationship between interest rates and metal price movements', *Review of Economic Studies*, 47: 161–81.

HMG (HM Government) 1990 *This Common Inheritance*, HMSO, London.

Hohmeyer, O. and Gärtner, M. 1992 *The Costs of Climate Change*, Report to the Commission of the European Communities, Fraunhofer Institut für Systemtechnik und Innovations-Forschung, Karlsruhe, Germany.

Hotelling, H. 1931 'The economics of exhaustible resources', *Journal of Political Economy*, 39 (2): 137–75.

Hueting, R. 1980 *New Scarcity and Economic Growth*, North Holland, Amsterdam (Dutch edition first published 1974).

Jevons, W. 1965 *The Coal Question: an Inquiry Concerning the Progress of the Nation and the Probable Exhaustion of Our Coal Mines* (third edition, first edition published 1865), Augustus M. Kelley, New York.

Keynes, J.M. 1972 'Economic Possibilities for Our Grandchildren' (first published 1930) in *Essays in Persuasion*, Vol. 9 of *The Collected Writings of*

John Maynard Keynes, Macmillan, London.

Lockwood, B. 1992 'The Social Costs of Electricity Generation', CSERGE Discussion Paper GEC 92–09, CSERGE, University of East Anglia, Norwich.

Malthus, T. 1970 *An Essay on the Principle of Population* (first edition, first published 1798) Penguin, Harmondsworth.

Malthus, T. 1974 *Principles of Political Economy: Considered with a View to their Practical Application* (second edition, first published 1836), Augustus M. Kelley, Clifton, NJ.

Meadows, D.H., Meadows, D.L., Randers, J. and Behrens, W., 1972 *The Limits to Growth*, Universe Books, New York.

Meadows, D.H., Meadows, D.L. and Randers, J. 1992 *Beyond the Limits*, Earthscan, London.

Mill, J.S. 1904 *Principles of Political Economy With Some of Their Applications to Social Philosophy* (sixth edition, first edition published 1848), Longmans, Green and Co., London.

Nordhaus, W. 1991 'To slow or not to slow: the economics of the greenhouse effect', *Economic Journal* 101, July 1991: 920–37.

O'Riordan, T. 1993 'Interpreting the Precautionary Principle', CSERGE Working Paper PA 93–01, CSERGE, University of East Anglia, Norwich.

Pearce, D. 1983 *Cost-Benefit Analysis* (second edition, first edition 1971), Macmillan, London.

Pearce, D. 1993 *Economic Values and the Natural World*, Earthscan, London.

Pearce, D., Markandya, A. and Barbier, E. 1989 *Blueprint for a Green Economy*, Earthscan, London.

Pearce, D. and Turner, R.K. 1990 *Economics of Natural Resources and the Environment*, Harvester Wheatsheaf, Hemel Hempstead.

Pigou, A.C. 1932 *The Economics of Welfare* (4th edition), Macmillan, London.

Ricardo, D. 1973 *The Principles of Political Economy and Taxation* (first edition 1817), J.M. Dent & Sons, London.

Rosenzweig, C., Parry, M., Frohberg, K. and Fisher, G. 1993 *Climate Change and World Food Supply*, Environmental Change Unit, Oxford.

RS and NAS (Royal Society and National Academy of Sciences), 1992 *Population Growth, Resource Consumption and a Sustainable World*, Royal Society, London and National Academy of Sciences, New York.

Schmidheiny, S. (with the Business Council for Sustainable Development) 1992 *Changing Course: a Global Business Perspective on Development and the Environment*, MIT Press, Cambridge MA.

Smith, V.K. 1981 'The empirical relevance of Hotelling's model for natural resources', *Resources and Energy*, 3: 105–18.

Smith, V.L. 1977 'Control Theory Applied to Natural and Environmental Resources', *Journal of Environmental Economics and Management*, 4: 1–14.

WCED (World Commission on Environment and Development) 1987 *Our Common Future* (The Brundtland Report), Oxford University Press, Oxford/New York.

World Bank 1992 *World Development Report 1992*, Oxford University Press, Oxford/New York.

WRI (World Resources Institute) (with UNDP and UNEP) 1990 *World Resources, 1990–91*, Oxford University Press, Oxford/New York.

WRI (with UNDP and UNEP) 1992 *World Resources, 1992–93*, Oxford University Press, Oxford/New York.

WRI (with UNDP and UNEP) 1994 *World Resources, 1994–95*, Oxford University Press, Oxford/New York.

INDEX